BRAZIL
AWAKENING GIANT

BRAZIL

AWAKENING GIANT

By Philip Raine

INTRODUCTION BY LINCOLN GORDON

PUBLIC AFFAIRS PRESS, WASHINGTON, D. C.

FOR ALICE

INTRODUCTION

Among the more populous nations commonly classified as "less developed countries," Brazil is the most likely to emerge in short order into full participation in the "First World"—the world of open market, industrialized, and consumer-oriented societies whose economies are increasingly interdependent. The Brazilian metamorphosis began in the 1930's, paused in the early 1960's, but has gathered prodigious momentum during the last five years. As this transformation moves forward, Brazilian influence is growing in the international arena, not only in Latin America and the Western Hemisphere, but also in the United Nations and the multiple organizations concerned with trade, finance, environment, and other global issues. In short, Brazil deserves, and is receiving, increasing interest and attention from the world beyond her borders.

On the economic side, the phenomenal sustained and continuing developmental boom, combined with the nation's wealth in natural resources, has enlisted the active participation of European and Japanese, as well as North American investors. Brazil is now the World Bank's largest client. Brazilian history, culture, and politics have become a major field of study for foreign scholars. There is a constant stream of both serious and casual visitors from the industrialized world.

Even the most casual visitor learns in a few days the fatuity of regarding Brazil as "just another underdeveloped country" or part of a supposedly homogeneous Latin America—a blend of charming but hopelessly backward Indo-Iberian cultures. The more serious visitor quickly learns that this is a nation of highly distinctive qualities. Brazil possesses a meaningful national history; an astonishing regional diversity within its huge expanse; a vast body of intelligent and energetic men and women in all classes of society; a creative cultural life; traits of personal and racial tolerance, adaptive capacity, and sense of humor which any society might justly envy; and a growing sense of national purposiveness.

There is, indeed, a danger that the visitor may swing too far from skepticism to blind enthusiasm. Having seen the splendors of Rio de Janeiro, Salvador, Ouro Preto, and Olinda; felt the modernizing vitality of São Paulo, Belo Horizonte, Brasília, Curitiba, and Porto Alegre; and the pioneering courage of the Amazon road-builders and the Mato

v

Grosso homesteaders, he can easily fall in love with the country. His romantic vision may persuade him that Brazil's resources and prospects are utterly without limit, that this is the El Dorado and new world super-power of the twenty-first century.

A more balanced view would at a minimum appreciate the dynamism of contemporary Brazil. There is nothing stagnant or static about it. Rapid change is not limited to the obvious and easily measurable aspects: population growth; urbanization; industrialization; electrification; auto-motification; growth in manufactured exports; expanded investment and output. It can also be seen in the enlargement of the middle classes; the modernization of agriculture (especially in the Center and South); the reform and expansion of education; the shift in patterns of consumption; the unfolding social, economic, and political aspirations; and the forging of a more independent foreign policy of world-wide scope.

On the other hand, it would be foolish to underestimate the continuing obstacles to full modernization. They include the desperate poverty of the overcrowded Northeast; the marginalized migrant peasants in the shanty towns of the cities; the claims of housing and urban infrastructure on a not unlimited capacity to save and invest; the tenacity of obsolete culture patterns in much of the countryside; the inertia of a massive and underpaid bureaucracy; and the increasing dependence on a favorable international environment for continued high rates of economic growth.

Philip Raine's *Brazil: Awakening Giant* provides a thoughtful introduction to a balanced understanding of this extraordinary country's possibilities, problems, and prospects. The author enjoys a thorough knowledge of Brazil's history in the forty years since modernization began under Vargas, and an intimate first-hand acquaintance with Brazil and Brazilians from his many years in the American diplomatic service in São Paulo, Rio de Janeiro, and Brasilia. He is especially sensitive to the interplay of traditional and modernizing social forces and to the nuances of evolving foreign policies He skillfully avoids the pitfalls of either the stagnationist or the romantic views.

The book does not purport originality as a general survey of Brazilian geography, history, politics, sociology, and the contemporary scene, but its references provide helpful guidance to the more specialized literature, especially the growing body available in English. The final two chapters are the author's own appreciation on foreign policy and on the general prospects for the future; they warrant especially close attention.

On the socio-economic side, Mr. Raine perhaps underestimates the drag of excessively rapid population growth on continued economic progress and especially on the achievement of greater social equity. On the other hand, he may overstate the resistance to agricultural modernization as the forces of industrialization, improved transportation and communications, enlarged educational opportunities, and spreading rural commercialization take hold (the current soybean boom is a dramatic illustration). On the political side, he expresses full confidence (which I share) in the ultimate liberalization and redemocratization of the present authoritarian régime, with wider political participation in the future than under the somewhat élitist democratic structure of 1945-64. Like other observers, Brazilian and foreign, he does not yet see clearly what uniquely Brazilian pathway may be blazed from here to there.

His analysis of foreign policy should be a sobering warning to those who lightly take for granted an automatic harmony between Washington and Brasília. It is a timely reminder that the United States cannot afford a new era of neglect in its attitudes toward Latin America in general and Brazil in particular.

LINCOLN GORDON

PREFACE

Brazil today is the keystone of United States hemisphere policy. To-morrow it may be the proving ground of its world policy. Both nations may find that their future greatness depends on their ability and willingness to work together as equal partners and with more under-standing and coperation than they have been able to muster in the standing and cooperation than they have been able to muster in the past.

Brazil has emerged as a force on the world scene. It has moved far ahead of the underdeveloped third world. Yet only a decade ago many questioned whether it would ever find its way into the twentieth century after nearly 500 years of isolation and somnolence. That it has found its way was acknowledged by President Nixon when, at a White House dinner late in 1971, he lifted his glass in a toast to Presi-dent Médici, saying "as goes Brazil so go the rest of that continent."

There has, of course, been considerable controversy in Washington as to how strongly American foreign policy should favor Brazil. In-fluential Senators and academics, among others, have criticized United States policy because recent military-controlled governments have used political repression, censorship and curtailment of civil rights while accomplishing "the Brazilian miracle." That "miracle" has wrought not only economic progress but basic reforms as well. In any case, there is no argument over Brazil's growing importance and it is im-perative that we fully understand this "awakening giant." The stakes are too high to risk repetition of the past errors of United States policy.

Recent studies devoted to specialized aspects of Brazil are highly useful, but they leave much to be desired in that their narrow focus complicates consideration of the nation as a whole by the non-scholar. On the other hand, works devoted largely to praise of economic gains do little to contribute to greater understanding.

My book tries to give a rounded picture of the Brazilian people in terms of how they see themselves and the rest of the world and what motivates them. To see Brazil solely through western-oriented eyes would be to miss the significance of a new way of life which has adapted western ways to fit a tropical environment.

Any realistic appraisal of Brazil must, therefore, take into account its physical environment and human elements, bearing especially in mind the fusion of Amerindian, European, and African races for despite this diversity a society with a unified sense of identity and a minimum of social friction has resulted.

Brazil's political institutions date back to colonial days and the Empire period which flourished almost to the beginning of the present century. Their relevance can be seen in the contrast between institutions in Brazil and those that sprang up under Spanish influence in other Latin American countries. Informal components of society such as pressure groups—often more weighty in making national decisions than formal organizations—are examined at considerable length.

The varied aspects of disruptive economic and social changes are also discussed. Some social scientists see these changes as inevitable consequences of the development process; others might be content to describe them as growing pains. Who could expect that a society deeply attached to the past could be transformed into a modern power without pain?

My Brazilian friends may, of course, wonder why I have given so much attention to the problems that abound in their society. These problems, it seems to me, must be taken into account if one is to understand the nation and appreciate the obstacles already conquered and those still to be faced.

Although this volume is necessarily limited to Brazil, the progress this nation has made may well serve as a model for other countries in Latin America and elsewhere. It is for this reason that I devote some analysis to comparative experiences in industrialization under democratic and authoritarian regimes.

Despite the broad scope of this book, it is far from all-inclusive. The rich fruits of a new culture which can be sensed in today's music, literature, and painting are mentioned only in passing. They deserve a volume to themselves.

It is clear that 1964 was a true watershed in Brazilian history, but it is not yet possible to say which of the nation's traditional characteristics and conditions will endure despite the sometimes ruthless methods used by successive governments to reform the country. In any event, the old must be known in order to measure the new for its probable durability. The urge for return to democratic procedures remains so strong, even among the military, that new forms of popular rule are inevitable. The present determination to change old patterns that were sometimes benign, but often corrupt, makes a return to the past exceedingly unlikely.

I first began to sense the epic quality of Brazil's modernizing process during the 1950's when I was stationed in São Paulo as American Consul. The ebullient confidence *Paulistas* felt as their economy began to undergo rapid expansion was in some ways distinctly similar to that of the American people during the industrial upsurge in the United States after the Civil War. The fastest growing city in the world, São Paulo today has over eight million inhabitants.

I lived in Brazil for ten years, first as a young man assigned to the U. S. Embassy in Rio de Janeiro at the time of the *Paulista* revolution in 1932, and again from 1955 to 1962 and from 1965 to 1967. During these years I traveled widely throughout the country. Moreover, my assignments as Political Counselor at the Embassy in Rio de Janeiro, as officer-in-charge of the Embassy Office during a pioneer year in Brasilia, and Deputy Chief of Mission in the Rio Embassy gave me unusual opportunities to become familiar with both foreign and domestic policies.

Many Brazilians helped me write this book. I will not attempt to name them; it would be ungracious to single out some and not others. People in all walks of life, in all classes and positions (both private and official), extended invaluable help through frank discussions from which I learned a great deal. I treasure their friendship and the memories of their many kindnesses. Several have provided me with indispensable information in recent years. I must express special thanks to Manoel de Nascimento Brito, managing director of the *Jornal do Brasil,* for furnishing copies of his outstanding daily. I am also grateful to Adolfo Bloch of *Manchete* and his editor Murilo Melo, as well as Luiz Alberto Bahia, editor of *Visão,* for informative publications which have enabled me to follow key events that have seldom been adequately reported in the world press.

I am also indebted to Dr. William Simonson, Director of the Inter-American Studies Center of Temple University, who read the manuscript at an early stage and made valuable suggestions, as well as my colleagues and students at Temple, whose discussions helped me sharpen my ideas. Dr. Rollie Poppino of the University of California at Davis also gave me encouragement and excellent advice. Dorothy May Anderson, geographer, editor and friend, did much to make the manuscript more readable. Angela Orlen spent many long days and nights deciphering my all but illegible handwriting, transforming manuscript into clean typescript. To both I extend thanks for their patience and interest.

PHILIP RAINE

CONTENTS

I: The Past as Prologue

Brazilians insist that they are different, and they are right. Brazil was created by Portugal, not Spain. The language is Portuguese, the culture is distinct, and the history of Brazil has been surprisingly separate from that of the rest of Latin America. None of the eighteen Spanish American republics can be treated as homogeneous entities, much less Brazil, a giant among them. Brazilians see their nation as a uniquely developing society destined to assume the role of a major power in a world that has not yet produced a modern, powerful nation of the tropics. An increasing number of leaders from all walks of life believe that their country has already reached the status of a major power and is moving on to higher destinies. The belief in itself is significant, since national power is in no small degree related to a nation's conviction of its importance.

Brazil probably is the only Latin American country with the potential to become a great power. It may be classified as one of the older developing nations which has already overcome obstacles such as ethnic divisions and the centrifugal force of regional independence from central control. Unlike some of the Spanish American nations with less tranquil histories, it has had time to develop a national identity with meaningful sentiments and symbols that penetrate below the upper and middle classes. A good deal of the uniqueness of the society derives from the conditions of "a new world in the tropics," but the tropical aspect is only a part of the total picture. Although the tropical plantation society of the past set many cultural patterns for the nation, other conflicting patterns now compete for a place in the sun. Brazil's "golden triangle," formed by the highly developed São Paulo, Rio de Janeiro, and Belo Horizonte areas, is worlds away from the backward tropical regions.

Immigration has made a substantial contribution to major change. The basically mestizo population of the coast has been broadened by a dynamic influx of Portuguese, Italians, Spaniards, Japanese, Germans, Russians, Lebanese, Syrians, and others. This fresh human capital, settling in the more temperate highlands behind the coastal plains and

1

in the south, has added a new dimension to the tropical nation. The immigrants have broken traditions and changed old social patterns, and like their earlier counterparts in the United States, they have come to symbolize the nation's progress. Leading economic and political positions in Brazil's changing society have gone not only to the sons of traditional Brazilian aristocrats but also to immigrants and their sons. Resourceful former members of the lower class are finding their way to high places in Brazilian society.

Heterogeneity provides the base for a strong, many-faceted nation, but it is national unity that provides the impetus for nation building. Unity is evident in the substantial religious hemogeneity, the national literature, the distinctive music, and—despite regional loyalties—the strong national political life. Perhaps the best expression of this national cohesiveness is found among Brazilian creative artists who no longer look to Europe for stylistic and formal models. They find their inspiration in the present and future of their own country, in a society motivated by high purpose and a sense of destiny.

Hemisphere Role

Brazil's potential in the southern half of the hemisphere can be compared to the position of the United States in the northern half. It is an integral landmass larger than the continental United States, a land of varied natural and human resources that form the base of Brazil's economy and its complex social structure. Its productive potential is greater than its size, fifth largest country in the world, would indicate. In Canada, which is exceeded in size only by the Soviet Union, the infertile Precambrian Shield comprises about half of the nation's territory; in Brazil only one area, the Amazon basin, is considered to be inhospitable. The difference in outlook for the two countries is that the unproductive part of Canada, like much of Siberia, seems doomed to a permanently marginal economic role, whereas most of the Amazon basin can be made productive through technology.

Brazil's 3.3 million square miles, spread some 1,680 miles north to south and a similar distance east to west, constitute almost half the landmass of South America. The most salient feature of the landscape, aside from the Amazon basin, is the huge, complex central highlands block, pushing upward to about 3,000 feet near the coast and tilting gently west and north. The Guiana highlands north of the Amazon are somewhat similar to the central highlands, but they comprise only 2 percent of the territory of Brazil and have not yet been fully explored. Because of such large elevated areas much of the country has a pleasant climate, although it is almost entirely within the torrid zone.

The 3,642-mile coastline has some of the finest harbors in the world, several of which—for instance, Angra dos Reis near Rio de Janeiro—are not yet developed but could shelter most of the world's navies.

Only two important rivers—the Amazon and the São Francisco—empty directly into the Atlantic. Because of the character of the central highlands, most rivers flow westward, often within sight of the Atlantic, to the Paraná or Paraguay rivers and empty into the Río de la Plata near Buenos Aires. Some of the larger tributaries of the Amazon, including the Tocantins, the Xingú, the Tapajós, and the Maderia drop rapidly from the central highlands into the Amazon or Solimões (the Amazon upstream from Manaus).

Some geographers have said that slow occupation and development of the interior is attributable to physical obstacles, especially the mountains on the coast and the westward flowing rivers, which made access to the coastal population centers difficult for those who lived inland. The establishment of the new capital, Brasilia, 600 miles in the interior, has changed the outlook. The capital is strategically located at the approximate geographic center of the country, near three important lowland areas—the southern part of the Amazon basin, the valley of the São Francisco, and the lowlands associated with the complex river system of the southwest whose waters eventually reach the Río de la Plata far to the south. Looking from Brasilia rather than from the coastal cities, geography presents no insurmountable obstacles to national integration.[1] Recent rapid development of the interior, including the Amazon basin, supports the Brazilian view. Soon "one of the blank spaces of the world" will be filled in.

Of the lowland areas, the vast Amazon basin (1.5 million square miles) is by far the largest. The river is navigable for more than 2,000 miles. The valley is unexpectedly narrow in many places, with the bordering lands rising high enough to assure a more salubrious climate than the sweltering heat at river level. The much smaller lowland area in western Mato Grosso is an extension of the Argentine pampas reaching as far north as the central highlands. It is good agricultural and pastoral land. The most highly developed lowland, however, is the strip of coastal plain that extends from Uruguay in the south to the long coastal plain of French Guiana in the north. In Rio Grande do Sul the littoral is relatively wide, turning to rolling grasslands that merge with the Uruguayan pampas. The long stretch north to Natal in Rio Grande do Norte is very narrow—in some places nonexistent, as along the coast between Santos and Rio de Janeiro, where the mountains rise from the sea. The climate ranges from subtropical to tropical. North of Ceará, the coastal plain widens considerably and merges with the Amazon basin. The long coastal plain was settled first, and it is here that some 85 percent of Brazilians still live. Virtually all the large cities are on the coastal plain, although some cities of the interior—for example, São Paulo, Belo Horizonte, Brasilia, Curitiba, and Londrina—are now growing at a more rapid pace than their coastal progenitors.

Brazil's dominant place in the southern half of the hemisphere is not due entirely to its location and varied physiography. Geopolitical factors have influenced development from the beginning. Portugal's earliest concern over the security of its New World colony spurred on its determination to drive out the French and Dutch claimants in the area. Later the goal was to push the colony's borders west and north as far as possible. Both enterprises were successful. Brazil now shares a common border with all but two of the countries in South America, Chile and Ecuador. Satisfactory boundry treaties with most neighbors were concluded by the first decade of the twentieth century. Another long-standing policy is the preservation of the *status quo* in the Río de la Plata area, *inter alia* to assure fluvial access to the Brazilian west. Brazil's determination to maintain this *status quo* has led to war against Argentina and Paraguay and to numerous interventions in Uruguayan affairs. Recent moves to break up landholdings of foreigners and to prevent nonpermanent residents from making future acquisitions in areas designated important for national security follows naturally from Brazil's geopolitical history.

National integration has been the overarching objective of all governments, but none has devoted more effort and resources to it than the military governments since 1964. In pursuit of this objective today, the most immediate aims are to develop the overpopulated Northeast economically and to develop the border areas and the Amazon region.

Status in the World

The map on p. 6, from *Geopolítica do Brazil,* illustrates a Brazilian perspective of the world. Situated near Africa and commanding the Western Hemisphere shipping lanes of the South Atlantic, Brazil was of great importance to the United States and the United Nations during World War II.

Brazil has a special interest in Africa, partly because Africa's nearest point is only a little more than 1,500 miles from its northeast salient and partly because a considerable part of its culture is drawn from Africa. Brazilians believe that the stability of countries on the west coast of Africa is important to the defense of South America, for which reason the following map shows Africa within "Fortress America."

For many years it seemed that serious physical limitations would prevent Brazil from achieving major nation status in the world. Many who did not know the country thought of it only in terms of steaming hot tropics. The great Amazon region was held to be all but useless because of leached soils; the arid Northeast was believed to be doomed to eternal poverty; and Brazil's petroleum supplies, as well as other resources, were considered to be inadequate for sound economic development. Well known geographers thought that within the foreseeable future only the populated coastal areas could be developed. In fact, modern engineering and scientific research in agriculture have proved that most problems arising from these physical limitations can be solved. Potentially productive areas with relatively rich soils have been found in the Amazon basin, and research on the utilization of poorer leached soils is progressing. Water for irrigation is available in the arid Northeast, but capital is needed to make more of the area produce as it does now only in good years. Petroleum production has increased from only 5,000 barrels a day a few years ago to about 175,000 barrels today, and the end to the rise is not in sight.

Most of the foreseeable requirements for minerals, except petroleum and copper, can be met for years to come from known sources, and much of the land has still to be explored.

As Brazil begins to exploit the resources of its vast interior, it sees itself on the verge of becoming a great world power. The last fifteen years have brought many changes, both physical and psychological. More and more Brazilians, not just those in the national government, look outward from the heartland rather than from the coastal plain. No longer is the interior thought to be remote and worthless. One part, called the *campo cerrado* (closed lands), is one of the world's largest untilled areas potentially suitable for food production. Today more and more wide highways are bringing the interior nearer to the country's main population centers.

The Past

A rapid review of Brazilian history goes a long way to explain the concept of the country's uniqueness, its dominant place in the southern hemisphere, and its potential as a world power.[2] This would have been difficult to foretell from its inauspicious first years. Its accidental discovery in 1500 by Pedro Álvares Cabral awakened no more than a short-lived interest at the Court of Manoel I in Lisbon. The Portuguese were then engrossed in their struggle for the riches of the Indies and paid little attention to the brazil-wood trade, the only noteworthy fruit of the discovery. It was not until thirty years later, when other nations began to be interested in the area, that Portugal moved to consolidate its claim to Brazil. It established the first colony at São Vicente in 1532, but did not send the first governor-general until 1549.

This neglect was less accidental than it was lack of conviction of the value of the empty spaces which the far from wealthy Portugal claimed, and the physical difficulties in taking possession. The Portuguese regime was loose—partly for this reason and partly because its colonial system was loosely managed. The various parts were allowed to develop more or less independently in contrast to the systematic, centralized regimes in the Spanish colonies. The complementary economies that developed served to hold the country together when independence came three centuries later. Probably at least as important in saving the nation from the fate of some of the Spanish colonies which suffered prolonged violence, economic disruptions and fragmentation after independence, was the steadying influence of the Braganza dynasty which set long enduring patterns of political behavior. For these and doubtless for more fortuitous reasons, all major changes have taken place with a minimum of strain on the nation's life. Probably more than any other single element the Empire experience gave Brazilians their basic patterns of accommodation and pragmatic adjustment to change.

Although Portugal had been the first in the field of overseas discovery, she had been overtaken by Spain, a larger and richer nation. Shortly after the first voyage of Columbus, Pope Alexander VI helped the two nations reach agreement on how they would divide the known and unknown world between them. This agreement was formulated in 1494 in the Treaty of Tordesillas, which established a longitudinal line west of the Cape Verde Islands—all the lands east of the Tordesillas line were to go to Portugal, all the lands west to Spain. Only a small part of the land that is Brazil today lay east of the line, but the treaty with Spain was of advantage to Portugal in preventing permanent colonization by other countries. Nonetheless, French, Dutch, and English explorers, traders and colonizers saw no reason why the Treaty of Tordesillas should be binding on them.[3] The French established a colony at Guanabara bay, where Rio de Janeiro now spreads, and the Dutch settled several places but found the northeast most to their liking. The French, Dutch, and English had footholds in the Amazon delta and other places in the north. It took the Portuguese until 1654 to drive out all these "pirates"; the Dutch, whose colonizing efforts in Salvador and Recife were the most successful, were the last to go. During this period and later, the Portuguese expanded their own claims far beyond the Tordesillas line.

Since Portugal lacked the resources needed to develop Brazil, as early as 1534 King João III divided the colony into fifteen hereditary *capitanías* (captaincies). They were granted to donatories, favored individuals who were to finance the settlements in return for the privilege of having wide governing powers and potential profits. But the captaincies were not well governed and to assure tighter royal control the King established the capital at Bahia and sent the first Governor General to assume central authority in 1549. The powers of the donatories were curtailed but not actually rescinded, and the hereditary captaincies did not revert to the crown entirely until the middle of the eighteenth century. Even so Brazil was so large that control was highly tenuous everywhere but in the administrative centers of the captaincies. The Portuguese pattern of control, quite different from the Spanish, seems to have been affected very little by the union of the Spanish and Portuguese Crowns from 1580 to 1640 under Philip II of Spain. Family loyalties and local ties were always more important to the colonials than allegiance to the central government, and they remain the basis of local democracy in rural areas today, as well as of the federal or pluralistic character of the government. The persistently strong sense of regionalism in contemporary Brazil dates from the period of the captaincies. The region first to be developed was the Northeast where sugar cane early became the basic crop supplying a strong demand in Europe and attracting new settlers. A century after discovery Olinda, the capital of Pernambuco, had 700 settlers and 50 sugar mills. Because the Indians proved to be poor workers, African slaves began to be brought in increasing numbers after 1580.

Active during most of the seventeenth century, the *bandeirantes* (flag bearers), including explorers, prospectors, trail blazers and slave traders, conquered the interior.[4] Organized in armed bands, they trekked inland in large numbers, often taking their families and slaves along. They were based in São Paulo; their quasi-military expeditions lasted months or even years. The *bandeirantes* sought precious metals, particularly gold, and Indian slaves, and in their search they pushed the borders of Portuguese territory farther and farther west. Since they often had to plant food crops to sustain themselves, some became semi-settlers. Behind them came the cattle raisers and, toward the end of the century, the miners.

Unions between Portuguese males and Negro and Indian slave women (Portuguese women were scarce in the colony) were fairly common in this period when the coastal plantations and towns settled into a relatively stable society. By the end of the century the economic foundations had been laid. The sugar-based economy produced an attractive way of life—for its masters—that was transferred almost intact to the coffee plantations in the next two centuries.

While *bandeirantes* were pushing Brazil's borders westward, the Portuguese were moving them farther south and consolidating all gains. In 1680, Colonia do Sacramento was founded near the mouth of the Río de la Plata, across the estuary from the Spanish settlement at Buenos Aires. This was the beginning of a Spanish-Portuguese rivalry over Uruguay and control of the Rio de la Plata that continued many years and several times led to armed conflict in the seesaw conquest and reconquest of territory. In 1750, Spain recognized as Portuguese possessions those lands west of the line of Tordesillas which were first occupied by the *bandeirantes*. In 1777, Spain and Portugal agreed that Brazil's borders would be established largely along the lines they follow today, with the Amazon basin recognized as Portuguese and Uruguay (then under Portuguese control) returned to Spain. In 1816, however, Brazilian and Portuguese soldiers reconquered Uruguay, and in 1821 it was annexed by newly independent Brazil. Uruguay did not gain its independence until 1830. Since then Brazil has continued to maintain a strong interest in the Rio de la Plata and has occasionally intervened in Uruguayan affairs.

In the last decade of the seventeenth century, *bandeirantes* discovered gold in Minas Gerais, touching off a gold rush that for the next century would make minerals the central fact of Brazilian life. Nearly 50 percent of the world's gold production came from Brazil, most of it from Minas Gerais. The discovery also touched off great economic and social changes in the eighteenth century, sometimes called the golden age of Brazilian expansion. A hitherto simple agricultural society, based on subsistence agriculture and a declining export of sugar, gave way to more complex development in which the mining of gold, diamonds, and tourmalines took up the slack and also made important infusions into the economy. Growth of the cattle industry in the interior and the rapid growth of cities, particularly Rio de Janeiro as a result of the mining boom, made a profound change in the economy and in social patterns formerly dominated by the sugar boom. The great mineral production, however, adversely affected the price structure and currency and distracted attention from the basic agricultural economy. As in most gold rushes, lawlessness and social disorganization accompanied the get-rich-quick fever. As the country's center of gravity shifted, the capital was moved from Bahia to Rio de Janeiro in 1763.

While Brazil was growing, Portugal had been declining in strength and prosperity and in 1703 had been forced to conclude the Treaty of Methuen with England. Among other concessions, the treaty gave England a virtual monopoly of Brazilian trade. It assured trade security in transit, but, according to João Ribeiro, caused a large loss of revenue, because most of Brazil's gold went to England.[5]

Not all the instability in Brazil during the eighteenth century was caused by commercial matters. Many Brazilians had learned of the intellectual ferment in Europe and in the Spanish colonies. In Pernambuco in 1710 the Brazilian aristocracy turned on the Portuguese merchants. This minor revolution had in it elements of incipient nationalism and overtones of defiance of the Crown. Some militant republican sentiment was evident, the best remembered being the plot headed by an army officer dubbed Tiradentes (literally tooth puller), which was supported by a number of Minas Gerais intellectuals. The plot was discovered in 1789; Tiradentes was executed, but his memory is still revered.

By the beginning of the nineteenth century, with little planning or help from the mother country, Brazil had outdistanced Portugal in wealth and importance. The Portuguese Court moved to Brazil in 1808 after Napoleon invaded the Peninsula. This did not end aspirations for independence and republican government, not even after Brazil was granted the status of a kingdom coequal with Portugal in 1815. Activity toward political independence, however, was minor; most of the discontent and conspiracy involved a quarrel over Portuguese liberalism as against Portuguese despotism and an effort to reduce Brazil to its former colonial status. The French and the American revolutions were important in shaping colonial opinion, but the divisions that led to independence movements in the Spanish American countries were generally less consequential in Brazil and aroused fewer passions.

On September 7, 1822, independence came to Brazil suddenly and without bloodshed. When João VI returned to Lisbon with his court in 1821, he left his son Pedro to rule Brazil as Prince Regent. Pedro refused orders of the Lisbon Convention to return to Portugal and declared Brazil an independent empire. Thus the Prince Regent became the new Emperor, Pedro I. He accepted a constitutional role after rejecting a constitution drawn up by a constituent assembly and replacing it with one in which more power was given to the monarch. The United States, in 1824, was the first country to recognize the new monarchy. Many problems plagued the early Empire. From 1825 to 1828 Brazil and Argentina were at war. One eventual outcome of this war was the creation of Uruguay as an independent nation, a buffer between the two giants on its borders. Pedro I was often criticized because he seemed more concerned with matters affecting Portugal than those affecting the future of Brazil, and in 1831 a military revolt forced him to abdicate. Nevertheless, Pedro I had successfully guided his country through the transition from absentee rule to independence.

When Pedro I abdicated, his five-year-old son was named to succeed him as Pedro II, and a Regency was established to rule until he reached his majority. The decade of the Regency was even more troubled than that of the first Empire. The Farroupilha Revolt (or war of the ragamuffins) in Rio Grande do Sul, which began in 1835, was not quieted until 1845. The military, savoring their first taste of successful usurpation and rebellion, were brought under control with difficulty by the energetic measures of a radical priest, Diego Antonio Feijó, who served as Minister of Justice. Some uprisings were royalist in nature, others republican and still others separatist (Pará in the north and Rio Grande do Sul in the extreme south). Some of the dissatisfaction and unrest was quieted by an amendment to the constitution, called the Additional Act of 1834, which gave the provinces greater autonomy than they had had under Pedro I. Constitutional reform during the Regency preserved Brazilian unity, albeit precariously, until Pedro II could be crowned. Yet dissent was so strong that many of the nation's leaders decided that the only way to save the Empire was to bring young Pedro II to the throne before his majority. This was done July 23, 1840. Despite some favorable results, as a first experiment in republicanism, the Regency was a failure, since it could not stop the internal quarrels and had to decree its own demise prematurely.

During the almost half century (1840-1889) that Emperor Pedro II ruled, Brazil was the most stable and liberal country on the continent. Civil dissent, based principally on strong federalist and some separatist sentiments, continued to disturb the country for the first nine years of his rule, but its intensity and frequency gradually abated. An 1841 law that took back some of the autonomy granted the provinces under the Additional Act of 1834 facilitated central control. A two-party system composed of Liberals and Conservatives, which was started under the Regency, worked smoothly, and despite the

Emperor's decisive control through the appointment and dismissal of ministers, eventually developed real meaning. Each party learned to respect the rights of the opposition, and perhaps more important for Brazilian development, the parties learned that it was not necessary to resort to revolution to change governments. The press was free, individual liberties were guaranteed, and the Emperor stimulated literacy and intellectual pursuits wherever he could. Pedro II, better known to many simply as Dom Pedro, has been called the philosopher king, but he took more pleasure in calling himself the "best republican in the nation."

During the long empire period, the agricultural economy shifted from dependence on sugar to dependence on coffee and rubber, partticularly coffee, first planted in equatorial Pará and brought south to Rio de Janeiro. From there it spread farther southward through Minas Gerais and the Paraiba valley to São Paulo, where for more than a century it became Brazil's most important crop. The change in the locale of coffee production contributed to a gradual change in society, when it was proved that *fazendas* (plantations) in the south could prosper more with free labor than with slaves.

Slavery had been an economically critical element of *fazenda* life. Both the Emperor and the British, who controlled most of Brazil's trade, tried in vain to abolish the slave trade. Brazil legally prohibited it in 1830, but the law was generally ignored. Later attempts to abolish the institution itself by gradual, limited means were equally unsuccessful. In 1888 all slaves were freed; their emancipation occurred almost accidentally when Princess Isabel, acting as regent in Dom Pedro's absence named an abolitionist as prime minister and thus made possible the passage of an abolition law.

The abolition of slavery was an immediate cause of the fall of the Empire. A less direct cause of Pedro II's downfall stemmed from his foreign policy, particularly his efforts to preserve the balance of power in the Río de la Plata. This policy led to wars with its neighbors to the south. In the War of the Triple Alliance (1865-1870), the most debilitating, Brazil joined Argentina and Uruguay against Paraguay, but Brazil bore the brunt of the fighting. Not only did the nation suffer economically but many of its military leaders smarted under their reduced status after the war and joined the growing ranks of the republicans. Following a series of quarrels with the Emperor during this period, the Catholic Church, which along with the rural aristocracy and the military had been a principle supporter of the Empire, lost interest in continuing its support. On November 15, 1889, a bloodless military *coup d'etat* deposed Pedro II and a republic was proclaimed.

The Empire had given Brazil political stability and the people a degree of freedom that was unusual for the times in Latin America. It also gave them a unique prestige deriving in large part from the court, which, as Karl Lowenstein put it, "shone as the Medici-Florence of South America." [6] This comment perhaps unwittingly gives an insight into the anachronistic character of the Empire in an otherwise republican Western Hemisphere and tells why its demise sooner or later was inevitable.

The change to republican government in Brazil was in no sense a popular revolution. The masses were hardly aware of the change. The coup was essentially urban based and bourgeois oriented, and although its causes were complex, effective organization and intellectual drive for deposing the Emperor came from young, reform-minded officers. Many changes had taken place in Brazilian society. Whereas before 1850 the commercial interests of the country were concentrated on the importation and sale of Africans, after 1850, when the slave trade became illegal, capital became available for other enterprises. Some manufacturing began; commerce picked up. A middle class made up of business men, public servants, and families of the military began to form. It was a new urban bourgeois society whose interests did not always coincide with those of the ruling aristocracy. The consensus favoring a changed political system originated in this middle class, an important sector of which was a newly educated elite. Law schools and medical schools had been established for sons of the rural aristocrats who did not go to Europe for their education. Later, after the middle of the nineteenth century, sons of the commercial and bureaucratic bourgeoisie began entering civilian and military schools. Even a few sons of the poorer middle class and the lower class could enter military schools, where many were imbued with Positivist ideas. It was this generation that sought a larger voice in national decisions and that eventually brought down the Empire.

Many of the precepts of Positivism which strongly influenced the military harmonized with the pragmatic side of the Brazilian character.

After the Empire fell Positivism exerted, as it did subsequently during the Vargas era and that of the 1964 revolution, a strong influence on the government. Comte, founder of the science of sociology, held that metaphysical abstractions about society as well as most religious social concepts were not adequate to deal with the world's social ills. He believed that the positive methods used in the natural sciences must also be applied to society. Comte rejected laissez-faire liberalism as an antiquated system resulting in injustice to the weak, and since he reasoned that a liberal democracy would not use the experimental and empirical methods of science to change a system which favored its leaders, he held that social planning must be imposed by a dictatorship. In the context of the existing monarchical order, these ideas were revolutionary. Positivism was first taught in the military academy in Rio de Janeiro in 1850, seven years before Comte died. It did not gain a wide following, however, until Lieutenant-Colonel Benjamin Constant de Botelho Magalhães, a mathematics teacher and a leader of the republican movement, became its ablest proselytizer, particularly among younger officers.

The first years after the Empire were stormy and frustrating. Marshal Deodoro da Fonseca, a leader in the revolt against Pedro II, took office as head of the provisional republican government while the Emperor himself was embarking for exile in Europe. Marshal Deodoro had young Positivists as his assistants, and his methods of governing were dictatorial both before and after the promulgation of the Constitution of the Republic on February 24, 1891, under which he became President. His hopes to establish a scientific republic were thwarted by a congress bent on dislodging the military from seats of power and installing a liberal democracy. Impatient with lack of progress and his inability to break the political impasse, Marshal Deodoro dissolved congress on November 3, 1891, and proclaimed himself dictator. Widespread opposition forced him to resign ten days later, and he retired from public life in disgust. One visible and enduring legacy of the early republic and the influence exerted on it by the Posivitists is the flag of Brazil, which is emblazoned with "Ordem e Progresso" (Order and Progress), the motto that symbolizes the heart of the Positivist philosophy.

Marshal Floriano Peixoto, who had been Vice President under Marshal Deodoro, served out the term of the first presidency. He was made of sterner stuff than his predecessor and was able to make visible progress in consolidating the regime, despite a civil war unleashed by naval officers who questioned his right to remain in the presidency. He ruthlessly kept in check other rebellious military and civilian elements, although he could not quell them altogether. It remained for his successor to bring the conflict to an end.

The Old Republic (1894-1930)

With the inauguration of Prudente de Morais of São Paulo, who assumed office November 15, 1894, as the first civilian president, the guiding principles of the 1891 Constitution became effective. This Constitution of the Republic was strongly influenced by the U. S. Constitution. The federal government consisted of the legislative, executive, and judiciary branches. Church and State were separated, civil marriages and freedom of worship were recognized. The provinces of the unitary monarchy became states of the federal republic and were given broad internal autonomy. They exercised full police powers, established customs barriers, and even made treaties, thus strengthening the tendency toward regionalism.

Meanwhile the political euphoria created among republican members of the upper class by establishment of the republic was transferred to the economic area, causing one of the wildest periods of speculation and inflation in Brazilian history. The period 1891-1893, called the *encilhamento*, saw paper values of corporation stocks increase five times. Railway lines expanded, telegraph service was extended to new areas. Easy credit—often granted merely for the asking by states which were now authorized to issue paper currency—made possible the establishment of large numbers of new banks and factories. When the bubble burst, the fall was as deep as the inflation had been high. Both new and old enterprises failed, and thousands of Brazilians who had been drawn into speculative ventures were ruined financially. Not until Manuel Ferraz de Campos Sales was elected president in 1898 were stern measures inaugurated to deflate the economy and bring expenditures into line with national receipts. Brazil's credit then rose rapidly in world markets. At this time the pattern was set for the next thirty years of oligarchic government based on the premise that Brazil's fortune rested on agriculture (on coffee in particular) and that governmental assistance should therefore be directed exclusively to plantation owners and to those engaged in related commerce. Virtually no encouragement was given to industry. The federal system, in this respect no different from the Empire, lent itself ideally to preserving the social system that gave all privileges to the economically strong.

Under the new order the national parties of the empire period began to disappear and were replaced by state parties and other groups controlled by local bosses. These, called *coroneis* (colonels), followed the orders of the landed aristocracy rather than those of the government. Thus, it was inevitable that the richest and most powerful states, São Paulo and Minas Gerais, dominated the economic and political life of the nation. The governments of the weaker states in the north remained content with a political autonomy under which the rural aristocracy preserved its feudal privileges while the economy and social conditions remained static or deteriorated. Political party activity degenerated from an institutional function to an opportunistic instrument serving only local elite interests. Although the military had gone back to the barracks not long after Marshal Floriano Peixoto left office, the question of militarism in government did not die. It was a principal issue of the 1910 presidential campaign in which the official candidate, Marshal Hermes da Fonseca, backed by the Rio Grande *caudilho,* Pinheiro Machado won over Rui Barbosa, one of Brazil's great jurists and constitutionalists. Ruy Barbosa, for the first time, took a presidential campaign directly to the people, and although he inspired considerable enthusiasm, he was unable to break down the system which had never failed to elect the official candidate.

By the time World War I broke out in 1914, the nation could show some material progress. Annual foreign trade had increased to more than $600 million, railroad mileage had more than doubled since the end of the empire period when 6,000 miles were in operation, and some industry had developed and survived. The population had grown from fourteen million to twenty-four million. The middle class had increased as state and national governments became more effective and commerce expanded. On the debit side was the failure to provide adequate educational opportunities (some 80 percent of the population was illiterate) and the failure to stimulate or to expand the electorate beyond its natural growth.

World War I brought many changes. At first, both imports and exports dropped. Soon, however, exports began to increase, and new industries were started to replace the loss of imports from traditional markets. As manufacturing grew more important it seemed that it might overcome governmental resistance to industry. Most of the new industries failed when peace came, however, as they were unable to compete with foreign sources and the government refused to protect them. The war broadened the nation's outlook on the world significantly. Brazil did not join the Allies until October 1917, but it was the only Latin American nation to take part in the Peace Conference and to have a seat on the Council of the League of Nations. After the flush of allied victory had faded away, serious dissatisfaction with the established order began to appear. Friction developed between civilian politicians and the military. The civilians feared a rising praetorianism, and the military believed that it was being unjustly maligned by political leaders. Among the military malcontents was a small but influential group of intellectuals who believed that the Positivist ideals of order and progress had been corrupted under the loose federal government and that Brazil was neither orderly nor progressing. A naval rebellion broke out in Rio de Janeiro in 1922, and more serious military uprisings in São Paulo and Rio Grande do Sul threatened the government. More representative of the underlying discontent were several quixotic protests in what came to be called the *tenentista* movement. Younger officers, mostly lieutenants (*tenentes*), revolted at Fort Copacabana in Rio de Janeiro and would not surrender, preferring to march to their death at the hands of government troops. Captain Luiz Carlos Prestes, one of the army's most brilliant officers, led a column of nearly a thousand men across the Brazilian backlands for more than two years in an attempt to ignite a popular uprising. He failed, but his exploits became legendary. The 1922 military uprisings did not overthrow the government, but they complicated its work and led many Brazilians to question the established order.

The Old Republic was able to withstand a postwar depression and numerous other troubles of the early twenties, because prosperity returned to the nation during the administration of Washington Luiz Pereira de Sousa (1926-1930). But in 1929, when the great world depression struck Brazil, coffee prices fell to an historic low in world markets; and since coffee represented 70 percent of exports, the entire economy suffered severe dislocations in which unemployment and discontent among workers ran high. Brazil was ripe for the persuasive arguments of leaders who had decided that the Old Republic had outlived its day.

The immediate cause of the 1930 revolution was an attempt by President Washington Luiz to install a Paulista as his successor when the Governor of Minas Gerais had every reason to believe that the office would go to him. Rio Grande do Sul joined Minas Gerais in opposition to the President and forced him to resign. Getúlio Vargas, a defeated presidential candidate from Rio Grande do Sul, was installed as head of new provisional government.

Modern Brazil

Modern Brazilian history begins with Vargas, who led Brazil for fifteen years as dictator (1930-1945) and for nearly four years as constitutional president (1951-1954). He was strongly influenced by Positivism, which guided his efforts to change the political, social, and economic order. Government was centralized, industrialization was stimulated, and coffee growers and other landowners (though not harmed economically) were shorn of political power by making the state governments responsive to the government in Rio de Janeiro. In the beginning at least Vargas was not particularly interested in changing the social order, but changes came as an unavoidable result of his policies. As industrialization moved ahead rural workers began to flock to the city, and soon social legislation had to be enacted to improve their living conditions. Vargas eventually decided that he needed support from the urban lower class to give his dictatorial government legitimacy. Only then did he move in earnest to improve the situation of the workers. During this period middle-class political power was minor, since Vargas had blocked reestablishment of a reformed liberal democracy. As the government expanded its activities, however, and as commercialization and industrialization created new opportunities for upward mobility, the middle class grew and prospered. Many of the middle class who could not find employment elsewhere were given jobs in the expanding bureaucracy, their loyalty to Vargas thereby assured. After quelling a large-scale revolution in São Paulo, in 1932, through which the Paulistas sought a return to liberal democracy and a larger voice in national affairs, Vargas instituted a constitutional government. Congress elected him president that same year, under terms that allowed him to keep power in his own hands. He did not find this solution satisfactory, and in 1937 engineered a *coup d'etat* installing his *Estado Novo* (New Society) with an authoritarian constitution resembling those of the regimes of Italy and Portugal.

World War II, in which Brazil fought on the side of the Allies with an expeditionary force in Italy, made the *Estado Novo* an anarchronism in a world in which Fascist forces in Europe had gone down to defeat. Vargas was forced to resign after a military coup in October 1945, and democratic procedures were reinstated and institutionalized in the Constitution of 1946. Meanwhile Marshal Eurico Dutra had been elected to the presidency. For all its lackluster, the short administration of Dutra was a welcome pause after a long period of effervescent change.

In 1950 Vargas was again elected president, this time by a large majority in a popular election. But postwar Brazil proved difficult for him to mange. He had grown older and had lost a number of exceptionally able assistants. He was honest himself, but corruption became common throughout the government. Changing social and economic patterns brought discontent at almost every level, and factors beyond his control stalled economic development, which had begun to depend more and more on assistance from other countries, particularly the United States. In 1954, the military again forced Vargas to resign; this time he committed suicide. Vice President João Café Filho finished out the term.

By midcentury Brazil was greatly changed from the depressed agricultural nation of 1930. Industrialization was moving ahead rapidly. Illiteracy had decreased from 80 to 50 percent; the electorate had expanded with women's suffrage and votes of new literates. The total population was nearly 60 million; the urban segment was overtaking the rural. Urban laborers had been organized into trade unions which were controlled by the government but which nevertheless made the government responsive to their material and political needs. Vargas had established two political parties. One, the *Partido Social Democrático* (PSD), the Social Democratic Party, first represented the interests of the rural elite and later the industrialists; and the other, the *Partido Trabalhista Brasileiro* (PTB), or Brazilian Labor Party, represented the interests of the working man. Other populist parties appealing to the urban masses sprang up. The *União Democrática Nacional (UDN)*, the National Democratic Union, became the party of the liberal constitutionalists of the upper and middle classes intransigently opposed to Vargas.

Under the PSD and PTB banners, Juscelino Kubitschek won the October 1955 presidential election by a narrow margin. The military was deeply split over events that had transpired before and after the Vargas suicide, and an important group within the army which had led the anti-Vargas forces sought to keep Kubitschek from assuming office, but a preventive military coup in November assured the succession. Promising "50 years progress in 5," Kubitschek did more to advance the industrialization of Brazil than any previous chief of state, especially in the areas of road building, power production, and capital-goods industries. He used nationalism as a basis for engaging the participation of the masses in the economic development of the country, and for the first time under a non-paternalistic government proved that they were as capable as any other people in mastering the techniques of modern industry. They built Brasilia, the ultramodern new capital in the wilderness, in four years. It was inaugurated in April 1960 and became the symbol of national pride and greatness.

The accomplishments of the Kubitschek Administration were costly, principally because they increased inflation and neglected areas of the economy other than those directly related to industrialization. Dissatisfaction with rising living costs as well as charges of corruption in the government contributed to the victory in October 1960 of the opposition candidate, Jânio Quadros. Quadros was a charismatic populist who, as mayor of the city of São Paulo and later governor of the state, pursued conservative policies. A broad sector of the population, 48 percent voted for him over three other candidates, had placed their hopes for a better Brazil in him. While President his domestic policies continued to be conservative, but his unpredictability and neutralist foreign policy aroused important opposition. He was unable to govern Brazil in the personal style he had found effective in lesser positions, and he resigned dramatically in August after only seven months in office in the expectation that he would be returned to office with dictatorial powers. His plans failed.

Quadros was succeeded by João Goulart, political heir of Getúlio Vargas, who had been Vice President in both the Kubitschek and Quadros administrations. He did not take office until September 1961, because of resistance from the military ministers who distrusted his leftist inclinations. Public opinion did not support the position of the military ministers, and congress worked out a compromise whereby a parliamentary system was installed. The President was given considerably less power than he had under the presidential system, and to the detriment of both political stability and the economy, Goulart fought more than a year to regain full powers. A plebescite in January 1963 restored the presidential system by a massive vote, but the promised political peace still did not come. The economy had all but lost its forward movement; inflation was running at a rate higher than 100 percent; development had come to a virtual standstill. The country was in turmoil. Radical, demagogic politicians had taken the plebescite as a mandate for their extremist views, and they began to call openly for changes in the social and political order. Growing dissension within the noncommissioned ranks of the armed forces led great numbers of Brazilians to fear that the nation would fall to the Communists or that Goulart intended to establish a syndicalist state similar to the Peron regime in Argentina. Few protests were heard when a civilian-military revolution ousted Goulart on March 31, 1964.

The governors and military leaders chose General Humberto Castello Branco to replace Goulart. He was elected President on April 15 by congress. President Castello Branco ruled under the terms of Institutional Act Number One, which gave him wide powers to suspend personal liberties and to speed legislation. This was the first time in the twentieth century that the military had formally taken political control of the country. Interventions in the past had been brief and were always followed by return of government to civilians. The new military revolutionary regime based its philosophy of government on the old Positivist motto "Order and Progress," but it was now called "National Security and Development." Its declared goals were to destroy the vestiges of "corruption and subversion" of previous regimes, to achieve economic stabilization, to hasten economic development, and to put into effect social and economic reforms intended to expedite the modernization process. Under strong pressure from the armed forces Castello Branco suspended constitutional guarantees in October 1965, and decreed Institutional Act Number Two. This Act empowered the President to deprive "subversive and corrupt" Brazilians of their political rights for ten years, to cancel mandates at will, and to intervene in the states with virtually equal facility. The Act also changed the political party structure from a thirteen-party to a two-party system. Castello Branco, a studious career soldier, apparently intended originally to turn over the government to a civilian at the end of a two-year term, but he stretched his administration to three years. By the time he left office an authoritarian regime had been established and had been institutionalized in a new constitution, the Constitution of 1967, which was approved, under duress, by congress. Most of the administration's goals had been reached, but under circumstances which made Castello Branco one of Brazil's most cordially disliked Presidents.

President Arthur da Costa e Silva, who had been elected by the congress and assumed office on March 15, 1967, promised to humanize the government. General relief at the change in administration and the President's willingness to listen to disaffected elements brought him wide support during his first year in office. Students, coffee growers, and industrialists particularly had suffered under Castello Branco. Some concessions were made to Labor, whose real wages had declined during the previous administration. Inflation was held to a manageable 25 percent and economic conditions improved. The political front, however, soon crumbled. The President's inability to control leftist and rightist extremists led to a confrontation between the armed forces and the congress which ended in December 1968 with the decree of the severely restrictive Institutional Act Number Five. Once again the government suspended constitutional guarantees and assumed exceptional powers to repress opposition. No time limit was set on the exercise of the exceptional powers, and Congress was recessed indefinitely. More than six months passed before Costa e Silva indicated that he intended to give the country a new constitution and to reopen congress. He failed to do so because on August 27, 1969, he suffered a cerebral hemorrhage and on August 31, a military junta formed by the three military ministers took charge of the government, ignoring the constitutional provision that the Vice President was next in line.

General Emílio Garrastazú Médici assumed office as President on October 30, 1969. He had been selected by a poll of all officers of general rank in the three branches of the armed forces and subsequently elected by the congress, which was reconvened for the purpose. A new constitution (actually the Constitution of 1967 with fifty-eight substantive changes that together were called an "Amendment to the Constitution of 1967") had been promulgated on October 17, and it became effective the day the new President took office. It gave the executive branch considerably more power, at the expense of the legislative branch and the state governments. It curtailed already severely restricted civil liberties even more, but it did contain several political reforms, including an improved party system and a provision for popular primary elections.

By the end of 1972 the new government seemed firmly in control, but many of the people were restless. The government had been under ceaseless attack by urban terrorists, but by using ruthless methods, seemed to have stopped them. Brazil was under an undeclared press censorship. Charges of torture of political prisoners appeared in the world press. The Catholic Church, whose demands for social reform and justice had become an embarrassment to the government, concurred in such charges. Though political stability was a distant goal, self-sustained economic growth seemed finally to have been achieved. The spectacular growth rates of 9.3 percent in 1968, 9 percent in 1969, 9.5 percent in 1970, and 11.3 percent in 1971, made possible by Castello Branco's unpopular measures, were among the highest in the world. After two years in office the new President, though known to be a militant anti-populist, had gained a certain degree of popularity, chiefly through the economic boom and his national integration program that promised social benefits for workers as well as to open up the Amazon region. In August 1972, just short of 150 years of independence, the population had reached 100 million.

The People and Society

Events of the past were produced by the land and the people, and the environment that together they created. In a country as large and as self-contained as Brazil, outside influence is relatively minor. To penetrate beyond the bare facts and try to understand the why as well as the what of history, one must know the people and the society they have constructed. Quoting from the French sociologist Roger Bastide in *Brazil: Land of Contrasts:* "All the notions [the sociologist] learned in Europe or North America are of no value here. The old is mixed with the new. Historical epochs are tangled together." Rigid concepts have no place; it is necessary to formulate "a kind of fluid notion capable of describing phenomena of fusion, of ebullience, of inter-penetration, notions formed in keeping with a live reality in perpetual transformation. The sociologist who wants to understand Brazil not infrequently needs to turn himself into a poet."

Like the United States, Brazil is a nation of voluntary immigrants.[7] In a population of 100 million, only about 75,000 are identifiable as pure-blooded Indians, descendants of those that Pedro Cabral found in 1500. Those who did not mix with the whites were driven farther and farther into the interior. Many were massacred. Their fate was not unlike that of the Indians in the United States. By the end of the sixteenth century, Portuguese numbered approximately 30,000 and Negro slaves nearly as many. In the following century, the whites increased to about 100,000, but because of heavy slave imports the blacks increased to almost double that number. White immigration had slowed down because economic opportunity for the Portuguese themselves was restricted by the already established sugar aristocracy and because Portugal discouraged foreigners.

The first mass immigration from Europe, the largest sustained trans-Atlantic migration the world had yet seen, began in the eighteenth century, following the discovery of gold. Increased economic activity and efforts of the Crown to populate Rio Grande do Sul brought still more immigrants, raising the estimated total white population to 500,-000 by 1800. Nineteenth-century immigration was encouraged largely to meet serious labor shortages. Even after the slave trade was pro-hibited early in the century, Negro slaves were smuggled in in ever increasing numbers. Efforts to attract white laborers had little success until slavery was abolished in 1888. By 1900 the population had in-creased to eighteen million, five times as large as it had been in 1800.

Portuguese immigration predominated until the last two decades of the nineteenth century. During that short period, more than a million Italians entered Brazil, as compared to little more than 100,000 Portuguese. Most of the Italians went to São Paulo, first to the coffee *fazendas* and then to the city; and many went to Rio Grande do Sul. Third in numerical importance were Spaniards, who kept largely to the southern part of the country. Nearly 200,000 Germans arrived between

1884 and 1963. They too, preferred the cooler southern areas where they could carry on diversified farming. Many settled in the hinterlands and formed ethnic colonies. More than 100,000 Russians (many of German origin) and Poles (very few of them integrated with other groups) also came during this period. The largest twentieth-century immigration came from Japan. Some began to arrive before World War I; more than 100,000 came between 1924 and 1933. A quarter of a million had arrived by 1953 and, unlike the Italians and Spaniards, few returned to Japan or migrated elsewhere. First concentrated largely in São Paulo, the Japanese moved on to western Paraná and eastern Mato Grosso. During their first fifty years, they maintained a self-sustained, closed society; but as economic opportunity expanded, they became very successful at commercial farming. Immigration as a source of manpower has become negligible in recent years. Since 1934, fewer than 50,000 immigrants a year, on the average, have entered the country.

Brazilian statistics on racial composition are not readily available and in any event should be used with caution, since less attention is attached to color in Brazil than in the United States. Thus, when 65 percent of the population in 1960 was counted as white, the meaning was that these persons were so accepted despite the light mulatto coloring of many.[8] Most Brazilian families have some Negro blood, the exception being those of recent immigrants. In 1960, 24 percent of the population was *pardo* (brown), which may mean white-Indian or white-Negro; 10 percent was Negro; and 7 percent yellow.

Because some of the slave traffic was illegal, accurate statistics on the total number of Negro slaves brought to Brazil do not exist. Estimates vary between three-and-a-half million and eighteen million, probably a figure nearer the former. They came from Portuguese Guinea, the Gold Coast (then called Costa de Mina), Angola, the Congo, and Mozambique. Many were Moslems with a relatively high culture, some with mechanical aptitudes and experience greater than their masters. Many from Angola first worked in agriculture but were later taken to the highlands to work in the mines, where their mechanical knowledge was put to use. Some who had worked in the diamond fields of the Gold Coast were used as prospectors for precious stones in Brazil.

The great majority of blacks in Brazil today remain in the lower strata of society, only a few are making their way up the social scale. According to the 1959 census, 11 percent of the population was black, 60 percent were employees, 0.97 percent were employers, and 24.5 percent worked for their own account.[9] These data do not indicate how many employees worked for the very small number of employers nor how important was the work done by the 24.5 percent who were self-employed. More indicative of the relative socio-economic status of the blacks is the fact that, according to the same census, only 448 of the 157,874 students who had completed university education were black, 0.28 percent of the total. 3,568 mulattos had university education. Later statistics would probably show an improved situation for blacks since higher education was available to some 500,000 in 1972, whereas in 1950 it was available to no more than a tenth that number.

The population explosion (2.8 percent annual growth rate in 1970) has created many new problems in a society in transformation. The increase in population derives more from a lowered death rate (10 to 12 per thousand estimated for 1960-1965) than from a higher birth rate, which has remained more or less steady at an estimated 41 to 43 live births per thousand. The forty to sixty-four age group increased from 13.9 percent of the population in 1960 to 17.2 percent in 1968.

These figures must be accepted with caution; complete and accurate data simply do not exist but there is no question that health programs have lowered the death rate.

Many concerned Brazilians believe that the population explosion is seriously retarding economic and social development because of the demand on resources by relatively unproductive parts of the population. Any statement of such concern runs into considerable resistance among a people who have long been taught that the nation's march to greatness is dependent on producing more citizens, or rather more hands to work the empty land. They believe that more people are needed to settle the virtually empty West and the Amazon valley and to man the increasing number of factories. This belief is particularly strong in the military establishment and also conforms to religious doctrine.[10] Despite the undeniable drag on development of a high population growth rate, a rapidly increasing population brings some benefits as well as serious problems to a sparsely settled developing nation. To oversimplify, Brazil, with about ten persons per square kilometer, needs more hands to build the nation, but it does not need undernourished hands like those in the overpopulated (or under-developed) Northeast. If economic growth rates like those since 1968 can be maintained the problem of an abnormally high population growth rate will be of less importance.

Large-scale interregional migration, which within the last thirty years has changed the face of Brazil from an overwhelmingly rural nation to one with a majority of urban dwellers, is stimulated by a variety of factors. For one thing, the adventurous spirit of the *bandeirantes* lives on. For another, natural disasters, such as droughts in the Northeast, periodically force large numbers of people to begin a new life elsewhere. More important are the new opportunities in industrial and commercial development in the cities and the fact that improved communications speed news of such opportunities to stagnant rural areas. Improved transportation makes it easier for people to travel to centers that may provide new sources of income, resulting in a vast migration to the cities. Most of this migration is carried out in stages. A family may move from a rural area to a nearby or even far distant small town, then to a small city, and finally to an area in or near one of the great metropolises. The 1940 census indicated that 8.5 percent of all Brazilians lived outside their native states; by 1950 the proportion had risen to 10.3 percent; and by 1960 to 18.2 percent.

Interregional migration has not yet perceptibly changed the strongly regional character of Brazil and most Brazilians, although the long-term influence must be significant. The people of one region are recognizably different from those of another by their attitudes, accents and dis-tinctive cultures. The persistent regional patterns are based on clearly differentiated geographic regions, which accounts for the early de-scription of Brazil as "many countries in one." This history of each region from the time of the autonomous captaincies onward has left its distinctive mark. The Northeast, whose early history was one of colonial wealth and rebellion against central authority, is still a patriarchal stronghold. Radical dissent is just below the surface, but now it comes from elements at the bottom of the social scale. Bahia, seat of the colonial capital, is notably moderate and is famed for its statesmen and orators. With his inimitable sense of humor, the Bahiano says *"Bahiano burro nasce morto"* (all stupid Bahians are stillborn). Known as the Scotsman of Brazil, the Mineiro of Minas Gerais is con-servative and industrious, and practices politics as the art of the posible. The quip that as between *Mater et Magistra* and *Das Kapital* the Mineiro prefers to read the *Diario Oficial,* Brazil's official gazette, reflects a strong dose of pragmatic realism. São Paulo has been called a separate, developed country. In moments of exuberent pride, the Paulistas call their state the locomotive that has to pull twenty-one empty cars—the other states. The frontier culture of Rio Grande do Sul is strongly influenced by its Spanish-American neighbors and its German and Italian immigrants. A separatist history of undisciplined *caudilhos* (military chieftains) makes Rio Grande do Sul reminiscent of Texas in United States history. These and many other examples of marked regional differences emphasize the great variety of attitudes in the large and diverse but generally unified nation that is Brazil.

Class relationships and basic cultural patterns have changed surprisingly little since the Empire's fall in 1889. Perhaps the most pessimistic diagnosis of the social condition is that advanced by the anthropologist Anthony Leeds, who observes that the division between "classes" and "masses" can be called "internal colonization" because it resembles most closely the relations between a colonizing nation and the people of the land colonized.[11] He believes this to be a condition in all those American countries, including the United States, where large native populations were conquered and where large slave populations were introduced in a social position equivalent to that of the conquered populations. He insists that in these circumstances the total societal system, in which the masses are the foundation and source of the internal economy of the classes, is much more resistant to change than are colonies, which provide an economy complementary to that of the mother country. He also contends that the modernizing process is complicated because the classes and masses, though occupying the same territory, cannot physically separate and then form an independent interrelationship. A far more optimistic view of the social condition in Brazil, one that is shared by most Brazilians, is the somewhat idealized hypothesis of Gilberto Freyre, who believes that a tolerant way of life with bland relations between races will prevail and will have a unifying influence on the nation.

In either hypothesis, the social structure is based on an elite and a lower class molded in a patriarchal form. The concept has its roots in the early days of the nation, when society was predominantly rural and the rural worker was either a slave or was otherwise entirely dependent on the *patrão* (broadly translated as rural employer and protector) for his well-being. The situation was not very different from that of the other Latin American countries, and historians generally agree that the Portuguese treated their workers relatively well. The patriarchal system was an acceptable way of life since it was better attuned to the monarchical than to the republican form of government in the Spanish-American countries. In any event it produced a tolerant way of life in a land which, although not producing prodigious wealth, was bountiful enough and benign enough to make starvation a rarity. Except in the drought-prone Northeast arid zone, nature has always been kind to Brazilians, making feeding and housing easy. In no other country of Latin American was there such a stabilizing environment.

Through the end of the nineteenth century and for several decades of the twentieth, the rural-based society remained a two-caste system based on the early Empire relationship between the white European master and his Indian or Negro slave. In some ways it was not unlike the English class system, and it also had many similarities to the life of the antebellum South of the United States. The upper class consisted of landowners, government officials and bureaucrats, members of the professions, and merchants. The lower class was made up of manual laborers and artisans. Abolition of slavery did not substantially change the relationship between the *patrão* and the rural worker, but the recent advent of a corporation type of agricultural enterprise has done so.

However the two-caste system may be judged by political and social standards of the United States, it had an important function in forming a stable society during the decades when violence was the rule in the rest of Latin America. It has been noted that in Japan and England attitudes of deference as well as obedience and loyalty to superiors and to the centralized government "seem to have helped ease the process of transition" from a traditional to a modern society.[12] The transitional process has by no means terminated in Brazil, and relationships between the upper and lower classes similar to those noted in England and Japan serve a similar function even today, despite the appearance of a large middle class and a large urban lower class.

II: The Brazilian Character and Culture

Some characteristics of Brazilians are commonly found throughout the country but many are local or regional in nature. In general, those that influence political behavior reflect the transitional state between a static, agrarian society and a modern, industrialized society. In addition, varying degrees of development in different regions make for differences in behavior and attitudes. One aspect of these differences can be seen in the still strongly entrenched family and class privileges of the older society as against the standards of merit and contractual relations of modern society found in the large urban centers. How slowly tradition and character change is evident from the persistence of both in juxtaposition even in the developed areas.

General Characteristics

Most of the Western Hemisphere's ideals and values derive from Western European culture, but important variations have developed. Culture and values of the United States are different from those of Great Britain; the Latin American countries have evolved distinctively from the Iberian pattern. Brazil resembles Portugal less and less. Nevertheless, for the vast majority of Brazilians values continue to be Portuguese, despite substantial contributions from the Negro and Indian elements of the population.

The family has been called the basic integrative institution of Brazilian society. Not only personal relationships but organizational behavior as well can be traced to values related to the family.

The family pattern in Brazil derives from the Portuguese model, but it has developed in a markedly distinct manner because of different social, economic, and more importantly, environmental factors. During the colonial period especially, when society was organized around plantations whose workers were slaves, the core of the social order was the large *parentela* (patriarchal extended family) headed by the owner and made up of innumerable persons who were related by blood or marriage. The unskilled, menial labor was performed by Negro or Indian slaves

who were part of the plantation property. Many of the employees or re-
tainers, even the slaves, sometimes enjoyed a relationship not unlike
kinship with the family. The most important of these ties was the
compadresco (godparent) relationship, which is far closer than the
godparent relationship in the United States. In addition, offspring of
male members of the family with slave mistresses, a common union in
colonial times, were sometimes recognized and taken into the family.
All formed part of this closely knit and complex plantation society dominated by the owner who was not unlike a feudal lord, particularly when
the plantation was so isolated as to be a world of its own. The custom
of male dominance came from Portugal, but the absolutism that characterized male supremacy in Brazil, with its virtual power of life and
death over the dependents of the plantation, was an outgrowth of
colonial rural life.

With economic progress and the emancipation of the slaves, the basis
for autonomous plantation life disappeared. Nevertheless, ideals of
family solidarity and behavior continue to be patterned after those of
colonial times, and the modern family is but a modification of the
colonial type. Ascriptive values, those derived from one's social status
at birth, predominate to an important degree. The status and role
of the individual in the total society is established by his family connections. Thus, businessmen will be expected to hire one of their own kin
for a place of trust even if he lacks ability rather than a qualified non-
kin. This also applies among members of the urban lower class, who
still rely more on kinship relationships than institutional representatives
to satisfy aspirations or solve problems. Today the model Brazilian
family consists of a large extended household that maintains close links
with numerous secondary kinsmen. The wealthier the family the larger
the extended household is likely to be. Its size decreases as the socio-
economic status descends, and the family of the lowest class in urban
areas is usually limited to husband, wife, and children.

Family loyalties are very much at the base of politics, particularly
at the *município* (roughly county) level where opposing families, concerned primarily with family interests, represent rival parties. In such
instances votes can be predetermined simply by counting the number of
relatives and others associated by bonds of loosely defined kinship.
Once in office, elected officials are expected to find positions for relatives
in need. No opprobium goes with this behavior; failure to be helpful to

relatives would instead generate criticism, since obligations to the family are held to be more important than those to the community.

Ever since the Empire, religious tolerance has been a mark of Brazilian society. Church and State were separated in the early days of the Old Republic. Brazil is the largest Catholic country in the world, but it also harbors the largest concentration of Spiritualists in the world, and São Paulo is the world capital of the Pentacostal sect. Protestant sects continue to grow rapidly in Brazil, whereas in other Latin American countries Roman Catholicism is largely exclusive. Some Brazilian Protestants hold high public office. (The Church as an institution is discussed in Chapter V.)

Not without reason, Brazil claims to be the greatest racial democracy in the world. The claim is largely true, but this does not mean that discrimination is nonexistent, despite Gilberto Freye's somewhat idealized concept of a tropical world where racial differences have little or no meaning and racial relations are bland. Brazilians contend they have no racial problem, despite the fact that great disparities exist between white and colored people. The problem, they hold, is economic rather than racial, and whatever discrimination exists is because of differences in wealth and position, not race.

It is true, as many Brazilians and foreign observers have pointed out, that "men of color" occupied high positions in and out of government during the Empire, serving in the senate, the chamber of deputies, and the council of state. One was the famed mulatto intellectual and engineer, André Rebouças. Negroes and mulattoes, sons of slaves, have risen to prominent positions as lawyers, physicians, and professors. All legal restrictions on the advancement of Negroes disappeared in 1888; but, as the sociologist Florestan Fernandes has pointed out, the Negro and the mulatto formed that "part of the population which had the least favorable departure point" in the stratification process that followed the disintegration of the slave-oriented social order of the Empire.[1]

Having started at the bottom of the social order when declared free, former slaves have not been notably successful in improving their position. Virtually no blacks are to be found in the upper levels of society today. Many who are accepted as whites throughout all levels of Brazilian society would be classed as Negro or mulatto in the more race-conscious U. S. The number of blacks and mulattos able to afford secondary and higher education is lamentably small in proportion to spread, the present white-Portuguese ideal may be replaced by the "new world in the tropics" ideal, and white Brazilians may find themselves in rigorous competition with blacks and mulattoes for the higher rewards of society.

An aversion to violence at the institutional level is one of the Brazilian characteristics not shared with other countries of the hemisphere. The qualification is important because Brazilians often are violent in personal relationships whether in "crimes of passion" in the city or family vendettas in the rural areas. The messianic movements of the Northeast backlands, the marauding bandits of the same area less than a generation ago, Jorge Amado's realistic novel, *The Violent Land,* all indicate a capability for personal violence of an extreme order. Nonetheless, the Brazilian preserves the belief that political problems can be solved by reason and through compromise. The aphorism "even in war leave a bridge over which your enemy can retreat" makes sense to the Brazilian. And even if the bridge needs to be gilded to encourage the enemy to retreat, that is preferable to wasting lives or creating hatreds that will come back to plague the victor.

Institutional nonviolence[4] might well result from the tranquil years of the Empire and the respect for law, order, and hierarchy that has become a part of the character. Brazilians seem to have a better sense of proportion than many other people on the importance and place of the political game in the scheme of things. Politicians seldom make personal enemies among their peers. The tolerant and patient Brazilian differs considerably from most other Americans, from both north and south, in his live-and-let-live view of the world. Many writers consider the "national genius for compromise" the key to the country's success in Europeanizing the topics.

Personal values widely shared by Brazilians are gentle manners, suavity in human relations, verbal subtleties in speech, and especially, avoidance of direct confrontations and categorical negatives. Not infrequently an affirmative is read into a reluctance to say "no." The apparent negative does not mean that he is insincere, as foreigners (especially Anglo-Saxons) might think, but rather that this custom forms part of a national code of behavior. Another aspect of the Brazilian character, equally difficult to understand, is *jeito.* To *dar um jeito* is to find a way to influence someone (often by hook or by crook), to go around regular channels rather than through them, or to seek or to give favored treatment. To many Brazilians it is far less interesting and challenging to do many things the prescribed way than to *dar um jeito,* which offers possibilities for a certain amount of adventure and the exercise of extraordinary talent.

Vianna Moog describes a highly negative variation of the "gentleman complex" which he calls *mazombismo.* The "gentleman complex," which makes a man look down on manual labor and enterprise not related to the land, is a universal characteristic. *Mazombismo* has more native roots. The term is derived from the name given in colonial times to Brazilians who, although of Portuguese parentage, were born in Brazil and formed a class to which few wanted to belong. He defines *mazombismo* as "the absence of determination and satisfaction in being Brazilian, the absence of taste for any type of organic activity, the lack of initiative and inventiveness, the lack of belief in the possibility of the moral perfectibility of man, the indifference to anything that does not produce a fortune rapidly and, above all, the absence of a collective ideal, almost total absence from the individual of the sentiment of belonging to the place and the community in which he lives." [5] *Mazombismo* has decreased but has not disappeared as a cultural phenomenon, despite the growth of a robust nationalism. *Mazombismo,* as well as the "gentleman complex" will disappear eventually as sons from the middle and lower classes, more motivated than some of the elite, enter the universities and make them more competitive.

Political Culture

An important characteristic influencing social and political behavior, is the sense of hierarchy inherited from the Portuguese. It is closely related to the *patrão* system of the Brazilian plantations. Its persistence accounts not only for the continued importance of the rural upper class but also in part for keeping political violence to a minimum, despite widespread social injustice. A sense of hierarchy also explains the continued existence of relationships associated with more primitive societies, such as the informal interpersonal relationships that prevail in the midst of modern corporations and managerial systems. Such informal relationships operate even among the increasing number of competent technocrats, many of whom gained prominent positions on a merit basis.

The most important *patrão* system characteristic is the sharp socio-economic distinction between the upper and lower classes combined with their intensely personal interrelationship. In this traditional relationship between the landed gentry and the rural peasantry, the peasant is almost completely dependent upon his employer, the *patrão,* whether landowner or merchant trader. The responsibilities are not unilateral, however, as both have duties and obligations. The peasant must produce for the *patrão.* For his part the *patrão* must not only pay wages to the peasant but also must provide for him a subsistence plot, give him credit between crop seasons, act as intermediary for legal matters or problems with the authorities, make purchases for him when he goes to the city, provide medicines and medical care in time of need, and see that he gets a decent burial when he dies. In short, the peasant finds security and protection in the relationship and in return gives his full loyalty to the *patrão.* Not infrequently a tighter bond resembling kinship is created through a *compadresco* relationship. This entails further obligations for the *patrão,* such as watching over the well-being of the godson even to the extent of giving him some education and later finding him a job.

The influence of the landed aristocracy penetrates much of the fabric of rural society, particularly in the North and Northeast. The eldest son usually inherits the land, the second son may become a merchant, the third a priest, the others local officials, and so on. Thus, an oligarchy of extended patriarchal families control the land, the commerce, and the local bureaucracy. Through the support of their extended families and members of the lower class who are dependent upon them, they send representatives from their own ranks to the state and national legislative bodies, where they work closely with other members of the same class to further their common interests. This pertains less to the South, where landholdings are run by their owners with a minimum of hired help or tenants.

The social pattern among the rural lower class is changing, partly because of changing patterns of land utilization. Absentee landownership, with managers running the enterprises, and corporate exploitation of the land in many places, including the northeast coast, are breaking up the relationship between *patrão* and peasant. In the more developed parts of the country the material lot of the rural worker may have improved under the corporation system, but this has not meant that the worker caught in the change which he does not always understand, finds this preferable to the personal relationship and security represented by the *patrão*. The less fortunate, with little knowledge of modern institutions or ways to seek political attention in their benefit, become the unthinking followers of political demagogues and look to them to advance their claims on society. Throughout the Northeast, particularly, the corporation has made the rural worker's situation generally worse than before, since the company no longer has any responsibility beyond paying the worker a minimum wage when he works.

The *patrão* system, the political socialization base through which many Brazilians early in their lives learn the importance of hierarchy, continues to be a strong cultural and political force. All the speeches on democracy by politicians and other leaders have done little to change the attitude of the lower class. Even in urban areas, where industry and commerce have changed basic life patterns profoundly, hierarchy has been maintained. Members of the middle class who have risen in the social scale adopt aristocratic ideals. Only when members of the lower class move into the middle class does this sense of the primacy of hierarchy begin to lose its place in accepted values.

Although not a peculiarly Brazilian phenomenon, the difference between upper and middle classes on the one hand and the lower class on the other is so deep and time-honored that meaningful relationships on a basis of democratic equality are all but precluded. This often means gross discrimination against members of the lower class, even by the public authorities. A member of the lower class in need of assistance from the authorities is not likely to receive help, despite his legal right to it, and he is not overly surprised when turned away.

In the bureaucracy, hierarchy remains of paramount importance. The principle also extends into other areas of political life, notably the armed forces and the Catholic Church. High-ranking military men consider it as of the highest value, to be preserved at all costs, though younger officers chafe under conservative attitudes of the general corps. President Goulart's encouragement of politically oriented associations of noncommissioned officers, frowned on by the commissioned officers, was one of the causes of his ouster in 1964. The Catholic Church has long held the hierarchial principle inviolate, but in recent years the Church has began to suffer erosive influences from within.

BRAZILIAN CHARACTER AND POLITICAL CULTURE

Personalism, reliance on personal qualities rather than p.... community organization, is a characteristic common to most of Latin America. It has important influences on politics in Brazil.

In general, personalism has tended to subordinate community efforts, and cooperative action has had little or no place in its culture. Although the pattern is changing among dwellers in *favelas* (urban slums) and among modernizing farmers, it is valid to say that personalism continues to obstruct social cooperation and accounts for over-dependence on the paternalistic state. In the political field, personalism means that less reliance is placed on institutions of the state than on a man for solving problems. This would indicate ineffectiveness in these institutions but equally relevant is the fact that on a more personal level it means that Brazilians give attention to the uniqueness of each individual—what they constantly refer to as his "spiritual" characteristics. Underlying most responses to political situations is the belief that direct personal communication is by far the most effective form of interaction.

Carrying this somewhat further, it means that ideologies, parties, and even issues are often significant only in terms of the persons associated with them. Politicians may and often do switch parties without significant effect on their political base. It has been said that the politician, so far as his constitutency is concerned, does not represent his supporters but rather that he embodies or personifies them.

A strong president has always been a Brazilian political idea. The powerful chief executive of modern Brazil is a direct outgrowth of the paternalistic, oligarchic, and hierarchic society and the long period under a monarchic form of government. The 1891 Constitution established a loose federal system, making state governors themselves depositaries of great power, and gave the president more power than the chief executive of the United States. His power was undisputed at the national level, his principal problems in its exercise arose in dealing with regional power that frequently was stronger than national. Vargas brought the state authorities under his control by using the exceptional powers he assumed after the revolution of 1930, and maintained through the dictatorship from 1937 to 1945. More than any other Brazilian president he approximated the father-figure role that Emperor Pedro II established in the nineteenth century. The 1946 Constitution returned some of the powers to the states, but the presidency remained one of the strongest among modern governments of the world.

This pattern has been strong enough to inhibit the development of an effective legislature. The congress has almost never taken the initiative in dealing with large technical problems, nor has it contributed importantly to national economic policy. Decisions in these areas have been left to the initiative of the executive.[6] Most politicians are content to deal with the individual political problems of their constitutents and have seldom been able to restrain the executive on larger issues, except by the negative route of blocking legislation. The failure of the political system effectively to satisfy national aspirations has contributed to a general disillusionment with the political process.

The voter seems less interested in how much power may have been given to his presidents, or how it was given, than he is in how effectively they exercise it. This seems evident from the early popularity of President Costa e Silva, despite the enormous powers he was given under the undemocratically promulgated Constitution of 1967. Seventy-six percent of respondents in a reliable poll thought he was trying to conduct a good government, though only 32 percent thought the accomplishments of the administration were good, and 45 percent thought them no more than acceptable.

The importance of the "formula," a compromise which can solve apparently insoluble situations, has been a special mark of the way of political life since the days of the Empire. As indicated above, the Brazilian in political life is highly pragmatic — a strong believer in the art of the possible. Ideas and ideologies have played only minor roles in the larger national decisions. Empiricism, improvisation, and above all, conciliation represent a basic conservativism of the society. That the elites by and large have been conservative but not reactionary, in contrast to the reactionary upper classes in other Latin American countries, has been an important factor in preserving unity.

Inequities between individuals and between regions, which are extreme in some parts of Brazil, produce only minor tensions. The capacity of the people to accept what some would call intolerable hardships and injustices in urban as well as rural areas has often seemed incredible to foreign observers. Part of the explanation is the paternalistic character of the ruling class, whose members have always seemed sensitive to genuine demands and often ready to concede them even before pressures reached dangerous points.

Political conciliation and compromise in Brazil is largely a process of working out differences between dominant groups in the polity rather than between dominant and subordinate groups. In the process, however, and apart from it as well, gradual concessions are made to modernizing the social structure, which means bringing benefits to the people.

Political Socialization

As economic and social changes take place, Brazilians broaden their participation in politics, in which interest was always widespread. Elections in rural areas were a time for protracted competition ending often in festivities, sometimes in violence as family political loyalties were called to the test. In urban areas political party and electoral activity brought forth a great show of civic industry, however slow it was to change the body politic to a more representative one. Before 1930, participants came from among the rival factions and the small urban upper and middle classes, many of whom made up the various elites or oligarchs with special interests. The political process was of highest importance to them since their way of life depended on it. Brazilians of the middle and upper classes have thus always been highly competitive in politics. Industralization has changed the earlier political patterns less than might be expected, because cultural patterns have been slow to change. Nevertheless, the urban industrial elite has become a more powerful force because its collaboration is necessary if the present modernization effort is to succeed. The shift in population toward the cities has forced presidents to be more responsive to popular demands because of the growing vote of the urban lower and middle class. And even though the lag in urban representation continues, at each election more and more representatives of the urban areas win office, including some who follow or lead the radical groups, which are made up principally of middle-class intellectuals and skilled labor.

Political participation through the vote has changed not only qualitatively but also quantitatively. Since an estimated 80 to 85 percent of Braziilans were illiterate in 1930, it is not difficult to conclude that few persons were interested in making direct contributions to the political process. The population in 1930 was near 35 million, but only 1,890,524 votes were cast in the presidential election. By 1945, when the population was about 45 million, almost 6 million votes were cast. This increase reflected a number of factors, among them more liberal electoral laws aimed at expanding the electorate including the franchise for women, growing literacy, and a growing middle class spawned by economic development with increasing interest in political participation. The percentage increase of voters to total population is impressive: from 6 percent in 1930 to 13 percent at the end of the Vargas dictatorship in 1945, to more than 15 percent in 1960. It had been even higher (just under 20 percent) in the 1958 congressional elections.[7] Turnout varied sharply according to interest in the election, from 83 percent in 1945 to 60 percent in 1955.

These data reflect real change in political participation, but they must be accepted with some reservation as to the degree of meaningful participation. The vote is mandatory, relatively few voters can be called "participants"—that is, citizens politically interested to the degree of having knowledge of and concern for factors and institutions related to policy formation. Most simply vote for an individual for reasons usually unrelated to the issues. Political scientists call them political "traditionalists." A large number are what political scientists call "subject"—those who show political interest largely in terms of its personal effects.[8] The difficulty in raising the number of participants has been discussed by Robert Scott, principally with respect to Mexico. Some of his findings are valid for Brazil and other Latin American countries. His hypotheses are based on parallel attitudinal polls taken in the United States, Great Britain, Germany, Italy, and Mexico.[9] The data show that successive governments with democratic objectives in Mexico have failed to build a modern political structure. The transition from the political "traditional" to "subject" appears to be a simple process, largely one of formal schooling and face-to-face contacts. The step from "subject" to "participant" is apparently far more difficult. Thus from 1910 to 1960, the percentage of "traditionalists" was reduced from 90 percent to 25 percent, but "participants" in that period increased only from 1 percent to 10 percent.

Unfortunately, data similar to that for Mexico are not available for Brazil. There are, however, data from attitudinal polls which, if not as searching as the Mexican, are useful as indicating trends. Such polls were taken in 1965 in São Paulo, Rio de Janeiro, and Recife.[10] They undoubtedly showed distortion ascribable to the time taken, less than a year after the downfall of the discredited Goulart administration when disenchantment with the political system was widespread and many were willing to give the military-controlled government a free hand. The respondents were largely urban, although an unspecified number of rural inhabitants near the cities were included. Even with these shortcomings, the polls are helpful in analyzing the political culture.

The number of respondents who were "very interested" in politics varied little from one region to the other—about 5 percent expressed themselves as so oriented, except in the *favelas* of Rio de Janeiro, where only 1 percent so claimed. Differences showed up in the "moderately" and "slightly interested" categories, as well as in the "not at all interested." In São Paulo, the most economically and socially developed state, 6 percent were very interested in politics, 19 percent claimed moderate interest, and 8 percent slight interest; 63 percent had no interest. In Rio de Janeiro, usually considered the most politicized city in Brazil, only 5 percent were very interested, 12 percent were moderately interested, 10 percent only slightly interested, and 73 percent of the respondents claimed to be not at all interested in politics. In a finer breakdown of categories, 91 percent of Rio de Janeiro slum respondents expressed no interest whatever in politics. The data for Recife, a city also believed to have a fairly high level of political interest despite a low rate of literacy, were not very different from those of the Rio de Janeiro slums, except that only 4 percent indicated a high interest in political affairs. These data may reflect a reluctance on the part of Recife respondents to admit to interest in politics, since the area was still laboring under repressive measures in the wake of the removal of a radical leftist from the governor's office.

The following table summarizes findings related to social class, occupation, and education:

The poll shows that those low in the social and economic order had little or no political interest. Presumably this was because of a low rate of socialization or because of alienation or political apathy arising from disenchantment with the system and its usefulness in satisfying personal demands or aspirations. The upper socioeconomic groups and the best educated, which in Brazil is to say the same thing, are those with the

Attitudes Toward Politics

	Very interested %	Moderately interested %	Slightly interested %	Not at all interested %
CLASS				
High/Medium high	23	23	16	38
Medium	6	18	11	65
Medium low/low	3	7	6	84
OCCUPATION				
Group 1 (professor, top management, large store owner, etc.)	15	33	13	39
Group 2 (middle management, teacher, journalist, Lt. Col. & Col. in army, etc.)	10	22	14	54
Group 3 (salesman, nurse, typist, small shop owner)	6	10	8	76
(Note: In groups 4 and 5, skilled and unskilled workers, 83 percent showed no interest)				
INSTRUCTION				
Illiterate	1	4	1	94
Primary complete	3	10	7	80
Secondary complete	8	21	13	58
University incomplete	27	27	10	36
University complete	11	47	11	31

Source: Instituto de Estudos Sociaes e Económicos poll, September 1965

most interest in politics. The variation in degree of interest among those in the instruction categories "university incomplete" and "university complete" may reflect a point of view among those who have completed university training, have found satisfactory careers, and see politics as a less pressing problem than those who did not complete their education.

An important question to which Robert Scott did not address himself in his study on Mexico is whether it is possible to establish a modern political structure in an economically underdeveloped society. There are grounds for holding that until a country is industralized and modernized it cannot long sustain a modern political structure, which demands the socialization that only a modern society can impart. Today's typical modern political structure is mass democracy. It is questionable if mass democracy exists elsewhere than in modern industralized societies. Costa Rica would seem to be the only exception in Latin America; it can be called a modern agrarian society if not an industrialized one. The viability of Uruguay's mass democracy is questionable; Chile's polity is still largely bourgeois controlled despite a socialist president. The masses may be politicized to a degree equivalent to "subject" before development, but as the transitional experience in Mexico tends to show, such politization may have little meaning. The Brazilian experience differs from the Mexican. Brazil has a democratic tradition of long standing which even the authoritarian governments since 1964 could not ignore. If this experience has been one of bourgeois rather than mass politics, it at least has given legitimacy to the system. The Vargas dictatorship eventually fell before the insistence of politicians, the press, intellectuals, and eventually, even the military on a return to democratic procedures, despite the dictator's effectiveness in mediating conflicting demands in a modernizing society.

The 1965 poll undoubtedly reflected a serious post-Goulart disillusionment with political practices during the 1961-1964 Quadros-Goulart period, as well as reluctance to admit to political interests during a period of political repression. Even so, admitted interest was lively by the standards of developing nations. That the political system was still far from a mass democracy was obvious from the large number in the lower class who expressed no interest in politics. This group comprises about 75 percent of the population.

The transition from "traditional" to "subject" in political participation in Brazil is likely to take on considerable impetus as a result of increased availability of schooling. Over 13 million children matriculated in primary schools in 1971, whereas only 7 million did in 1959. Enrollment in secondary schools in 1971 increased at an average annual rate of 12 percent from the less than 1.5 million who attended in 1961; and at a rate of 11 percent in higher education courses from the 117,000 who had enrolled in 1960. How many of these better educated citizens will become political participants remains to be seen. The Mexican experience will be useful in observing such developments.

In any event, the hierarchic-paternalistic political system is moving toward a more modern structure. The change is slow, and because of the persistence of some of the important cultural patterns in the political process, it is not likely to antedate industrialization.

Nationalism

The single most powerful force in Brazilian politics today, along with the drive for development, is nationalism. This may be because in a world where nationalism became a strong force in the nineteenth century and moderated as nations passed their identity crises, it was late reaching Brazil. In a diverse, strongly regional nation so large that it is hard for its nationals to visualize as a whole, the development syndrome—the new economic base for nationalism—appeared only after 1930. Before then few outside the army and the Church thought in truly national terms, even though an institutional base had been established as a sort of binding element for separate regions with a high degree of autonomy.

Some politicians and many leftist intellectuals have been so strident in their xenophobic nationalism that the basically strong nationalism of the armed forces and their influence on national developments have often been overlooked. This nationalism is largely confined to matters considered vital to national security, such as limiting the extraction of strategic minerals, reserving to the state the control over petroleum and power resources, and keeping certain industries that are useful in national defense either in government or national hands. The military usually sees foreign policy from a nationalistic point of view.

The nationalism of the politicos, who have found it an important issue in urban areas where populism has taken hold, is of post-1930 vintage.

Vargas was the first strong economic nationalist. In this he was helped not only by statist inclined *tenentes* but also by urban conservatives who were beginning to see their country's potential and the growth of their enterprises as linked to a united, strong, inward-looking polity. His administration was the first effectively to communicate the concept of nationalism to the people. Subsequently, intellectuals formulated the so-called ideology of national development, which was taken to the people in varying forms by politicians in and out of government. It had its greatest impact under Kubitschek, who postulated development based on opening up the great undeveloped interior at a time when industrial expansion was at a peak and brought benefits in one form or another to most of the country. The intellectuals also developed the semimystical concept of the *"tomada de conciencia,"* defined as a human condition related to awareness of the need for achievement of national development. Based principally on internal factors, this concept has become an important element of the political culture.

The extreme leftists and Communists, with a scattering of extreme rightists, have won radical urban votes by using attacks on the United States to keep the nationalist issue alive. Anti-Americanism seemed more important to the radicals than constructive nationalism, but this did not negate the fact that hate or fear can unite a nation as much as can constructive action. The premise has historical support: fear of Spanish-American neighbors played a part in unifying Brazil during the Empire, and even the peace-loving Pedro II believed that the Paraguayan War would serve to strengthen Brazilian nationalism. However, until 1969 at least, radical anti-American nationalism as a tactic had only minor success, because of the general conviction that U.S. assistance is necessary to development. Leftist ultranationalists find it hard to break through the long-held conviction that the interests of the United States and Brazil run parallel. That concept is doubtless changing as recent military-controlled governments adopt more nationalistic postures and policies.

A more strongly based and potentially more far-reaching form of nationalism, because not all of it is irrational, is in the field of foreign affairs. Nationalism—or the national interest—served as the basis for the brusque change in Brazilian policy during the Quadros and Goulart regimes after 1960. At the base of this break with the past, which until then had been characterized by closest ties between Brazil and the United States, was the lagging economic development in Brazil and the reluctance of the United States to assist financially to the extent the Brazilians thought necessary for effective progress. The new Brazilian position was more sophisticated than parochial approaches of the past; it was preoccupied with the growing division between the developed nations of the northern hemisphere and the underdeveloped nations of the southern half of the world. The new nationalism had strong international overtones as Brazil sometimes took upon itself the role of spokesman for the more backward nations, supporting the have-nots. That it was partly international in concept did not lessen the rejection of the outsider in order to stimulate national unity.

This growing concern with Brazil as a nation is gradually overcoming regional and class disparities that tend to be barriers to a stronger sense of unity and nationalism among the masses of the people. Several other factors also serve to decrease the importance of regional and class disparities. The Brazilian is conscious of his national culture and political unity uncomplicated by questions of race, ethnic origin, or religion. He has a profound sense of belonging to one people with a common past, a people with problems which transcend the regional, and he believes in a common bright future when his country will have achieved the status of a modern, powerful nation with a high standard of living. Because social mobility is real, if limited, even members of the lowest class in urban centers believe that their participation, or perhaps their children's participation, in that bright future is possible.

Although the social structure is distorted and many general and political-cultural traits are anachronistic, until the 1964 revolution the Brazilian polity functioned extraordinarily well, due allowance being made for time and place. Obviously, injustice to the lower class, as defined in present-day terms, was general, but the time and values were different and were acceptable. By standards of the time, Brazil was a successful and relatively stable democracy. A number of factors kept popular discontent to a minimum. Principal among them was the *patrão* system which helped not only to preserve the hierarchic principle and to discourage questioning the social system but also maintained loyalties which served a similar purpose. For those who were ambitious the system was sufficiently open to make room for a man with intelligence and initiative. This meant that many lived on hope for better days as the nation began perceptibly to grow and produce new factories and roads.

Before 1950 barefooted workers were common on São Paulo streets. Today it would be difficult to find one. By midcentury every Brazilian could believe that he lived in a great nation that would one day give education and a living wage to all its citizens. Despite the repressive treatment meted out to the political and intellectual elites by a succession of military governments since 1964, the lower and middle classes have not lost hope in their future.

The political instability under Goulart, just before 1964, and the insistence of the revolutionary governments since then on changing the characters on the political scene, has unquestionably reduced participation by voters and dampened interest in a formerly lively electorate. But Brazilians in the more advanced states have always been interested in politics, and it is not speculating too much to expect a return to days when it can be said, as it was in the past, that Brazil is overdeveloped politically.

Many of the important political-cultural traits contribute to maintaining a stable polity. The ideal of nonviolence, conciliation, and compromise, a strong belief in the hierarchic system, and racial and religious tolerance all contribute to easing tensions arising from an interplay among elite groups, as well as between upper and lower classes. How much these traits will delay modernizing changes is not clear. They do make it possible to bring about changes with less disruption than in many other nations throughout the world. Other aspects of the traditional society will have to change. Overdependence on ascriptive values of family and class privileges to the detriment of more universal standards of merit must change. The erosion of the paternalistic system is a gradual change that should hasten a salutary decline in personalism, which would influence the voter in giving more weight to issues than to charisma. Finally, progress itself and national achievement, by removing frustrations and a nagging sense of inferiority, will make exalted nationalism and xenophobia increasingly irrelevant. Issues can then more easily be decided on their merit than by unreasoning emotion.

III: The Framework of Government

Political structures and institutions the world over almost never are identical with political functions. In most countries the legislature has become less and less a lawmaker and more a clearing house for mediating conflicting interests. It is called on to bestow legitimacy on laws and rules already made effective by executive agencies. In many modern societies the executive branch has tended to assume the role of innovator and source of laws and rules. The judiciary, through its review power, has also become a principle lawmaker or, in some cases, an abrogator of laws by legal interpretation. Brazil is no exception.

Other anomalies are not hard to find. It has long been held that constitutions of Latin American nations may be nearer poetic ideals than effective charters establishing restraints on political action. Although one of their considerable virtues has been the maintenance of democratic ideals, many were modeled on systems unsuited to the particular political culture and stage of political development. In the case of Brazil, political activity has varied relatively little from constitutional norms. A great deal of the country's strength and unity derives from its long-established and stable institutions and from the basic cultural pattern of respect for the law and legal institutions, which has been passed down from the time of the Empire. As the country has developed, the structure has become more differentiated to meet newer and more complex problems of government, reflecting a basically pragmatic and increasingly achievement-oriented society. This and similar statements must, of course, he qualified to take into account numerous aberrations arising from the 1964 revolution.

Constitutions

The powers of the various branches of government as well as the prerogatives enjoyed by institutions at the various levels of government are set in broad outline in the national constitution. Each state has its own constitution which must not conflict with the national charter. Brazil is today ruled by the 1967 Constitution as amended by a military junta in 1969. It has had only four other constitutions. The Empire Constitution promulgated in 1824—two years after independence— was in effect until the Empire fell in 1889. Two years later the Constitution of the Old Republic was promulgated. This second constitution was the law of the land until the 1930 revolution annulled it. The 1891 Constitution was replaced in 1934 by a third constitution, but this charter lasted only until Vargas proclaimed the dictatorship in 1937 at the same time offering a constitution intended to institutionalize the new order. The 1937 document did not become operative. Only after Vargas was removed from office did a liberal democracy return under the Constitution of 1946. The 1946 Constitution, the country's fourth, guided the political life of the nation until the revolution of 1964 and was replaced in 1967 by the constitution now in effect.

The Constitution of the Empire set patterns of government which had much in common with the English parliamentary system. The constitutions of the Republic drew heavily on the Constitution of the United States and later on those of European social democratic orientation which outlined civil and economic rights in great detail. But whatever the inspiration for the various charters, the constitutional issues have remained constant. Above all has been the issue of unitary versus federal systems of government; most other important issues derived from the question of how far the central government should encroach on powers traditionally exercised at the regional and local levels. A separate but related issue, because the powers of the national executive are involved, is that of the balance of power between the executive and the legislative branches. The taxing power has also been a contentious issue.

The Constituent Assembly called by Emperor Pedro I shortly after independence drew heavily on the British and French constitutional models to write the new Brazilian charter. As drawn up, this constitution gave the provinces some autonomy. Pedro I rejected it and ordered a revised constitution which left him with considerably more power. An important amendment to the 1824 Constitution, made during the Regency after Pedro I had been forced to abdicate, was added in 1834. It granted limited legislative powers to the provincial assemblies, but under Pedro II these were revoked and the central government was again strengthened.

The 1824 Constitution established a unitary state. The provinces and municipalities were administrative subdivisions under the direct control of the central government. A council of state was established but was purely advisory, except during the period of the Regency. Nevertheless, individuals were granted a broad range of rights, including religious liberty. Many of these rights were carried over in subsequent constitutions. One of the unique provisions of the 1824 Constitution was a fourth moderative power, which gave the Emperor authority to conserve "the independence and harmony of the other political powers." Under it he had the authority to choose the senators, call and recess the legislature and dissolve it at his will, and designate and dismiss cabinets and cabinet ministers. Most historians credit Pedro II with using this fourth power to represent the interests of the lower classes, very few of whose members participated in the political process.

The Constitution of the Republic, promulgated in 1891, had the Constitution of the United States as its principal model. It provided for a presidential system with clear separation of the three powers and with checks and balances among them. It provided for individual rights and liberties, most of which had been in the Constitution of 1824. They could be suspended (they were often ignored in the back country) during a state of siege declared by the congress, or during its recess, by the president. Church and State were separated and religious liberty was guaranteed. The legislature was established as a bicameral body. The judiciary was made independent and was assigned power of review over legislative and executive acts. Members of the federal supreme court were appointed by the president with senate approval.

Perhaps the most radical change, besides the transition from monarchy to republic, was that from a unitary to a federal system. The powers of the federal government were broad, but all rights not specifically given to the federal government or denied to the states were left to the latter. Extreme decentralization resulted, with the states assuming the power to levy duties against each other, maintain virtual armies, and in other ways to act as independent political entities. This federalization gave rise to the system called the *"política dos governadores"* (politics of the governors) under which the president, working and making deals with the governors, controlled the elections. Members of congress were beholden to the governors and represented not the national interest but the interests of the states—

that is, the interests of the families who had installed the governors, and through them, the people. As the power of the president to intervene formally in state affairs could only rarely be used, the governors were only weakly controlled by him.[1] The president was selected in congressional caucuses with the president himself exercising a strong voice in the final choice of his successor. Despite the changes to a republican constitution, legislators and government officials came largely from the same families and social classes that had staffed the bureaucracy of the monarchy, and the power of the rural *fazendeiros* (plantation owners) increased rather than decreased after 1891.

Another, perhaps fatal weakness of the Constitution of 1891, and of the Constitution of 1946 to a lesser degree, was the incongruity between them and the social and political reality. The principle of separation and balance of powers embodied in both predicates wide participation, without which such constitutions become dead letters. At the time of the fall of the Empire, participation in the sense of influencing political decisions, was limited to a handful of political activists; and even by 1930 when the population was 35 million, less than 2 million voted. It speaks for the non-violent nature of the Brazilian system of conciliation and compromise that these constitutions lasted as long as they did.

The Old Republic held together under its first charter until the Vargas revolution of 1930. Vargas ruled without a constitution until pressure, particularly from São Paulo, led him to promulgate a new constitution in 1934. In many respects this Constitution of 1934 was liberal, but it also reflected the influence of the corporate system prevailing in Portugal and Italy at the time, including functional representation. Individual rights were fortified by progressive social and economic provisions that served as models for future charters. Other provisions increased the power of the presidency at the expense of the states.

The 1934 Constitution was in effect for little more than three years. It was abrogated when Vargas assumed dictatorial powers in 1937 and decreed a new constitution which gave greater social and economic responsibilities to the central government. The principle of functional representation was retained. The document was intended to give some legal basis to the Vargas revolution, but the plebiscite which was to approve or disapprove it was never held. Vargas ruled largely by decree.

The second republic came into being with the liberal democratic Constitution of 1946. Both lasted for twenty years and effectively expired together. Only six amendments were made between 1946 and 1964, and only three of these were of some importance. Two involved the parliamentary system under which Goulart was allowed to assume the presidency in 1960; the third had to do with the tax system. Pressures for change had built up so strongly that fifteen amendments were passed in little more than two years after the 1964 revolution, most of them of major importance.

In an effort to institutionalize the 1964 revolution, Castello Branco imposed a new charter which gave the executive new powers to control the country's political and economic life. Not only did he hope to rationalize the numerous amendments and other acts of congress hastily passed but also to legitimize expiring extra-legal acts decreed after the revolution and without which the powers of the executive branch would have been greatly diminished. Congress made changes in the draft, but none that would subsequently lessen the executive's powers was permitted. The government had enough votes and party discipline was strong enough to prevent passage of any but government-approved changes, which were limited largely to those dealing with individual liberties. Of the three branches of government, that least affected by the Constitution of 1967 was the judicial. However, the courts were prohibited from reviewing acts of the 1964 revolution.[2]

The principle of leaving to the states those powers not reserved for the federal government remained, but its importance was decreased by lengthier enumeration of rights of the central government and by imposing numerous restrictions on state actions. Thus, the tax system, formerly controlled by the union and the states, was placed almost entirely under central government control.

Despite congressional approval of the 1967 Constitution, serious doubt persists as to its legality. By any standard the Constitution was approved under duress. It gave many new powers to the executive but it was still inadequate to meet a crisis engendered by a confrontation between congress and the military establishment over the immunities of a deputy who had attacked the armed forces.

Institutional Act No. Five of December 13, 1968, unilaterally decreed by President Costa e Silva, arrogated to himself the power *inter alia* to recess congress and to suspend the constitution and its guarantees for an unlimited period. He exercised those powers the same day, and until October of the following year, Brazil was governed by an executive with unrestrained powers. President Costa e Silva became incapacitated in August 1968 and was succeeded by a military junta made up of the Ministers of Navy, Army, and Military Aviation who simply ignored the Vice President's right to the succession.

On October 17, 1969, this military junta promulgated an amendment to the Constitution which provided for fifty-eight changes. The junta assumed authority to do so without reference to any other body and justified such procedure on the consideration that "the recess of the National Congress having been decreed, . . . the Federal Executive Power is empowered under Institutional Act No. Five to legislate upon all matters," and, on the assumption that "the elaboration of constitutional amendments is a part of the legislative process," declared the unchanged articles still to be in effect and the "modifying and suppressive amendments . . . [to be] . . . now adopted." The amended Constitution came into force on October 30, on the day General Garrastazú Médici, the newly selected President, assumed office from the military junta. It extended the powers of the executive to an unprecedented degree.

The 1967 Constitution as amended in 1969, grants the president powers to suspend *habeas corpus* proceedings, deprive any Brazilian of his political rights for ten years on grounds of "corruption or subversion," and to decree the forced retirement of judges, civil servants, and university professors, among others, for similar reasons. No defense or appeal procedures are provided for. These powers stem from Institutional Act No. Five which is retained as a transitory constitutional provision whose duration remains unspecified. Moreover, the powers of congress were further restricted by various provisions such as those depriving its members of immunity from "crimes against honor or those set forth in the National Security Law;" making them subject to loss of mandate if their conduct threatens "existing institutions" or if they practice "acts of party infidelity." Ordinarily, only the president may now call special sessions of congress, and such sessions are restricted to consideration of the subjects for which they were convened. Congress is prohibited from publishing pronouncements of its members which constitute "war propaganda, subversion of the political and social order . . . or . . . crimes against honor." The powers of the National Security Council, usually controlled by its military members, were increased.

The amended Constitution establishes that governors will be indirectly elected in 1970 but thereafter elected directly. Subsequently, indirect elections were extended to 1974. Powers of the states are further reduced: legislative assemblies in the states are no longer empowered to propose constitutional amendments. An additional cause for federal intervention in the states is "to put an end to corruption of public power." Additional causes for intervention in municipalities are established.[3]

Not all the changes can be termed regressive or repressive. Several are long-delayed reforms which could establish a basis for a more democratic process once the present authoritarian character of the government is modified. For example, the requirement for the establishment of political parties is reduced, making a limited multiparty system. Article 39 provides for calculating the number of deputies on the basis of voters rather than inhabitants. This is an important reform which can eventually give more political power to states with a high rate of literacy (suffrage is restricted to literates), reducing the power of politicians from backward states which have been strongholds of the rural aristocracy. Another reform is a new formula for setting the number of deputies to be elected. The minimum for each state is reduced from 7 to 3 and the total number from 409 to 280.

The constitutional crisis which has shaken Brazil since 1964 has as its base the fact that increasing responsibility has fallen on the executive to direct the modernization process. The growing influence of the urban commercial leaders and industrialists, served by corps of technocrats whose opinions more and more influence national decisions, made inevitable shifts in political power. The new needs had to be formalized in law, and the most effective way to change the balance of power was through the constitution. The relationship between executive and legislative powers was crucial to the problem since the executive was forced to think in national terms while the legislature continued to represent regional interests, the most powerful of which were still dominated by the rural oligarchies. The old constitutional system had its strengths not the least of which was that the legislature was often a bar against presidential abuse. It was particularly effective under Quadros and Goulart. On the other hand congress exercised its decision-making role sometimes constructively, sometimes negatively. The negative side of the coin was most patent when urban-oriented presidents unsuccessfully sought modernizing legislation from a still rural-controlled congress. The contrast was highlighted during the first nine months of the Castello Branco administration when congress worked under time limitations for debate imposed by the executive. It enacted more than 150 laws proposed by the executive in that period. Many were revolutionary in their modernizing scope and in the past could never have passed congress so expeditiously. In addition, congress approved in quick order important international agreements that had rested for years without action in committees. The legitimacy of procedures followed to adopt and change the constitution since 1964 is another aspect of the constitutional crisis. The 1969 Amendment is so authoritative and usurps so many of the powers traditionally granted to the states and the legislative branch, it is unlikely to survive the reestablishment of democratic procedures. Many of the powers usurped by the central government will remain, but a more democratic constitution will come eventually.

The Presidency

Qualifications for the president and the vice president—that they be native born, thirty-five years of age, and currently exercising their political rights—remain the same in the 1967 Constitution as in earlier ones. The principal change came in the manner of elections: from direct to indirect. To avoid having a president and a vice president from different parties, the amendment to the 1946 Constitution requiring that the vice president be elected automatically on the same slate as the president was incorporated into the new charter.

Under the 1967 Constitution the president is to be elected for five years by an electoral college comprised of members of the federal chamber of deputies and the senate and delegates appointed by the legislative assemblies of the several states. Voting is to be public and nominal. States are represented by three members of the legislature and additional ones for each 500,000 voters, no state to have less than four delegates. Election is by absolute majority of votes, failing which after two ballots, a simple majority suffices. The president cannot succeed himself in office.

In the event of a presidential impediment or vacancy of the office, the presidency is assumed by the vice president, who otherwise has few formal responsibilities beyond serving as president of the national congress (when it meets in joint session). If the vice presidency becomes vacant the order of succession is first the president of the chamber of deputies and next is the president of the senate or the president of the supreme court, who hold office pending the calling of a new election within thirty days.

The president has executive, administrative, legislative, and even quasijudicial powers in relation to pardons and commutation of sentences. He is commander-in-chief of the armed forces. His other principal powers are to decree a state of siege, to intervene in the state governments under conditions prescribed in the constitution, and to make a wide range of appointments. The last gives him control of important patronage.

The balance among the three powers shifted perceptibly in favor of the presidency under the 1967 Constitution, but the not inconsiderable checks on the abuse of the power of the president remained more or less intact. Thus, he cannot succeed himself, nor can a relative to the third (formerly second) degree. He is subject to impeachment by a vote of two-thirds of the members of the chamber of deputies; he is also subject to trial by the supreme court for common crimes, and by the senate, for crimes against the constitution.

Other checks of a less formal nature are important. Although the president has been granted the exclusive power to introduce money bills and the congress is prohibited from increasing them, the latter must approve the bills and can reduce them. The president still requires the support of congress for legislation which he cannot decree, and most decrees must be approved subsequently by the congress. The senate must approve key appointments. In addition to the power to try the president for common crimes under certain circumstances, the supreme court can declare his decrees and actions unconstitutional. Thus, the key to his legal powers is control of the majority party.

As recent history would indicate, perhaps the strongest restraint on the president is exercised by the armed forces. The president is legally commander-in-chief, but in fact his relationship with what can be called the ultimate power of the military depends on many factors of a variable nature. This is particularly true in light of the fact that as a matter of principle the Brazilian armed forces hold loyalty to the constitution to be higher than that to any particular administration.

Not to be discounted are the restraints placed on the president by the democratic traditions that have been the ideal of the people since the time of the Empire. Even Vargas found it necessary to establish the appearance of a constitutional base for his government.

Under the 1967 Constitution as amended, the ability of the president effectively to use all the powers conferred on him still depends on his personality and his political and leadership abilities, as well as his ability to administer an increasingly complex and often unwieldy structure that is subject to countless pressures of varied interests. The Brazilian looks to him to be a strong president who makes the principal national decisions and initates new programs of government. He enjoys extraordinary freedom from most pressure groups because the influence of most such groups is limited by their dependence on the government in one form or another.

Presidents since 1964 have followed constitutional precepts so long as the body politic responds as desired. When the military feared loss of control it changed the constitution or interpreted exceptional behavior as within constitutional bounds. Restraints on the presidency from 1964 through 1972 were largely ineffective.

The president's immediate staff is made up of members of the civil and military households. The heads of both households are considered to be of cabinet rank. The civil household is headed usually by the principal political adviser and executive assistant who bears the title Chief of the Civil Household. Assistant chiefs head sections charged with specific functions such as liaison with congress, government departments, and the judiciary. The office is that of political coordinator, not only at the national level but also at the state and municipal levels. It has its own press chief as well as a protocol officer, usually on loan from the Foreign Office. The responsibilities of the chief of the civil household vary from one administration to another and can be enlarged or reduced according to the willingness of the president to delegate his own powers. It is patently a key position, and the success or failure of presidents can sometimes be laid to the ability of the man who is chief of the civil household.

The chief of the military household also holds a key position, though normally of less importance than his civilian counterpart. He advises the president on military matters, attends to his physical security, and provides liaison with the military services. With the increasing importance given to national security by the 1967 Constitution and supporting legislation, the importance of the position of chief of the military household has increased accordingly. This trend was reflected in legislation increasing his responsibilities as the secretary-general of the National Security Council.

The cabinet is composed of seventeen ministers of state who head the executive departments, plus the chiefs of the civil and military households and the director of the National Information Service (NIS, more or less a counterpart of the CIA in the United States), which has public-relations responsibilities in addition to those of gathering information. As of 1969 the active ministries were: Justice, Navy, Army, Foreign Affairs, Finance, Agriculture, Education and Culture, Labor and Social Welfare, Air (military but with civilian responsibilities), Health, Industry and Commerce, Mines and Energy, Planning, Interior, Transportation, and finally, Communications. An additional ministry for Science and Technology had yet to be organized five years after it was established in 1967.

Ministers for the armed forces since the downfall of the Empire have been almost exclusively military officers. The creation of a Ministry of Defense, to be headed by a civilian over three military chiefs with cabinet rank for the three services, has been discussed, and first steps toward establishing such a ministry were taken under the Administrative Reform Decree-law 200 of February 1967.

Ministers of state are appointed by and are responsible to the president, but they can be required to appear before and to give information to congress. They must countersign Acts of the president and may be tried by the congress if accused of unconstitutional behavior.

The 1946 Constitution listed the National Security Council (NSC) in the section under armed forces. The 1967 Constitution devotes a section to national security under the chapter on Executive Power. The former left the responsibilities of the NSC to ordinary legislation; the newer document as amended is specific as to its powers and responsibilities. The NSC "establishes the permanent national objectives and bases for national policy." It designates areas and municipalities considered vital or important to national security.[4] The Constitution provides for prior approval by the NSC on matters related to a) land concessions, opening of highways, and installation of means of communication; b) construction of international roads, bridges, and airfields; and c) establishment or exploitation of industries related to national security. The NSC authorizes the presence of foreign labor organizations and the affiliation of national unions therewith. Membership of the National Security Council is made up of the president, the vice president, the ministers of state, and the chiefs-of-staff of the armed forces. Provision is made for additional members through subsequent legislation.

In addition to the executive departments of government headed by ministers of state, Brazilians are served by a multitude of agencies which form part of the complex administrative apparatus. Decree-law 200 of February 25, 1967, was a slowly hatched, much compromised but yet sweeping reform measure designed to rationalize a system which had often grown without plan, generated from pressures of one form or another. Some thirty different bodies came under the direct authority of the president before the reform; they have been reduced to eleven. About forty additional agencies were coordinated through the presidency. Among them were the *Departamento Administrativo de Pessoal Civil* (DAPC) — the administrative department of the civil service, which not only administered the civil service but also exercised budgetary control over it; the National Atomic Energy Commission; the Tariff Commission; the General Staff of the Armed Forces, slated eventually to become a Ministry of Defense; the *Superintendencia do Desenvolvimento do Nordeste (SUDENE);* an agency to aid development in the backward Northeast and the *Superintendencia do Desenvolvimento do Amazon* (SUDAM), a similar newer agency for the Amazon.

A more varied group of agencies came under indirect authority. Included were such commercial and industrial enterprises as the mixed-capital (very little private) Volta Redonda Steel Mill; PETROBRAS, the petroleum monopoly; the Brazilian Coffee Institute, a government corporation; the mixed-capital Cia. Vale do Rio Doce, an enterprise which mines and exports iron ore; the similarly organized Bank of Brazil whose credit facilities in the agricultural field, for example, made it more important in many respects than the Ministry of Agriculture.

Others like the Getúlio Vargas Foundation carried on economic, political, and other research as well as the training of officials at all levels to improve administration. Decree-law 200 places these semiautonomous enterprises under the general supervision of appropriate agencies.

Overlapping of functions and responsibilities often make coordination of administrative policy difficult. Ministries sometimes work at cross purposes (a not uncommon phenomenon in most governments), but the principal problems arise from the many free-wheeling autonomous and semiautonomous agencies which are difficult to coordinate whether by the presidency or the responsible ministry. Some, like PETROBRAS, which has a strongly nationalistic history, gain a political independence that makes them virtually untouchable. Immediately after 1960, when the new capital was established but was still not prepared to function, the existence of two capitals added greatly to the difficulties of coordinating and maintaining efficient government.

The Brazilian suffers many of the universal abuses of bureaucracy, but some checks have been devised to keep them under control. Thus, the government is liable for injury caused by any of its employees to third parties. Budgets, contracts, and certain actions of government agencies are subject to approval by the slow-moving but competent Tribunal of Accounts.

The civil service, which makes up a good part of the bureaucracy, has a long and, by Latin American and also by broader standards, not undistinguished tradition of service to the country. Employees have protection as outlined in the constitution. They acquire tenure after two years employment if they were hired on the basis of competitive examination. Once tenure is acquired they can be removed only for cause based on judicial sentence or administrative process in which they have been granted adequate defense. If jobs are abolished the incumbent must be retained on the rolls at full salary until another comparable job is found. This is the provision which has complicated administrative reforms of both past and present. The problem was met temporarily by Costa e Silva in Institutional Act No. 5 which suspended civil service rights.

The administrative reform of 1967 did a great deal to establish clearer lines of authority. Its principal effect after two years was to rationalize the government structure and to give authority to the minister of planning to reform the civil service and to improve government administration in general. Some progress was being made with the help of the authority accorded in Institutional Act No. 5.

Legislative Branch

The Brazilian congress is bicameral: the senate is made up of three senators from each state, the chamber of deputies has proportional representation. Members must be Brazilian born, in possession of their political rights, and over twenty-one years of age for the chamber and thirty-five for the senate. Legislative sessions are from March 31 to November 30. The internal administration of each house is established by its membership, but business is conducted by a steering committee made up of officers elected annually by each of the bodies who work with the majority and minority leaders for that purpose.

Legislation can be initiated by individual members or committees of the congress or by the president. As noted before, the areas of public finances, creation of new positions, setting the strength of the armed forces, and the administration of the Federal District and territories are responsibilities of the president; the 1969 amendments broaden this power to include legislation affecting civil servants' status and granting amnesty affecting political crimes. The congress must meet in joint session to consider presidential vetoes, which can be of the entire bill or specific items. Two-thirds vote of the membership present is necessary to override a veto. This right was freely exercised before 1964 but has been used infrequently since. Both houses must approve treaties.

Deputies are elected by popular vote and with proportional representation. The chamber of deputies elected in November 1966 for four years was composed of 409 representatives of the states and territories. Under the 1969 Amendment of the 1967 Constitution the number is reduced to 280, no state to have fewer than three deputies and the territories to have one each. Representation is fixed in proportion to the number of registered voters according to the following criteria: three deputies for the first 100 thousand; one additional for each additional 100 thousand to 3 million; one additional for each 300 thousand to 6 million; and one additional for each 500 thousand over 6 million. Alternates to the deputies are selected from the unsuccessful candidates of each party in the order of number of votes received.

In addition to its legislative functions the chamber of deputies has exclusive power to initiate impeachment proceedings against the president or cabinet ministers and to require a financial accounting from the president if one is not voluntarily submitted within sixty days after the opening of the session.

Each of the twenty-two states is represented by three senators elected for eight-year terms. One-third and two-thirds, alternately, of the senate is renewed every four years. An alternate is elected with each senator. The senate has exclusive power to judge impeachment charges against the president or cabinet ministers, and it has the power to judge supreme court justices and the attorney general of the republic in crimes of responsibility. The senate has the exclusive power to confirm certain presidential appointments such as the attorney general, judges of the tribunal of accounts, and chiefs of permanent diplomatic missions. It also has exclusive power to approve foreign loans made by the states or the Federal District as well as other foreign agreements. It suspends the execution of any law or decree declared unconstitutional by the supreme court.

An informal survey of most of the 1966 Congress made by Carlos Castello Branco, a leading journalist, shed some light on the composition of Brazil's legislature. Of the 409 deputies, 176 were lawyers by profession, 37 were medical doctors, 35 industrialists, 30 large land-owners, 26 businessmen, 21 engineers, 20 military men, 12 civil servants, 7 professors, 7 economists, 6 Catholic priests, 5 journalists, 5 notaries public, 5 radio announcers or reporters, 4 dentists, 3 bankers, 3 contractors, 2 accountants, 2 Protestant pastors, 1 pharmacist, 1 laborer, and 4 undeclared. Among these, a number have banking and farming on a relatively large scale as secondary occupations. Of the senators, 25 were lawyers, 9 industrialists, 7 doctors, 5 businessmen, 3 professors, 2 engineers, 2 from the military, 2 bankers, 2 journalists, 2 economists, 1 civil servant, and 1 large-scale farmer.[5]

The great majority are thus from the middle and upper classes. In fact, 165 deputies and 27 senators declared themselves to be independently wealthy. As for political orientation, 363 deputies and 65 senators declared themselves to be either centrist or conservative; 36 deputies and 1 senator claimed to be leftist. These claims must be accepted with reservations since the political climate discouraged admission of leftist tendencies. The revolutionary government formed in 1964 was successful in removing or preventing the election of most demagogues and far leftists. It was less successful in controlling the use of economic power, in elections, an announced goal of the revolution.

Judicial Branch

The Brazilian judiciary continues to be held in high esteem within and outside the country. Brazil is credited with one of the highest juridical cultures in Latin America. Although no university was established in Brazil during the Empire, law schools existed early in the nineteenth century. The great majority of the country's jurists, statesmen, and political leaders are graduates of law schools, almost all of which today form part of universities.

The legal system is based on continental Roman law, but it includes a number of Anglo-Saxon practices, such as the wide use of *habeas corpus* and the use, in certain cases, of the jury.[6] Statutory rather than case law is applied in the courts, based on detailed legal codes.

According to the Constitution as amended in 1969, the judicial power of the union is exercised by the federal supreme court, the federal courts of appeal and by federal judges, military courts and judges, electoral courts and judges, and labor courts and judges. Judges have life tenure and cannot lose office except as a result of judicial sentence.[7] Laws or other acts, such as decrees, may be declared unconstitutional by the vote of an absolute majority of the court's members.

The supreme court is composed of eleven justices[8] appointed by the president with the approval of the senate from among native born Brazilians thirty-five years of age "of notable juridical learning and of spotless reputation." It has the power, *inter alia,* to try certain high government officials (including the president), to litigate lawsuits in which a foreign state or agency and Brazilian federal or local government entity are involved, and to hear cases between the union and a state, cases involving conflict of jurisdiction between judges or courts, extradition, *habeas corpus* in certain circumstances, and writs of security (*mandados de segurança*) against acts of certain high officials. It hears a variety of appeals from lower courts.

The federal court of appeals, seated in Brasilia, is composed of thirteen judges selected with the same criteria applicable to supreme court justices. Eight are selected from among magistrates and five from among lawyers and members of the public ministry. Provision is made for the creation in subsequent legislation of two additional federal courts of appeal in the states of Pernambuco and São Paulo. Federal courts of appeal have original jurisdiction over appeals in criminal cases, writs of security against acts of a minister of state, of the president of the court or its panels, the federal police chief, or a federal judge; *habeas corpus* in certain instances; and conflicts of jurisdiction between subordinate federal judges. It hears appeals from cases decided federal courts of appeal.

A new departure was the creation in the 1967 Constitution of federal courts in the states, territories, and the Federal District to try a variety of cases involving federal law. This addition to the federal system was an outgrowth of dissatisfaction with the action of state courts in handling cases involving national legislation. Judges are appointed by the president from among Brazilians "over thirty years of age, educated and of good moral character," through examination organized by the federal Courts of Appeal.

The states are empowered to organize their own court systems within the lines set forth in the constitution. Jurisdiction given to the newly created federal courts in the states reduces the formerly important role of the state courts. Each state has an appellate court of justice, and on the local level each municipality has at least one trial court. The Constitution lays down a number of restrictions on membership, e.g., entry into the career magistracy is by competitive examination conducted by the court of justice with the participation of the sectional council of the Order of Lawyers of Brazil, a private association not unlike the Bar Association of the United States; and standards are set for promotion and remuneration. On proposal by the court of justice the states may create or name magistracies without life tenure, temporary justices of the peace, and state military justices.

The supreme court has always been conservative, although some of the justices had close ties to the pro-Vargas forces before their forced retirement in 1969. Most were appointed during the Vargas era and its successor regimes. When President Castello Branco enlarged the supreme court from eleven to sixteen, he gave it better balance. Costa e Silva weighted it heavily in favor of its conservative members. Once the court had acquired a fully conservative character, its membership was reduced to eleven by the October 1969 Amendment. Its constitutional interpretations have generally been broad and it has shown a reluctance to declare legislative or executive action unconstitutional. This extends even to the power of the president to legislate by decree. Occasionally in its history the supreme court has yielded to strong pressures; at other times, as under the Vargas rule, it refused to accede to his demands. Vargas ended by ignoring the court and, of course, there was nothing that it could do to enforce its rulings.

Supplementing the regular court system, military, electoral, and labor courts have been established to deal with cases in those specified fields. The provisions regarding the military courts in the 1967 Constitution have been outlined in greater detail than in the previous charter. Thus it is provided that the superior military court shall be composed of fifteen judges appointed by the president for life, with senate approval. Three are to be selected from navy flag officers, three from general officers of the army, three from among general officers of the air force, and five from among civilians. The superior military court and such lower courts of the same nature as may be established hear cases involving military persons charged with military crimes and also, under certain conditions, civilians charged with crimes involving national security or military institutions, with right of appeal to the federal supreme court. The superior military court is empowered to hear in first instance cases of this nature against state governors and their secretaries of states.

The most important of the special courts are the superior electoral court and the lesser regional electoral courts, involving electoral judges and electoral boards. The electoral courts were created by Vargas with the objective of making elections more honest and meaningful by taking them out of the hands of the politicos. They have administrative as well as judicial functions, including a part in the formation of national parties.

The organs of labor justice are the superior labor court, regional labor courts and boards of conciliation and judgment. The superior labor court is composed of seventeen judges, eleven of whom are magistrates for life. Six are temporary judges representing employers and workers equally. The labor courts were established to give the workers more sympathetic and more knowledgeable treatment.

Completing the judicial system is the public ministry headed by the attorney general (*Procurador Geral*) of the republic who is appointed by the president and approved by the senate but is not a member of the cabinet. The public ministry is made up of career attorneys (*procuradores*) who represent the federal government in cases involving the public interest. The states also have public ministries whose members are required to be selected on a competitive, career basis.

Tribunal of Accounts

Not actually a part of the judiciary and with attributes set forth under the constitutional provisions related to the legislative branch, financial and budgetary control, and reports to the congress, the tribunal of accounts supervises the execution of the federal budget, audits accounts, and approves federal contracts. Justices who are ministers of the tribunal have rank equivalent to that of justices of the federal courts of appeal but are not required to have legal backgrounds.

State Government

Brazil's twenty-two states draw up their own constitutions, but they must conform with the national charter. They have structures closely akin to that of the federal government. Governors are elected by universal suffrage[9] as are members of the unicameral legislative assemblies. The governors have secretaries of state comparable to ministers of state in the federal government, although their number is usually considerably less in poorer states. Each of the states has an independent judicial system, but state courts no longer have jurisdiction over cases involving the federal government, certain labor matters, or foreign countries. The state militarized police are considered auxiliary forces and reserves of the army. All powers not conferred on the federal government or on the municipalities belong to the states.

Municipal Government

In many respects the municipal governments—governments of the *municípios*[10]—parallel the federal and state governments. The 1967 Constitution established that "Municipal autonomy shall be ensured: By direct election of a mayor, vice mayor and city councilors (*vereadores*) held simultaneously throughout the country on a date other than the general elections for governor, the chamber of deputies and the legislative assembly; [and] by self-determination in all matters concerning their particular interest . . . ." However, state governors, with the approval of the legislative assemblies, are to name mayors of state capitals and other cities that are predominantly watering spas. The president of the republic is to approve gubernatorial appointments of mayors of municipalities declared by law to be of importance to national security. Sixty-eight mayors were initially designated under this provision. They include border areas, areas containing important mineral deposits, national industrial establishments like the Volta Redonda Steel Mill, certain military establishments, and others whose inclusion appears to be less reasonable. To rectify past abuses, city councilmen, whose number is limited to twenty-one in any city, are to receive compensation only in cities with a population over 200,000.

The states are empowered to determine the number and size of municipalities, which usually comprise a city or town and its rural surroundings, and this power has been used occasionally for partisan ends. Generally speaking, however, *municípios* are created when population centers grow large enough to warrant independent existence. In 1950 Brazil had 1,894 municipalities; by 1960, 3,000; and in 1966, 4,000. In urban centers and in modern rural areas municipal political processes are usually democratic. In remote parts of the country the old *coronel* system, under which the mayor owes his office to the local political leader, is still operative.

The federal government has found it politic to establish direct relationships with the municipalities rather than through the state governments. Quadros established a national service for municipalities within his civil household and appointed representatives in various parts of the country, thereby undermining the power and authority of the state governors. The Brazilian Association of Municipalities, with headquarters in Brasilia, was founded in 1948 and is an active special interest group both in the congress and in the executive branch. It holds regular national meetings and sends representatives to international conferences.

The *município* is considered the base of Brazilian democracy. Early constitutions reserved to municipalities all privileges, rights, and powers not specifically reserved to the state or federal bodies. In effect this made each state a confederation or—as T. Lynn Smith says in his classic study *Brazil, People and Institutions*—an "agglomeration" of little sovereignties. Like the states, a municipality could tax goods passing through its territory. Federal and state authority was often tenuous or virtually nonexistent. Local authority was controlled and exercised by the dominant family or clan. Control by this family or clan was absolute in many areas, but as indicated earlier, in others it might be contested by two or more rival clans. Perdo II made it a practice to alternate power from one group to another during the empire period, but this type of political education could not be effected under the decentralized Old Republic, nor even during much of the more centralized Vargas period.

Another less obvious feature of the municipality, arising from the existence of rural and urban areas within virtually all of them, is the conflict of interests between groups from the two different areas. The urban seat of the municipality usually wants schooling, policing, social assistance, and public utilities—most of which are of little interest in the agricultural sector. The latter wants access roads, bridges, irrigation, and other aids to rural development. Eventually, throughout much of the country the urban sector came to control politics and the public purse through a preponderance of votes in the municipal chambers.

The Territories and the Federal District

The remaining units of government are the four federal territories (Amapá, Roriama, Rondonia, and the island of Fernando de Noronha), whose governors are appointed by the president with senate approval; and the Federal District, whose mayor is similarly appointed.

Centralism vs. Federalism

As has been noted, a principal issue throughout the history of Brazil has been centralism vs. federalism. The swing to extreme decentralization under the Old Republic brought Brazil to the point of total disintegration. The Vargas revolution of 1930 changed the system by giving the federalist union a greatly increased role in the political process. The trend toward modified decentralization established under the 1946 Constitution was reversed by the 1964 revolution, whose innovations were institutionalized in the 1967 Constitution.

The principal changes in relationship between the federal government and the states under the 1967 Constitution have been outlined above, but beyond the matter of division of powers under the constitution, several aspects of the relationship should be noted. The strong current toward local autonomy or states' rights is based in regionalism and arises from the fact that the states are cohesive entities whose capitals are the cultural, historical and, above all, political centers of the regions. Local elections have always excited more interest than national, and although voting is mandatory in both, voting in state and municipal elections usually is considerably heavier.

The matter of federal intervention, under which the president may depose a state governor and replace him with one of his personal choice, has often been a contentious issue in the country's history. In recent times the bitter struggle between President Goulart and Governor Carlos Lacerda of Guanabara almost reached the stage of intervention but was frustrated by congressional and public opinion—not to mention military opinion. Nonetheless, Goulart could harass the Governor through such means as withholding revenues and failing to approve agreements with the United States Agency for International Development. The subsequent revolutionary government intervened to eject the Governor of Pernambuco and those of other states during its early months. Later it removed the increasingly difficult to manage Adhemar de Barros, Governor of São Paulo, who had been one of the pivotal figures of the revolution. Until this point, interventions after 1946 had been very infrequent. The 1967 Constitution establishes grounds for intervention but maintains some curbs on possible abuses by requiring *ex post facto* approval by Congress.

Perhaps as effective as any of the powers of persuasion granted the federal government over the states and municipalities is the taxing power. The 1946 Constitution assigned large percentages of revenues to the federal government, thus giving the central authority a dominant role in the relationship between nation and states despite the fact that the states together collected as much revenus as did the nation. Most of the total revenue came from a small number of the richer and better administered states. Apart from that collected for its own use, São Paulo in some years contributed 60 percent of the total federal revenues. Both the states and municipalities were empowered to levy and collect a variety of taxes of their own. Under the Constitution of 1967, this power has been narrowed considerably, with the states and Federal District allowed only to tax property transfers and levy a one-time tax on the circulation of goods. They must otherwise depend on revenues collected by the federal government, part of which, or in some cases all of which, are earmarked for the states and municipalities. No formulae are established in the 1967 Constitution for distribution of these revenues, which were to be set through separate legislation. The municipalities are entitled to the taxes levied by the federal government on rural land within their territories, and a part of the income taxes collected by the federal government as well as whatever they may receive from earmarked percentages of other taxes which go to the municipalities. They themselves can tax only urban land and buildings as well as such services as are not included in the tax competence of the central government or of the states, which are defined in a supplementary law. The merchandise circulation tax, which may constitute about a third of municipal revenues and is not subject to federal discretionary distribution (but subject to review of expenditures) has given municipalities a degree of autonomy they did not enjoy before.

As has been suggested, the formal structure of government in Brazil is not identical with political functions, but historically the identity has been close. As the country modernizes, new ways have had to be found to carry out the increasing number of technical and administrative functions of a more centralized government which early in the modernization process took over the operation of railroads, the merchant marine, petroleum production and refining, power production and distribution, and a variety of other industrial enterprises. The traditional bureaucracy was not equipped to handle these functions. A number of specialized, regulatory agencies for industrial, agricultural, and mineral enterprises were therefore established. These agencies were empowered to make decisions affecting the establishment and financing of new and old industries, rules governing their operation and foreign allocations, which amounted to the power of life and death over many of them. New regulatory and administrative functions were thus allotted to new agencies, which exercised their authority outside the formal structure established by law.

Not only is the government in a state of continuing transition as development needs spawn new agencies or new rules to perform new functions, but the revolutionary governments since 1964 seem determined to make basic changes in traditional relationships in their effort to modernize Brazil within a concept of "national security and development." The form which this revolutionary change will ultimately take, has not been defined. Most of the present structure is likely to be retained but with some further shift of power from the states to the central government and from the legislative and perhaps judicial branches to the executive. Political, cultural and practice argue for the continued importance of the municipality as the democratic base of Brazilian politics.

IV: Political Parties and the Electoral Process

To carry the description of political institutions further into the realm of political behavior, it is essential to understand not only the formal aspects of elections but also the role of parties in the political process. The principal function of political parties is to bring some degree of order to the election of representatives who are to carry out the will of the people in the government. Part of this function ideally includes aggregrating the interests of members most effectively for consideration by those who make the laws and regulations. They need to know possible alternatives in formulating policies. Another important role of parties is to bring more citizens into the political process in an orderly way, that is, through political recruitment and socialization.

The record of political parties in Brazil has been spotty. Whereas parties have sometimes served their prescribed roles in the early stages of development, later on many have fallen under the control of an entrenched leadership that becomes less interested in progress than in retaining power and maintaining the *status quo*. The effort of the revolutionary Costa e Silva government to make party organization more democratic by requiring primary elections in 1969 reflected a generalized conviction that the parties, controlled by political oligarchs, had failed to make an adequate contribution to democratic political development.

Political Development

The aphorism that Brazil was as overdeveloped politically as it was underdeveloped conomically is a reflection more of the competitive nature of political activity than of its quality. The political system which came into existence with the 1946 Constitution broke down in 1964 under a strain made too heavy by too many unresolved conflicts. The pro-Vargas/anti-Vargas dichotomy occupied the attention of politicians to the exclusion of constructive activity. Quadros's brand of leadership and Goulart's ineffective leadership, which followed on the heels of the first important break with paternalistic governmnt under Kubitschek, were serious political setbacks. The old paternalism returned and eventually the political process broke down. Inflation increased at a rate that threatened to pauperize the middle class and leave the rest of the economy in chaos; economic stagnation brought all development processes to a halt.

The euphoria engendered by the Kubitschek administration, and the hopes it had raised for increased popular participation and escape from the trap of economic and social underdevelopment, died as Goulart and the radical left tried to cover up economic failure with promises of radical social and political reform. Conciliation, which from its earliest history had brought Brazil through a series of crises and thus had maintained the unity of the nation, was no longer effective as a political instrument. Frank Bonilla wrote in 1961 in a penetrating if harsh study:

"It is hard to deny that the forms of domination elaborated by the groups who have traditionally held power here and in large part continue to do so have been singularly effective in mitigating and controlling violent social conflict. . . . In no other country in Latin America do such staggering inequalities. . . seem so little productive of individual tensions and resentment or of intransigent, regimented, collective strife."

Aware that this could not be ascribed to mass apathy or fatalism, Bonilla went on to observe:

"The disposition to yield among groups at the top, though not extravagant, seems often more than apparent pressures from below would reasonably demand, just as the disposition to accept small concessions among lower groups seems often out of line with the urgency of their need or their apparent power at a given moment. In short, there is an element of civility, a capacity and a disposition to work out disputes peaceably in Brazilian political life that one would hardly expect to find in conjunction with such harsh inequities, the generally low cultural level, the sad record of corrupt and irresponsible government, and the vulnerability and rudimentary organization of political institutions." [1]

The civility and capacity to work out disputes peaceably had disappeared by early 1964 when the military, with the approval of great numbers of civilians, removed Goulart from office. The military controlled government established then still had roots in the old politics, despite the fact that the 1946 system was basically inadequate for development needs. Only extraordinarily capable leadership could have maintained it. The consensus for rapid economic development had become so pervasive as to generate unacceptable political instability when the pace of development slackened. Executive powers under the 1946 Constitution were not strong enough to force the passage of unpopular measures without which development would bog down. Nor could an executive branch whose freedom of movement was restricted by a conservative congress solve other conflicts which arose concomitant with industrialization.

Except that more power had been concentrated in the hands of the executive after 1964, the political system that had its roots in the municipalities and states was still operative in large areas of the country. The locus of power during the Old Republic could almost always be found at the state and municipal level. This was the time when the *"política dos governadores"* prevailed and power rested with the dominant families of the state, represented by the *coronel,* or political chieftain. He gave the system its name, *coronelismo.* Often the system was highly competitive, with rival families engaging in violent conflict, particularly in the backlands. Differences in political parties in remote areas were usually oriented more toward a family than an ideology.

The elite in many other Latin American countries traditionally have been dependent on the military to maintain power. The oligarchs of Brazil, such as the coffee-plantation owners and others, held power during the Old Republic through the use of electoral machines which had real grass roots. The idea that Brazil is overdeveloped politically perhaps owes its origin to this fact. The president was at the top of a pyramid. A unifying factor to a degree, he was nevertheless dependent on the support of the strongest state organizations, those of São Paulo and Minas Gerais. The dominant state party was just below, and at the base was the *coronel* whose family, friends, and dependents made up the oligarchies. The oligarchies have been described as states within states in which all three powers—legislative, executive, and judicial— were concentrated. Municipal governments were headed by a mayor and his minions who were installed by and depended on the owner of the land, the *coronel* who was chief of the clan. In addition to handling municipal business, his job was to make life as difficult as possible for rival clans. The power of some clans was restricted to the municipalities, but others controlled a number of municipalities, and a few families disputed state power and had a direct voice in national affairs.

Obtaining votes in rural areas was, and to a degree still is, a matter of transportation, feeding and clothing, and of giving small favors to assure proper voting on election day. Before 1930, the *coronel* controlled areas having some 70 percent of the of the population. By 1970 such control reached only half this figure, as Brazil had become almost 60 percent urban.

The system which encouraged the *política dos governadores* was largely dismantled after the revolution of 1930, but the power of the rural element in politics was not destroyed. Groups changed and urban areas gained power at the expense of the rural *fazendeiros,* but the rural element of the Social Democratic Party, for example, was strong enough to decide the presidential elections of Dutra in 1945, of Vargas in 1950, and of Kubitschek in 1955. As for the rural voters, many eventually escaped the control of the *coronel,* but at the expense or moving outside the protection of the patriarchal system. Corporate agriculture broke down old patterns in many places and the *coronel* now competes with radical rural labor leaders, often priests who seek to bring to the disinherited better living conditions along with the gospel.

In addition to simply changing the owners of the electoral machines of the Old Republic, Vargas began a process which eventually broke the stronghold of the rural oligarchs over the entire political process. Not only did the central government assume more power but changes in political practices which came with industrialization and urbanization were also responsible. He also recreated national parties. Even today the political parties tend to be controlled by politicians more concerned with regional than national interests. This is not surprising, considering their role in the past, but it has worked to retard national development.

Vargas first organized and assumed control over the urban classes as an element of a corporate state. World War II saw accelerated migration to the urban centers, and this broadened the political base. Urban dwellers obviously could not be controlled by the techniques employed by the *coronel* in rural areas. The new politics of Brazil became urban politics, which grew stronger as the traditional rural brand lost strength and importance. Since this shift of power is basically an urban phenomenon, it crosses regional lines and applies in Recife and Belem as it does in São Paulo and Rio de Janeiro.

The essential difference between urban and rural politics stems from higher literacy rates in urban areas, which means that more votes are cast there in proportion to the total population. Because of the higher rate of literacy, far more developed means of political communication can be employed in urban areas. Greater concentration of voters makes campaigning less expensive and opens the field to populists. On the social and cultural side, as has been observed, family ties are weakened, resulting in a more independent electorate. And since urban areas are less likely than rural areas to become the exclusive political preserve of any political boss, political socialization finds more fertile fields. At the same time, as in most countries throughout the world, concentration of voters breeds demagoguery and opportunistic politics as well as constructive populism. In the Brazilian system, where personalism often carries more weight than party labels, it is possible for the demagogue or charismatic figure to win a large following even without party backing. Politically moderate São Paulo gave Brazil its Adhemar de Barros, who in little more than a decade built a personal following into the fourth largest party in the country. Jânio Quadros, without personal financial resources or genuine party backing, rose from city councilman to president of the republic in twelve years. Until the reversal caused by the 1964 revolution, however, politics had tended to grow more and more populist, and politicians from urban areas could ignore this fact only at the peril of losing office. This trend will accelerate as a consequence of the constitutional amendment of 1969, under which representation is based on the number of votes registered rather than on population.

Elections

With a number of qualifications Brazil's record on elections has been good. An increasing number of the electorate does vote, despite continued high rates of illiteracy which automatically disbar about 30 percent of the population of voting age. Voter registration increased 200 percent in the twenty years before 1966, during which time the population had increased only 83 percent.

All literate registered adults over the age of eighteen have the right and legal duty to vote. Only persons over seventy and invalids are not required to register. All registered voters must vote, except those excused by law because of illness or absence from domicile and those specifically deprived of political rights. Most enlisted men in the armed forces are exempt. In 1964, sergeants and other noncommissioned officers, after acrimonious and sometimes rebellious activity, were given the right to vote and to be elected to office.

The Brazilian electorate has increased far more rapidly than the general population. The first election in modern Brazil, that for president in 1945, when the population stood at 45,215,000, saw 6,200,005 citizens vote out of a registered total of 7,459,849 voters. The turnout was 83 percent, 16 percent of the population registered, and 13.4 percent of the population voted. In the presidential election ten years later, when the population was estimated to be 58,456,000, a total of 9,097,014 of the 15,243,246 registrants voted. Only 59.7 of the voters turned out, but 26.1 percent of the population had registered, and 15.6 percent voted. A decade and a year later when the population was estimated to be 86 million, in the congressional election (the president was indirectly elected) voters totalled 17,285,556, whereas 22,407,959 has registered. 75.8 percent of those registered turned out to vote; 26.05 percent of the population had registered, and 20 percent had voted.

The literacy factor is less important as a bar to expansion of the electorate than might be expected. More important is its distorting effects in the political process. One of ex-War Minister Marshal Henrique Lott's main campaign issues when running for president against Jânio Quadros was the vote for illiterates. In recent times the most consistent proselytizer for a vote for all adults was Goulart. It was a popular issue but Congress was always able to defeat constitutional amendments designed to change the rules.

On the literacy issue, as on many others, the Brazilian genius for accommodation was put to work. Although new proposals to drop the literacy requirement were defeated, election laws and regulations were steadily made less stringent until in 1965 the electoral code required as a proof of literacy only that the potential voter date and sign the application for registration. This was estimated by electoral officials to have qualified 50 percent of those previously disbarred from voting.[2] Adult literacy campaigns past and planned will doubtless make it possible for many of the remaining potential voters to meet the lowered requirements.

For many years to come, however, the Brazilian electorate is likely to be smaller in proportion to total population than in more developed countries. Since nearly 50 percent of the population is under the voting age of eighteen—a phenomenon confined to countries with very high population growth rates—the voting adult population must necessarily remain relatively small.

São Paulo, Minas Gerais, Guanabara, Rio de Janeiro, Rio Grande do Sul, Paraná, and Santa Catarina had 13 million voters in 1966, representing 60 percent of the electorate. Of this number São Paulo had just short of 5 million, or nearly 20 percent of the total electorate. Minas Gerais, second in number of registered voters, had just over 3 million, 14 percent of all voters. This does not mean, however, that São Paulo and Minas Gerais control 34 percent of the congressional representation. The system of apportioning seats in the chamber of deputies makes these states — the most advanced in virtually all respects — politically underrepresented. A similar situation can be found in the United States where urban districts were disfavored in relation to the rural vote until a supreme court decision forced state action to rectify the imbalance. Thus São Paulo has 18.3 percent of the total vote but only 14.4 percent of the seats in the chamber of deputies. Since present (1972) congressional representation is still based on a minimum number of deputies per state, proportional to total (not voter) population and with decreasing representation as population increases, the largest, most developed states fail to exercise political power commensurate with their importance. Because of these factors, political bosses and other elites in the more backward states find it easier to maintain their political hegemony (again not unlike the situation in the United States). The significance of this becomes clearer when it is considered in relation to the Northeast states of Alagoas, Maranhão, and Pernambuco, where the percentages of voting populations were 11.1, 11.7, and 14.2, respectively. For generations political control in these states has rested with a few families. On the other hand, in the more urbanized, developed states of Minas Gerais, São Paulo, Rio de Janeiro, and Guanabara 19.3, 23.8, 24.7, and 29.1 percent, respectively, of their populations voted. This distortion will presumably correct itself eventually as elections are held under the new constitutional provision for representation based on registered voters instead of population.

An additional factor distorting proportional representation is the system of representation in the senate, where each state is allotted three senators.

As for the effectiveness of the provision of law that requires registered voters to appear at the polls, the record is good. Despite a fairly wide variation since 1945, taking due account of factors such as "phantom voters," the percentage held steady at nearly 80 percent until 1966, when it dropped to 75 percent.

Elections, as any civics text demonstrates, should be the heart of every democratic political system. The effectiveness of the electoral system in bringing into office representatives of the peoples' choice should be an important factor in judging the system's ability to perform its prescribed function. As indicated before, Brazil's electoral system is effective, even though it fails in some respects because of abuses and in others because many citizens lack civic education.

The new electoral code was promulgated by the revolutionary Castello Branco government in July 1965. Many of its provisions repeat those of the basic code of 1945, revised in 1950, 1955, and 1962. Modifications have been made since then by constitutional provision and by decree.

The new legislation on political parties under the Constitution of 1967 effectively reduced their number from thirteen to two by raising the requirements for establishing legal status. Interparty alliances which had fostered endless political deals were prohibited in proportional representation elections. Electoral courts were given broader supervisory powers over local party organizations. Pretenders to public office were required to run from their own constituencies. In an attempt to strengthen party discipline, the government decreed that federal and state legislators would have to be chosen from the same party. And to prevent such crises as developed after the Quadros resignation, running mates of successful presidential and gubernatorial candidates were to be automatically elected. The 1969 Amendment to the Constitution attempted to strengthen the party system even more by making party disloyalty grounds for removal from elected office in the legislature. By lowering the requirements for establishing parties, it once more became possible for more than two parties to function legally.

To come into existence and continue to exist, parties need strong national grass roots. To survive, a party must poll at last 5 percent of the total vote in a general election for the chamber of deputies, distributed in seven states with a minimum of 7 percent of the vote in each. This requirement of the 1969 Amendment is a considerable reduction from the 10 percent needed under the Constitution of 1967 which, in effect, institutionalized a two-party system.

The electoral courts were given wide supervisory powers over the election of party officers and convention delegates and control over a party fund which, among other things, was to be used for political education and party information activities. Its funding came from federal tax revenues and from fines levied by the electoral courts. Party officials could hold office no longer than four years and candidates had to be selected through primaries or party conventions. Primary elections were not required, however, until a supplementary decree in mid-1969 made them mandatory.

The electoral code of 1965 did away with the old ballot, still used in rural areas, and introduced a new ballot to be used in all elections. The change was intended to stimulate straight ticket voting. The code retained the provision, effective since 1947, which bars the Communist Party by prohibiting "the organization and the registration of a party whose program or action is contrary to the democratic system based on the plurality of parties and the guarantee of the fundamental rights of man." The constitution prohibits any political party from having "ties of any nature" with foreign parties.

Several other reformatory provisions were included in the electoral code, among them the requirements that candidates must be backed by a party, poll watchers must represent a party rather than a candidate, and party representatives may accompany voters at registration and even receive registration documents on their behalf. These provisions strengthened the formal role of the political party. The provision of the 1969 Amendment demanding adherence to party directives by legislators at all levels on pain of losing their seats was designed to strengthen parties even more. To limit the influence of wealth, the code provided that parties could not receive assistance from foreign sources or from any corporation with financial links to the government. Campaign expenditures were limited for the first time, and because of chronic inflation, were set at multiples of the minimum wage in effect at the time. Thus, senators were limited to expenditures totalling 200 times the minimum wage, and deputies were limited to 100 times that amount.

Under the 1967 Constitution the president and vice president, who formerly held office for five years, were to be elected to four-year terms; the 1969 Amendment returned the term to five years. The electoral code had originally provided for direct elections, but the Castello Branco government decreed election by an electoral college.

In the not unlikely event that direct election of the president and vice president eventually returns, the system employed would likely be that approved by the constitutional amendment of July 1964. This required an absolute majority, failing which the name of the candidate with the highest number of votes is to be submitted to the congress for a vote of confidence which would have the concurrence of more than 50 percent of the members. If the vote of confidence is not forthcoming, then a runoff election is to be held between the two candidates receiving the largest number of votes. This amendment sought to avoid political crises of the nature engendered by the election of Juscelino Kubitschek in 1955, when he received only 35.6 percent of the vote. Senators are elected by direct vote for eight-year terms. As before, elections held every four years were alternately to elect first one senator from each state and then two, thus theoretically adding new blood to the senate every four years and keeping a residue of experience in each state's senatorial representation. The entire chamber of deputies is to be elected every four years, with candidates running at large. Numerous efforts to install the single-member district system were unsuccessful.

Beginning in 1970, governors and vice-governors, previously elected for four or five years, depending on the state's constitutional provision, were all to be concurrently elected every four years in direct elections. All the states have unicameral legislative assemblies. Their members are chosen every four years by the same system of proportional representation applied to national, as well as municipal, elections.

Except for those in state capitals, watering spas, and other cities designated important to national security, mayors are popularly elected. Municipal councilmen or alderman are also chosen in popular elections. The Federal District, however, is governed by a mayor appointed by the president of the republic.

One of the most successful features of the Brazilian electoral system is the unique role of the electoral courts. They are charged by law with administering the entire electoral process. Generally enjoying the confidence of the people, they have given prestige to the judiciary equaled by few countries of the Western Hemisphere. Their role is both administrative and judicial.

Operating at the national level, the superior electoral court has original and appellate jurisdiction to decide all electoral issues.[3] It has, in addition, complete administrative authority over the entire electoral system and process. It sets dates for national elections not otherwise set by law and announces all election results.

Regional electoral courts exercise jurisdiction in each of the states, the Federal District, and several territories. They follow uniform rules set by the superior electoral court but are given discretion in some matters such as setting dates for elections not otherwise set by law and dividing the state into electoral zones. Within the electoral zones, electoral judges appointed by the regional courts have supervisory authority. They register voters, designate polling places and appoint their officials, process complaints, and conduct trials for electoral frauds or crimes. An electoral board made up of the electoral judge and two other members receives ballots, counts the votes initially, and certifies the winning candidates to the regional electoral courts.

At the lowest electoral level is the polling places, which is administered by a president and two other officials. The polling place serves a territory with a minimum of 50 voters and a maximum of 300, except that in capital cities the maximum may be 400.

Much progress has been made in voting procedures to assure that the voter has as free a choice as possible and that his vote once cast is accurately counted.

Before 1955 separate ballots were cast for each candidate. These ballots, supplied by the candidate, contained the name of the candidate, his party affiliation and the office for which he was running. The first ballot reform, in 1955, provided for a single official ballot for the presidential and vice presidential election, furnished by election officials at the polling station. In 1958 the single ballot was extended to include all majority elections and was extended again in 1962 to include proportional representation elections in all state capitals, as well as the entire states of São Paulo and Guanabara. The 1965 electoral code provided for the use of the single ballot throughout the country but, to assure election of government candidates, the Castello Branco government chose to reverse itself in the

1966 election by allowing use of separate ballots, furnished by the party or candidate, in rural elections. This reversal of a previously approved reform measure gave new life to the weakening political *coronel*. However, the states of São Paulo and Guanabara and twenty-five cities with populations over 100,000, including state capitals, were allowed to use the single ballot. Another innovation for the 1966 elections was the tied vote (*voto vinculado*) which required voters to select state and national deputies from the same party.

Vote counting is not unlike that in other countries, but final counts are delayed by the size of Brazil, the slowness of communications, and occasionally by the bureaucracy. In the larger cities the results come in as fast as anyplace not using voting machines, but counting votes in more remote parts of the coutry is so slow that many states have exceeded the thirty-day limit for reporting official results. The electoral code requires that final tabulations must be completed within ten days, paving the way for numerous requests for extensions.

A national election day is usually a peaceful and festive occasion and has impressed observers as a genuine civic exercise, when as many as 250,000 official election workers man the approximately 70,000 voting stations throughout the country. More than 2,000 electoral boards are on duty and something like half a million poll watchers look out for the interests of their party's candidates. Barbecues, drinks (nothing stronger than beer can be sold on election days), and free rides to the polling station in candidates' trucks are regular aids to getting out the vote.

Political Parties

When the Castello Branco administration in 1965 radically changed the political party system that had served to channel most of Brazil's political activities for the preceding twenty years, questions were raised as to how durable the new party system might be. But agreement was general that the old system had outlived its usefulness and had so degenerated as to have contributed to the breakdown of the democratic system established under the Constitution of 1946.

The system of national parties begun by Vargas in 1945 and officially established by the Constitution of 1946 was well designed to meet the needs of the society he had done so much to change in the previous fifteen years. Because the Old Republic had abandoned the manipulated but reasonably effective two-party system of the Empire, a highly centralized political system under which the Emperor periodically alternated the parties in power and made changes from the national level down through the municipal level, parties as national entities had ceased to exist. They became state machines whose principal objective was to channel the political activity of rival rural elites, whose interests were generally economic and seldom included the needs or aspirations of the middle class, let alone those of the lower class. When the people eventually became convinced that this system was anachronistic and a drag on progress, a thesis widely held by the *tenentes* of the 1920's, they supported the 1930 Vargas revolution. The revolution changed political styles and eventually paved the way for a new party system.

Most of the traditional rural elites that Vargas favored were drawn into the newly formed *Partido Social Democrático* (PSD), the Social Democratic Party. Their rivals, weaker and fewer in number, joined the *União Democrática Nacional* (UDN), the National Democratic Union. Its principal strength was among the anti-Vargas, reform-minded, liberal constitutionalists of the urban middle class. To bring the newly organized working class into political life in an orderly way, and incidently to undercut the Communists, Vargas encouraged the establishment of the *Partido Trabalhista Brasileiro* (PTB), the Brazilian Labor Party. Like the unions themselves, which were paternalistically organized and controlled by the government, the Labor Party was a hierarchical structure which paralleled and in effect consolidated the labor union structure.

Unfortunately, the party system established by the Constitution of 1946 inadequately provided for the great increase in the electorate. Party registration became so easy that the system of a few parties, apparently envisioned by Vargas, was strained to the point of allowing as many as fifteen parties to operate at one time. Many were personal machines, usually comprised of leaders with small followings who sought social status and personal gain.

The larger national parties in Brazil, like their counterparts in other countries of Latin America, were controlled by elite groups and reflected the paternalistic, hierarchical structure of society.[4] Many of the small new parties represented neither elites nor interest groups. They had no appeal to large numbers of voters, but in the aggregate they controlled enough votes to make elections and political deals a principal preoccupation of all parties, even the large ones. None of the parties represented power centers of similar interests strong enough to assure unquestioned control. Given the already dispersed bases of power and the struggle for power among numerous elites, resolution of conflict among them became even more difficult. The growing power of the urban and industrial elites, whose members entered the PSD and the UDN, principally, made inroads on but could not overcome the influence of their rural peers. Inability to resolve these conflicts left the way open for the demagogue, as well as the populist. Their similar techniques were to play on the failure of the system to reconcile differences and improve social conditions, and to build a following large enough to create a new party, often a splinter group from a larger party.

The parties contributed a democratic facade and the machinery to get out the vote but were seldom strong enough to avoid crises or to oppose military intervention when it occurred. Beset by the ills of personalism, fragmentation, provincial outlook, political expediency, voter apathy, and, in the early 1960's failure to facilitate reform that might have hastened modernization within a democratic framework, the political party system bears its share of responsibility for the failure of democratic processes in 1964. Party weakness invited military intervention to prevent a breakdown of the entire political system.

The strong attraction of voters to individuals rather than to ideas and principles has often been pointed to as a principal factor in the deterioration of the party system established by the 1946 Constitution. Hermes Lima, a mild socialist who was Foreign Minister and briefly Prime Minister under Goulart, has noted that Brazillians use ideas as campaign material, not for establishing ways of life.[5] This is not surprising in a society in which one of the principal bases of political power has rested on a particularistic, clientelistic system flowing from a still strong paternalism. As the social system is structured hierarchically, so is the political party system. As a result, ideological parties have always had only slight appeal in Brazil.

Parties became more and more pragmatic after 1950. Coalitions perforce became the rule as dissidents and recalcitrants jumped party lines or created new parties with no real ideological or politically pragmatic *raison d'etre* beyond personal aggrandizement. New groups seeking political expression, most of them labor oriented and dissatisfied with the PTB after the Vargas decline, lost effectiveness in the dispersion of a dozen parties. Elections assumed paramount importance because so much time had to be devoted to maneuvering and planning complex political alliances. Rival parties at the national level were often forced to accede to coalitions made by subordinate groups at the state and municipal levels. Among the larger parties, political leaders formed an elite fraternity of their own. As competition mounted and it became more costly to run for office, more were beholden to those who had helped finance their campaigns—a problem that plagues most political systems but which was acute in Brazil. Even the PTB was no exception. A number of leaders sought to give it an ideology like that of labor parties in other democracies but found that task hopeless. Not that it did not work for workers' interests, but its principal aim was to win and control the urban labor vote for the benefit of the political leaders seeking not only political power but increased social status.

The PTB was long a moderate party with radical and conservative wings. As the urban-labor vote grew, the PTB grew in size, sometimes outvoting the UDN. Many PTB leaders lost their political rights after the 1964 revolution and other party members were removed from positions in government agencies. Nonetheless, the Vargas tradition continued strong among the lower and middle classes, and the PTB or a successor organization should be one of the first to reestablish itself under the terms of the Constitutional Amendment of 1969 or subsequent legislation.

The UDN maintained its role as the principal anti-Vargas party, with a program for political reform but with less interest in social and economic reforms. Among its most active members were some of the now aging *tenentes* who had broken with Vargas on the issue of the dictatorship. Other leaders were the *bachareis,* prestigious lawyers whose profundity and wit enlivened congressional debates but attracted few popular votes. The UDN lost its chance to capture political control of the country after the Vargas suicide in 1954, but it did furnish political leaders after the 1964 revolution. By that time, however, its power was severely limited by the military dominance of national political life.

Ideologically—if the word can be used for parties which had a minimum of ideology—the UDN, with principal support among professional, intellectual, and commercial elements of the middle and upper classes, and the PSD had many common interests centered in the preservation of the social system. The PSD's strength, however, was largely in rural areas (although it later gained the support of most of the industrial elite), whereas the UDN was largely supported by the urban middle class. But even with the political system in jeopardy during the Goulart regime, the two parties could not work together for long in the face of the overarching pro-Vargas/anti-Vargas dichotomy.

The ten other Brazilian political parties active at the time of the 1964 revolution were of minor importance, except the *Partido Social Progressista* (PSP), the Social Progressive Party, whose strength was based in São Paulo on the personal popularity of its several times elected Governor Adhemar de Barros. This populist politician won nearly 25 percent of the vote in presidential elections. Of the remaining parties, only three—the *Partido de Representação Popular* (PRP), descended from the fascist Integralists; the *Partido Socialista Brasileiro* (PSB), the Brazilian Socialist Party; and the *Partido Democrata Cristão* (PDC), the Christian Democratic Party—can be said to have had significant ideological aims, albeit insignificant voter strength. Only PDC appeared to be filling a need for a socially oriented, progressive Catholic party which could articulate the demands of non-Communist, reformist elements that found the UDN too rigid to attract popular support. Although it grew, it never achieved the importance of other Christian Democratic parties in Latin America, probably because in the years immediately preceding the 1964 revolution the party's extreme left wing, members of the *Grupo Compacto,* tied itself closely to Goulart. These radicals went far beyond even his leftism to try to force revolutionary solutions to Brazilian problems. The failure of the ideological oriented parties to gain broader support can be explained by their inability to help their constituencies materially, unlike the large national parties whose leaders were close to the sources of power and thus were able to guarantee satisfaction of the aspirations of many clients. Only highly skilled laborers, some intellectuals, and few *técnicos* (technocrats) seem to have any real interest in ideological political action in Brazil.

The following table shows the relative strength during five terms in the chamber of deputies (the more representative of the two chambers at the national level) of the fourteen political parties that were active in Brazil from 1945 until all political parties were abolished in 1965.

PARTY REPRESENTATION IN THE BRAZILIAN CHAMBER OF DEPUTIES

Party	1945	1950	1954	1958	1962
PSD—Social Democratic	151	112	114	115	122
UDN—National Democratic Union	77	81	74	70	94
PTB—Brazilian Labor	22	51	56	66	109
PSP—Social Progressive	4	24	32	25	22
PR—Republican	7	11	19	17	5
PDC—Christian Democratic	2	2	2	7	20
PTN—National Labor	0	5	6	7	11
PST—Social Labor	0	9	2	2	8
PL—Liberation	1	5	8	3	3
PRP—Popular Representation	2	2	3	3	4
PSB—Brazilian Socialist	0	1	3	9	4
PRT—Republican Labor	0	1	1	2	3
MTR—Labor Reform Movement	0	0	0	0	4
PCB—Brazilian Communist	14	—	—	—	—
Without party	6	0	6	0	0
Total seats	286	304	326	326	409

Given the workings of the electoral system, the minor parties were of far greater importance than their national representation indicated, which, of course, explains their continued existence and their importance to the larger parties. Parties were required to register in all states in which they intended to run candidates in a national election. Very few parties were able to maintain organizations in all states, and local parties, sometimes regionally based, found their registrations sought after by other parties at election time, either for rent for a temporary period, so to speak, or in coalition.

Under these circumstances the party system failed to control nominations adequately and thus simplify alternatives for the electorate. Party jumping and the great number of candidates, many of them well known, served to confuse the voter and to erode the prestige of parties. The nature and extent of change in party loyalties is illustrated by the shift that took place in the chamber of deputies between the 1962 elections and the 1964 revolution without an intervening election. In early 1964 the PSD representation had shrunk from 122 to 119, the PTB, then in power, had grown from 109 to 119, and the UDN had added one deputy to its 1962 total of 94.

The party system became a negative factor when it could make little contribution to executive efforts to modernize the country socially and economically. This is not to say that political change to improve the process could not have been brought about through improved legislation sponsored by energetic leaders, but it was not, and it fell to the authoritarian revolution to make political reforms. The parties did contribute to the general development of the nation by bringing some of the emerging groups into the political process, though not very effectively, and by supporting the government's economic development efforts. They also made it possible for party elements legitimately dissatisfied because of entrenched noninnovative leadership to go elsewhere to seek office or combat such leadership. The effectiveness of the party system was lost, first, by unwillingness to give the executive additional power, and second, by loss of control over the system through party fragmentation and a breakdown in party discipline. Some UDN members, for example, encouraged military intervention when the party could not otherwise gain control. For all its failures and weaknesses, the Brazilian Labor Party played an important role in the country's political development by bringing important new lower-class groups into the political process. It also attracted large numbers of leftist, reform-minded, liberal elements, thus keeping in legal, nonrevolutionary channels many who might otherwise have been won over by the Communist Party had their only alternatives been the conservative PSD and UDN. The Brazilian party system failed for reasons related to the incongruity of a system that can operate democratically and effectively only with a high level of political participation but which instead operated as a system run for the elites and controlled by them. In this respect the Vargas changes had been more personal than institutional.

The failure of the national political parties effectively to represent much more than the narrow interests of conflicting elite groups, thus preventing united party action, led eventually to the formation of several informal fronts composed of deputies and senators. These fronts attempted to unify cross-party class and ideological activity in congress, paralleling groups outside the congress. The strongest and most vocal grouping was the *Frente Parlamentar Nacionalista* (FPN), or National Parliamentary Front, which sought to mobilize support for basic reforms. Made up largely of the more radical PTB deputies and leftist deputies from other parties, with a sprinkling of senators, it worked in and out of congress, attempting to polarize the electorate and to force a polarization within the government. It sought radical solutions to problems on which a preponderantly conservative congress was acting slowly or not at all. Occasionally the FPN applied pressures on President Goulart when he seemed to be seeking accommodation with center groups. At its peak, in 1961 and 1962, during its short-lived existence, the FPN claimed the support of 120 members of Congress, but many of the ties were very tenuous.

To counteract the propaganda of the FPN, the *Ação Democrática Parlamentar* (ADP), or Democratic Parliamentary Action, was formed by a number of conservative deputies, mostly from the UDN. Although it claimed over 150 members of congress, its voice was never as loud as that of the FPN, but it was successful in damping down pressure tactics from the radicals.

An attempt at creating a legislative bloc aimed at achieving moderate reforms was made early in 1964 by San Tiago Dantas, Minister of Foreign Affairs and Minister of Finance in the Goulart government. His instrument was the so-called *Frente Única* which aimed to be a coalition of moderate reformists. More broadly based than the FPN, it failed because the radical left wing of the FPN refused to allow Dantas to assume leadership of the movement. The Communists gave it their support.

With the failure of conventional politics to make headway with Brazil's growing economic and political problems, and with the accelerated move toward violent solutions, the parliamentary fronts lost meaning and their membership gradually declined.

A new party statute was promulgated in July 1965. Only some of the provisions had gone into effect and no changes had yet taken place in party registrations when the Institutional Act No. Two of October 1965 changed the prevailing system by abolishing all parties existing at that time and requiring temporary registration under the new party statute. The result was a two-party system consisting of the government *Aliança Renovadora Nacional* (ARENA), or National Reform Alliance, and the opposition *Movimento Democrático Brasileiro* (MDB), or Brazilian Democratic Movement. No additional groupings could qualify for party status. Realignments resulted in 259 federal deputies opting for ARENA and 150 for MDB.

The requirements for registration under the 1965 party statutes were complicated and difficult. The 1967 Constitution made some changes: for a party to continue in existence, it was obliged to have won 10 percent of the vote "in the last general election for the chamber of deputies, distributed in two-thirds of the states, with a minimum of 7 percent in each of them, and also 10 percent of the deputies, in at least one-third of the states, and 10 percent of the senators." These requirements were so rigid that the government had to overlook them even to register a second party in order to establish the two-party system favored under Castello Branco. To meet widespread dissatisfaction among the parties, the Costa e Silva government devised an electoral mechanism which permitted *sub-legendas,* or separate tickets for factions within parties, for municipal and state elections. As many as three factional tickets were permitted within any party, but all votes were to go to the winning party candidate. This clumsy mechanism aimed at satisfying the demand for more than two parties should have disappeared when the requirements for establishing parties was lowered by the Amendment to the Constitution of 1969. However, as no new parties came into being and the MDB continued a precarious existence while most of the political competition took place within ARENA, the *sub-legenda* still proved useful.

After the political breakdown of December 13, 1968 (the second military intervention after the 1964 revolution) the government made a number of political changes, pending contemplated modification in the party statutes as well as constitutional reform. Complementary Act No. 54 was promulgated on May 20, 1969, for the ostensible purpose of postponing elections scheduled in Mato Grosso and Goias.[6] The Act also set dates for political party conventions to elect municipal party leaders. The elections, as set forth in Article 2 of the Act, were to be public and "only those electors inscribed therein, and members of the respective political party may vote and be voted for in each municipality." The importance of the measure was to institute primary elections on the basis of a strengthened political party system. Complementary Act No. 54 was designed to correct the undemocratic process for selecting party leadership at the local level, whereby candidates for political office all continued to be designated by state and national directorates. Voters had little voice in their selection. This system perpetuated the old structure of party oligarchies that had changed but little in most states from the time of the 1930 revolution. In 1972 the new system was still in a period of unstable transition.

Communist Parties

The orthodox Brazilian Communist Party, (*Partido Comunista Brasileiro* (PCB), reputedly the largest and best organized Communist Party in the Western Hemisphere, is usually dismissed by most Brazilians as unimportant and without capability to assume a larger role in the country's life. "Brazilians are anti-Communist" is the usual phrase employed to dismiss them as a danger, and the description through 1972, at least, was accurate. Yet the fear of Communism played an important part in the overthrow of the Goulart regime in 1964, less because Brazilians believed Goulart was a Communist, or that they really feared a Communist takeover, than because of growing infiltration of Communists and Communist sympathizers in many sectors of Brazilian public life. Leftist extremists had found places in the bureaucracy, labor unions, student groups, and even among non-commissioned personnel of the armed forces.

From the time of its formal foundation in 1922, the PCB was permitted to act as a legally constituted party for only two short periods, but it was active politically virtually from the time of its establishment until 1964, when it was forced so far underground that it became a negligible factor. The power and prestige of the Communist Party, which has usually been far greater than its number of supporters and adherents would indicate, derived from the high regard in which its leader, Luíz Carlos Prestes, has been held. Prestes was one of ths untranquil *tenentes* of 1922 who sought political, social, and economic change to benefit the lower class. As leader of the legendary *"Coluna Prestes"* over most of its 6,000-mile march, his fellow officers considered him one of their brightest and most capable members. Converted to Communism in 1930, he spent some time in the Soviet Union, returning to Brazil in 1934. He was in the country during the 1935 revolution, one which served to give the armed forces a symbol of anti-Communism when they annually repair to the graves of the victims of the attempted coup to honor the memory of their murdered fellow officers. Leonido Basbaum sharply criticized Prestes' judgment in launching a revolt without support from the people. Taking further aim at Prestes' leadership, the former Communist official noted that "Unfortunately, as the facts would later show twice over at least, Prestes' concept of the proletariat was more sentimental than scientific." [7]

In this criticism may be found a diagnosis of the essential weakness of the Communist Party in Brazil. Like other ideological parties, it never had large support from the people. During its short period of legality from 1945 through 1947, it emerged as the fourth largest party, with fourteen deputies of a total of 286 and about 10 percent of the vote in the presidential election. Much of this apparent strength can be laid to the electoral system which allowed votes for Prestes, still revered as the "Knight of Hope," to accrue to other Communist Party members. The party's registration was cancelled when a second set of party statutes were discovered in 1947. These statutes placed it in the category of parties whose program or action is contrary to the democratic regime.

If the PCB had little popular support, whether in legal or illegal status, it had disproportionate political weight because the party system then operative put a heavy premium on election support from disciplined groups. Even conservatives saw little wrong in making deals with the Communists for financial or other considerations in the years before the Cold War reached its peak. The Communists operated openly most of the time, if not as a legal political party, and members were permitted on other tickets. They were reported to have a membership of some 30,000 in the 1960s; they had probably many times that number of sympathizers who, if they did not see Communism as the only way to social reform, liked some part of the Communist program. Communist strength was always somewhat difficult to assess because it adopted nationalism and national unity against "North American imperialism" as a principal tactic. Many, especially students and radical church activists, consider collaboration with Communists for reform purposes both legitimate and desirable. It has thus become difficult to separate the true nationalist, whose slogans and arguments often sound similar to if not identical with those adopted by the PCB, from the hard-core Communist.

The unorthodox, violence-oriented *Partido Comunista do Brazil,* the Communist Party of Brazil, was formed in 1962 under the leadership of Mauricio Grabois, João Amazonas, and others who broke with Prestes in protest over his cautious tactics that reflected the new Soviet policy of coexistence. (The Communist Party of Brazil is known by the same initials as the orthodox Brazilian Communist Party, PCB.) The new *Partido Comunista do Brazil* found the revolutionary tactics of the Chinese and Fidel Castro more to their liking than those of the orthodox, "revisionist," Soviet-oriented followers of Luiz Carlos Prestes. Prestes' campaign for legality was seen by the splinter group as a surrender of revolutionary principle. The dogmatic position of the new party did not attract many followers. Membership reportedly never rose higher than a thousand, even after another important leader, Carlos Marighella, broke with Prestes in 1967 and joined the *Partido Comunista do Brazil*. Marighella was killed in a shootout with the police early in 1970.

Some of the uncharacteristic terrorist activity that began in Brazil after 1966 was credited to the unorthodox Communists. From principally nuisance bombings in the beginning, activity moved into other areas as the terrorists gained experience and boldness and included attacks on isolated police stations, military installations, and television stations. Some coordinated guerrilla activity got under way. Information on the subject was scarce, except when the authorities were successful in breaking up several groups still in the planning and training stage. Since at least one of the student groups had also adopted violent tactics, as had extreme rightist groups reacting against leftist activity, it was sometimes difficult to distinguish one from the other.

Prospect

Brazil's election system before 1964 was and in some respects still is, a model of democratic procedures among developing nations; and the structure may even improve under the reform-minded, military-controlled government. This does not, however, guarantee a working democracy. One of the principal reasons a democratic polity has not developed is the failure of the political parties to perform their roles and expected functions adequately, because their leadership has often been more responsive to personal and class interests than to popular interests. They have little mass support. With few exceptions, the parties have been almost powerless to prevent military interventions, some of which were justified as necessary in order to correct civilian political failure and corruption. As we shall see, political parties occasionally encouraged military intervention into politics.

Several probabilities emerge from the variety of diagnoses and prognoses about the political party system in Brazil:

1) The municipality will remain the basic political structure.

2) Short of a change in the socioeconomic structure of landownership and land utilization, present party leadership will change slowly. Many present leaders at all levels are being removed, but, having learned the political game, some may be expected to return at a more propitious time.

3) It will be many years, if ever, before personalism loses its place in Brazilian politics. The party system formalized in the 1966 Constitution changed old habits and ways of politiking. After 1946 the *coronel* who formerly whipped the vote into line with little beyond a call to loyalties and terror, now offered favors, jobs, and other forms of competitive compensation to get votes. These tactics are not basically different from forms of politiking in most parts of the world. They are more the rule in Brazil, where the urban recruit still looks to a *patrão,* often a political broker, to get him a job, promotions, or other favors. Only the highly skilled workers who fit the universal patterns of radical, ideologically motivated political participants seem to be exceptions.

4) It is not likely that primary elections will change the basic political structures unless further reforms are made. These would include a change to the electoral district voting system in order to avoid abuses made possible by heavy financial expenditures in elections as well as a universal application of the single ballot to replace the election slips furnished by candidates. Such reforms would make it easier for the system to function more democratically.

Election reforms may help build a more viable and more democratic polity than the authoritarianism of the military-headed governments since 1964, but until the socioeconomic system is changed or its anomalies corrected, reforms are more likely to be palliatives than cures. Nevertheless the Brazilian political system cannot operate effectively until the pattern of society has actually changed. The country has grown economically and has modernized to a notable degree under a system that enjoyed a high degree of legitimacy and stability,

even if it did not fit patterns of mass democracy in developed nations. Brazil is likely to continue on this viable if imperfect path
to modern democracy unless the system breaks down because of the
inability of its military rulers to adjust in acceptable degree to civilian
aspirations.

V: Groups in the Political Process

One way to look at the political processes of a nation is through the groups that most influence them. In developing countries, the character and degree of influence exercised by the important groups in developing countries is often a reflection of the country's stage of development. In Brazil this can best be seen among the larger institutional groups—the bureaucracy, the military, the Catholic Church, and labor. All directly shape the life of the nation. Other groups exercise a more subtle and indirect influence. Political scientists often call them pressure groups and may classify them as associational if they are formal, or as nonassociational if they are informal. They may have economic or political objectives. Students, for example, may act as members of a large formal group with which they are associated in order to improve their condition as students. They may and often do have political objectives, as do students who act informally in small numbers. Businessmen act in groups for the common good, but some of them also work in their capacity as heads of large family banking, commercial, or industrial empires strictly to benefit the interests of the smaller group. Although communications media are not interest groups in the usual definition, they are included here because their influence on political behavior is often very similar to that of other pressure groups.

The selection of groups to consider here has been made more or less arbitrarily on the basis of observation of their importance in the body politic. Different ones might be selected by other observers, depending on their analysis of the power structure. The Brazilian educator, Anisio S. Teixeira, for example, saw the pre-1964 power structure as dominated by what he calls the "cupola," or the governing group, which may change rather frequently, and the fixed bureaucracy, which is much more stable. They are supported and influenced by the oligarchies, which are the coffee interests, heavy and light industry interests, military and civil servants, the merchant marine, highway builders, personnel of banks and social security agencies, and workers on the railways, ports, and highways. In Teixeira's model the Church exercises influence at all three levels of what he designates as the "classes," which are made up of cupola, the bureaucracy, and the oligarchies. He estimates that the "classes" constitute 40 percent of the population, the other 60 percent being the "masses." [1] Anthony Leeds generally agrees with Teixeira but suggests the need also to consider a number of "rather amorphous interest groups or categories," including churchmen, primary and secondary school teachers, self-employed professionals, and members of some unions and other types of associations.[2]

Although Teixeira's model was useful at the time it was constructed (during the Goulart administration), several of his oligarchies, such as the bank workers and highway builders, have been shorn of the exceptional power status they enjoyed. Nor are they likely to regain their former power, whatever type of government replaces the present military-controlled regime. On the other hand, the status and influence of the more stable, conventional groups have not changed radically.

The Bureaucracy

Even responsible officials of the Brazilian government do not know the number of people on the government payrolls. A 1966 census indicated that civil and military personnel totaled 685,000, of whom 29 percent were military.[3] Adding other government employees who work under the labor code rather than Civil Service, the total figure is closer to a million. In any event, according to the chief of the *Departamento Administrativo do Pessoal Civil* (DAPC), the three-quarters of a million civil and military personnel in 1968 were budgeted to receive the equivalent of $1.4 billion, something over 60 percent of the total budget. This averaged nearly $200 per month, a salary that would put its recipient in the middle to upper-middle brackets in Brazil; but in fact, 95 percent of the federal employees were paid less than $110 per month. In Rio de Janeiro this equalled the rent for a small apartment. These figures are high for a population of less than 90 million, but it should be noted that they include employees of the merchant marine and other government enterprises such as railroads, electric power generating agencies, and the petroleum and other independent agencies, which in the United States are privately owned.

Even with a tradition of service and capability under the Empire and the Old Republic, the bureaucracy found it difficult to absorb the infusion of new personnel during the Vargas period. Not only did Vargas expand existing services to meet requirements of a modernizing nation, but new legislation brought the government into new fields. Social welfare and trade unions alone required a large administrative apparatus. But over and above the requirements for new personnel, the practice of making appointments for political purposes came into its own under Vargas. It was one of his principal tools to control opposition. This establishment of the so-called *cartorial* state also reflected a need to find a place in society for elements of the emerging middle sector that the slowly expanding economy could not absorb.

The political use to which the federal civil service has been put is illustrated by the rise and fall in the number of civil servants in proportion to the total population. The climb has been generally steady, as in all countries as governments modernize, and has become more complex as more services have been performed for the nation. The first big rise, from 1.46 civil servants per 1,000 inhabitants in 1937 to 3.33 in 1938, probably reflected the need to police the dictatorial *Estado Novo*. More securely in power by 1941, the proportion then dropped to 2.16 only to rise again during the war years. The Dutra administration slowly reduced the proportion but not the number. Curiously, during the second Vargas administration, perhaps because economic conditions were poor, the rise in new employees was modest and the proportion to population actually decreased. Increases during the Kubitschek administration were modest until the development program moved into high gear in 1958, when the percentage of civil servants per 1,000 population increased to 3.75, and, in 1960, the Kubitschek administration's last year, to 5.26. Under seven months of Jânio Quadros and two and a half years of João Goulart, public employment rose to unprecedented highs despite deteriorating economic conditions.[4] More than 300,000 new civil servants were added to the rolls during those years, bringing the total to 676,554, or 8.73 per 1,000. The revolutionary governments since 1964 have reduced the proportion but not the total number, which continued to increase. Even the extensive dismissals of partisans of Goulart were hardly noticeable statistically.

Given its size and strategic position at many of the controls of government, the bureaucracy has become a highly important element in the governmental and political process. It not only administers but often initiates government policy. Possibly because of the persistence of kinship patterns, among other reasons, the Brazilian bureaucracy became one of the most important channels for the exercise of influence by interest groups, unlike the bureaucracies of other countries where political parties and the legislature serve in that capacity. To know the "right" people in the bureaucracy became the accepted way of resolving problems of large and small import. Because of its size and generally higher educational level of its employees, whose family and political connections are customarily above average, the bureaucracy itself is a significant pressure group with vested interests. The protection it receives under the constitution and administrative laws and practices has strengthened it.

It would distort the true state of affairs in the bureaucracy to dwell too long on its shortcomings, since in many ways it continues to serve the nation at a higher level of efficiency and dedication than the bureaucracies of most Latin American countries, to say nothing of other parts of the world.

In addition to the obvious relationship of size of the bureaucracy to political activity, notably patronage, much importance has been attached to the political orientation of civil servants in the middle and higher echelons. Many are long entrenched, conservative in point of view, and either effectively controlled or still strongly influenced by the landowning upper class that traditionally controlled important power centers and, concommitantly, the mechanism of government.[5] That the archaic structure of the bureaucracy was unsuited for dealing with the needs of a fast developing society is evidenced from the large number of independent agencies established by Vargas and Kubitschek to operate outside the restrictions of the antiquated departments of the government. The Administrative Reform Law of 1967 tried to rationalize these unsatisfactorily controlled but operatively necessary agencies. How effective this reform will be and for how long, remains to be seen. Some scholars have reached the conclusion that it is virtually impossible to establish and maintain an effective, modern bureaucracy in an underdeveloped society and that the bureaucracy improves definitively only as the other processes modernize. Meanwhile, the bureaucracy will function as administrator and also as one of the more important decision-making instruments of the government.

The Military

Until 1964, the role of the armed forces in nation building and modernizing was, on balance, salutary and constructive. The balance after 1964 was less clear. Their role during the Empire and in the abdication of Pedro II, as well as in the early years of the Old Republic has been outlined. In effect, President Deodoro resigned when his military dictatorship bcame no longer viable; and after his successor, Marshal Floriano Peixoto, had with vigor put down civilian and military revolts, the military returned to the barracks. But this did not mean that it had permanently foresworn interest in political affairs. The government was given back peacefully through democratic procedures to civilian control when Prudente de Morais was elected president; but the army, the preponderant element in the armed forces, had assumed part of the moderating power formerly exercised by the Emperor. This was done in the guise of its role as guardian of the constitution and meant that the army arrogated to itself the power to serve as arbiter between contending civilian political forces whenever differences became so serious as to threaten the national stability. It meant also, but less frequently, that individual officers or small groups of officers would see their role, as did the young officers influenced by Benjamin Constant, as assuming responsibility for righting real or imagined civilian failings. This outlook led to gross insubordination until civilian control was firmly entrenched again, and even then it could not be stopped altogether.

When the *tenentes,* many of them outlawed, joined the Liberal Alliance and took leading roles in the military action preceding the successful 1930 revolution, the senior officers at first were prepared to fight to keep the legitimate president in power. When it became evident that opinion strongly supported the revolution, however, the army bowed to popular will and forced President Washington Luis to quit. Civil strife was avoided. Vargas was a strong civilian president, but his philosophy of government did not differ greatly from that of the young, reform-minded officers who believed in "Order and Progress." They had an important activist role during much of his first fifteen years in office, although many were opposed to the extent of his dictatorial rule. Thus, when São Paulo rose in arms in 1932 in a "constitutional revolution" aimed at reestablishing republican government, the army was clearly divided. Large forces supported the uprising. Subsequently, Vargas was careful to win military support before making important political moves, legal or illegal. When he established the dictatorial *Estado Novo* in 1937, he had solid military support yet in 1945 military intervention forced him from office. One of its objectives was to reestablish democratic procedures. Five years later it required the agreement of the military for Vargas to run for president, apparently conditioned on his promise to maintain the *status quo* or at least to make changes in a legal, orderly fashion. In 1953, a group of colonels presented the President with a manifesto that led to the dismissal of the Minister of Labor despite the fact that many other officers, although agreeing to the justice of the complaint, opposed the political methods used. In 1954, military insistence that Vargas again leave the presidency led to his suicide.

The armed forces were divided over the seating of President-elect Juscelino Kubischek in 1955, with some apparently plotting to keep him out of the chair. A preventive coup headed by the War Minister assured his assumption of office. In 1961 the armed forces were divided again over the seating of Vice President Goulart after the Quadros resignation, but a compromise formula prevented civil war, at the same time giving the military ministers a face-saving device to withdraw their opposition to seating him. The army removed him in 1964, this time assuming unprecedented control of national life.

All the major military interventions in civilian government not only have had the support or acquiescence of public opinion, but in several instances have also responded to popular wishes. When military interventions failed, as in 1961, it was because the articulate public opposed them.

This record summarizes a history of deep military involvement in civil affairs. As Ronald Schneider observes, "between 1900 and 1950 the Brazilian armed forces were an even more active factor in the politics of the nation than were their Argentine counterparts . . ."[5a] Interventions from 1930 to 1964 were also numerous and yet an important distinction must be made between Brazil and Argentina in this respect. The profound currents of reform among the younger and middle grade officers is one facet of the difference. Another and perhaps more enlightening difference is that military interventions in Brazil until 1964 must by and large be considered as part of the political process consequent on the assignment of a moderator role to the military in the constitutions of 1891, 1934 and 1946. Therein the military was established as an institution charged with maintaining law and order and guaranteeing the normal functioning of the three branches of government. These constitutions made the military obedient to the executive power, but with the caveat that they were to be obedient "within the limits of the law." Judges of what constituted legality were not designated and the military has made its own decisions. This usurpation of power—as it can be called in liberal democratic terms—was only rarely abused. In any event, virtually all interventions after 1930 were so strongly backed by public opinion as to have acquired legitimacy. As Alfred Stepan notes in a first study on the Brazilian military to use modern techniques of political science: "what has been called 'pathological interventionism' in terms of the liberal model becomes the normal functioning of the political system in the moderator model, whereby civilians look to the military to perform a moderating role at certain times." [5b] In 1964, the military was supported by public opinion but soon abandoned its historical role as moderator, under which interventions lasted no longer than needed to transfer power from one civilian group to another, to become ruler and reformer.

In 1968 the army, air force and navy numbered about 234,000 men of whom 70 percent were in the army. Of the approximately 20,000 career officers in all three services, 13,373 were army officers. These figures make the Brazilian armed forces the largest in Latin America, but proportionate to population and expenditures they are not outsized. Defense expenditures were $6.00 per capita in 1970 and represented 2 percent of GNP. This compared to $20.00 per capita and 2 percent of GNP in Argentina and $34.00 per capita and 6 percent of GNP in Cuba. Like defense expenditures in most countries, published budgets by no means represent total outlays, but the comparisons are reasonably accurate.

Another point worth noting is that about 15 percent of all Brazilian officers are colonels or generals compared to 16.4 percent of officers in the United States army. As *The Economist* survey of Brazil (September 2, 1972) observes, military rule today is a corporate system, not a one-man, or even small group rule, largely because of rigid retirement and transfer rules which prevent the formation of "baronies within the barracks." Division commanders are forced to retire at 64 and full generals retire at 66. They serve a maximum of four years in any post.

The constructive aspects of the role of the military have not been confined to the political field. From the days of the Empire and the Old Republic, the army as an institution and through its individuals have made important contributions to economic and social modernization. Not only did the army serve the nation on its farthest borders, but the garrisons in the hinterland did much for community development. Illiterate recruits have been taught to read and write and often have been given sufficient technical training to acquire a trade. The army built roads and railroads and set up communications networks where none existed before. The air force made an important contribution to national integration and development through mail, passenger, and air cargo services to outlying areas.

An unusual facet of the military role in Brazil has been the technological and administrative contribution to national development, both private and public. Educational standards in the three services are high. The army early concentrated on producing engineers who for long were the best in the country. Many officers have spent fifteen of their twenty-five years in the army in service schools. Military officers on detached service have traditionally worked in civilian government agencies, often heading such organizations as the petroleum monopoly PETROBRAS, the Volta Redonda National Steel Mill, the merchant marine, the Postal and Telegraph Service, some of the national railway companies, price-control agencies, and the National Motors Plant, which manufactures trucks and motor cars. Many more officers, after early or regular retirement, entered all phases of private industry. It is not too much to say that certainly until midcentury and perhaps later, the military was technically superior to the civilian establishment. To a great degree, this reflected the country's inadequate civilian educational system.

As already noted, members of the armed forces, active and otherwise, have served as catalysts or have assumed an active role in social and political reform. The *tenentes* of the early 1920's sought to change the antiquated system, and they helped make possible the modernization under Vargas. Most of the social measures he adopted were espoused by the *tenentes*. The more "formal" successful interventions have never been reactionary; that of 1964, which led Castello Branco to the presidency, probably spared Brazil a violent explosion from which it might have taken generations to recover. Despite serious shortcomings in the social and political areas, the Castello Branco administration instituted many necessary reforms that previous civilian administrations had been unable or unwilling to effect. The record of General Garrastazú Médici is not likely to be as good on this score; nor will it be entirely negative.

Castello Branco was by no means a generally esteemed president.

The military before 1964 had been so popular among Brazilians of the lower and middle classes that the Communists never found it profitable to attack them. A poll taken in the mid-sixties showed a generally favorable disposition toward the armed forces with the highest acceptance among the lower classes. The reason is not only the army's tradition of civic action dating back to the last century but also its history of avoiding violent confrontations with the lower-class urban groups, thus differing from the armies of Argentina, Chile, and Mexico, where the military is often highly unpopular. The army has always left police action to the state and local police, acting only when the police lost control and serious disorders threatened.

The difference in public attitudes toward the army in Brazil and those of some Spanish American countries has other explanations as well, chiefly related to the character of its officers and soldiers. Brazilian soldiers are almost all one-year recruits. Even if some individuals were so disposed, the officers as a group have never created a militarized elite or caste, being essentially middle class in outlook. They have always been sensitive to public opinion; even after 1964 strong currents in the armed forces opposed their new role, and those in power made many concessions to minimize civilian dissatisfaction.

An important aspect of the military in Brazil's historical development in that the army has served as a channel for upward social mobility. Before the middle of Pedro II's reign, only the sons of the rural aristocracy and a few scions of the Court and upper bureaucracy could attend European universities or the few Brazilian centers of higher education such as the law schools in Rio de Janeiro and Recife. Sons of the less affluent middle class, the commercial and bureaucratic bourgeoisie, had to content themselves with attending the military and central technical schools where the Comtian doctrine of order and progress was spread among the young officers and students. The contribution of the younger officers toward breaking the rural aristocracy's monopoly over Brazilian political processes was significant. Many today favor agrarian reform. A study of the make-up of the officer corps sheds some light on this. In the 1941-1943 period, 19.8 percent of cadets at the Brazilian Army Academy came from the traditional upper class and by 1962-1966 this representation had been reduced to 6 percent. Among these only 3.8 percent were the sons of large landowners in 1941-1943 and 0.5 percent in the period 1962-1966. The record for lower class origins of officers is more difficult to ascertain because of lack of satisfactory data. Nevertheless, 9.0 percent of the cadets in the 1962-1966 period could be considered to be from the lower class. This percentage is unlikely to increase rapidly because entrance requirements at the Academy have been raised in an effort to professionalize the officer corps through specialization in the sciences. Nearly 80 percent of officers come from the middle class.[5c]

The role of the military in Brazil has other institutional aspects. The military forms the most cohesive of the major national groups and is the least affected by regional interests. That it is probably the most national-minded group is apparent from its preoccupation with national integration, which it considers important to national security. In the minds of some high-ranking officers, national integration takes precedence over economic integration, although they are not mutually exclusive. The distinction is that such officers would give higher priority to a road that had little or no immediate economic utility but linked the frontiers of the country to the important centers than they would give to building or improving a road that might be economically more useful. It is as guardians not only of the constitution but also of the national security that the military has been most insistent on establishing its role since 1964. In the view of the military, politicians can operate freely in an environment coincident with constitutional limits of law and order so long as national security is not threatened. No administration has survived the withdrawal of military support.

Writing about the Empire period, Joaquim Nabuco once noted that John Armitage, official historian of the period, always attributed to Brazilian military disasters the most salutary effects on civil order. He noted that in circumstances of "constant ill fortune of Brazilian arms" interest among the population in seeking military careers was lessened and there was a tendency "to incline the energies of the new generation toward civilian careers, which preserved Brazil from complete anarchy." Rui Barbosa made the threat of militarism the theme of his campaign for president in 1909. Other writers have pointed to evidences of praetorian characteristics among ranking officers at various periods of Brazilian history. But on balance the Brazilian military has been unique among Latin American nations in its adherence to legality, its consciousness of its role in a civil society, and its economic and social contributions toward building a strong nation.

There were fewer reasons to question the role of the military before 1964 than after. The change that began in 1964 has its roots in the work and studies at the *Escola Superior de Guerra,* Brazil's national war college, home of the so-called Sorbonne Group of officer-intellectuals, many of whom studied in military schools in France before World War II. The *Escola Superior de Guerra* seems fated to become even more influential in shaping the nation than did the schools at which Benjamin Constant taught young officers. The objectives of order and progress have not changed greatly, although Comte is all but forgotten by most Brazilians.

Founded in 1948 and modeled after the United States National War College, the *Escola Superior de Guerra* early became a haven for more introspective, studious, high-ranking officers (only colonels and officers of equivalent or higher rank attend). This is in keeping with the character of the institution as planned and outlined shortly before its establishment in a preliminary study (until recently, secret) made by Generals César Obino, then Chief of Staff of the Army, and Oswaldo Cordeiro de Farias, who was to become the first Commandant. "Security," the study noted, "depends essentially on the general development of the Nation. In size, population, and resources, Brazil possesses all the basic requisites to become a great power. However, national progress is being achieved at a[too] slow rate because of obstacles which could be changed or removed . . . ." [6] One of the principal needs according to the study, was to create a select group, or elite, capable of assuming "the responsibilities of leadership and administration of the national effort of construction." Two basic causes were seen as responsible for blocking national solutions for the country's problems: a) the failure on the part of the governing elite to learn to work together and b) the "precarious" decision-making process. The proposed school would work to meet these problems. Apart from its purely military functions, the *Escola Superior de Guerra* has adhered closely to the philosophy which inspired its founding.

Both civilians and military attend the Superior War Course and the Intelligence Course. The civilians usually outnumber the military. They are selected from among leading industrialists, journalists, professionals, jurists, members of congress, diplomats, professors, or high-ranking government officials—in short, from the most outstanding of the elite. Subjects taught generally relate to the development of national power and security. The themes selected for study during 1969 were the following:

1) The Brazilian model of development as seen through inter-action between private and public efforts.

2) Science and technology as stimulating and conditioning elements of development and national security.

3) Regional divisions of Brazil considered for planning purposes with a view to autonomous development.

4) Expansion of telecommunications and effects on national security.

5) The student movement; study of national student organizations; interrelationship of the national and international student movement and its consequences. Recommendations for solutions.

6) Civil defense.

7) Mechanisms for coordination of plans for research and strengthening of the potential of the armed forces.

8) Elaboration of an outline of military policy for the armed forces.

In the international field, special attention is given to the need to strengthen Latin America against what *Escola* doctrine (national doctrine as well since 1964) considers the three fundamental antagonisms of our time. a) ideological opposition between East and West; b) increasing economic disparity between developed and undeveloped nations; and c) "the dramatic division" of the world into nuclear and non-nuclear powers.[7]

The *Escola* has been called more a center for national leaders than a war college. The students work in groups, preparing studies on varied subjects, sometimes of such pertinence and high quality that they serve as bases for national policy. The new elite group created by the *Escola* holds together through an active alumni association and refresher courses. Its members and graduates, not necessarily working together as a group, largely controlled the decision process under the presidency of a former deputy commandant, President Castello Branco. Its influence continued into successor administrations, despite the fact that Presidents Costa e Silva and Médici were not graduates of the *Escola* and were believed to hold views contrary to many of the concepts held by members of the Sorbonne Group.[8] In practice the general philosophy of the Sorbonne Group has been to favor moderately nationalistic policies, to encourage economic development largely through private enterprise, to encourage social change at an evolutionary pace, and to favor expansion of the state's role in the economy when necessary to increase national power and national security.

The role of the *Escola Superior de Guerra* has been questioned less for its objectives and teachings, than for the extension of its influence into civilian governmnt. Questions were seldom raised before the revolution of 1964, but since then, while a succession of military-controlled governments have held power, activities of the *Escola* have come under closer scrutiny. Much of the polemic revolves around national security and how far the armed forces are prepared to go in maintaining and furthering national security in the broad concept defined and adopted by the *Escola Superior de Guerra* as follows: "National security is the relative degree of guarantee, which, through political, economic, psycho-social and military acts, the State at a given time, gives the nation over which it has jurisdiction, for obtaining or maintaining national objectives in the face of existing antagonisms." [9]

How far this concept has been carried is evident from the statement made by President Castello Branco at the inaugural session of the 1967 class that development and security are linked by a relationship of mutual causality. That is, what affects one affects the other. The danger of continuing confrontation between military and civilian elements in Brazil rises far less from its traditional role as moderator than from the acceptance by the military of the responsibility for national security which, in its view, is directly affected by the nation's "political economic, psycho-social and military acts." Thus, the national security law, partly based on doctrine formulated at the *Escola Superior de Guerra,* can be used to prosecute individuals for a variety of actions which can be interpreted as threatening national security but which are considered to be normal in traditionally democratic societies. The restrictive press law passed during the Castello Branco administration is closely linked to this national security concept.

Writing in 1965 on the philosophy of the *Escola Superior de Guerra,* Umberto Peregrino, a retired general and formerly head of the military library in Rio de Janeiro, observed that when the ruling elites (then closely identified with the *Escola*) "lose their capacity to recognize the legitimate national interests, while the people still preserve them," the State is likely to become a totalitarian, an authoritarian, or a police state.[10] Another critic, likely to have wider influence, was the National Conference of Brazilian Bishops, a committee of which in 1968 issued a working paper which called the ideology of national security a "fascist" doctrine. Yet the logic of the national security and development concept made any change unlikely in the near future.

National Integration and Manifest Destiny

One of the great strengths of the military has been that it was never a monolithic structure but rather reflected parallel differences in the main currents of opinion in the body politic. But more than any other group the military holds the conviction that Brazil is destined to become a world power and that it is incumbent upon the nation to hasten and prepare for the event. This nationalism of the armed forces has a variety of connotations that have made themselves felt most strongly in the fields of economic development and foreign affairs. Vargas said that Brazil could not become a world power if it did not have the industrial capacity to produce most of its armaments, and part of the industrial drive ever since has been predicated on that idea. As a matter of national policy, the basic industries, wherever possible, have either remained under state ownership or are privately owned by Brazilians. In several instances where private Brazilian capital has been lacking, the government, with strong military support, has invested heavily, as in the steel, petroleum, electric power, and iron ore industries, to the exclusion or severe restriction of foreign capital.

The rationale for the petroleum monopoly, for example, was outlined in 1959 by General Castello Branco, then the Deputy Commandant of the *Escola Superior de Guerra,* to a visiting group of officers from the United States National War College during a briefing at the Brazilian school. When queried about why the government did not permit foreign companies to drill for oil, Castello Branco explained that Brazil had long been concerned over its dependence on foreign oil and believed that sizable resources could be found within the country. Large private oil companies of other countries had been invited to explore but had refused until Brazil on its own made important discoveries. The private companies' subsequent requests to explore were denied. Castello Branco added that the nation would never permit foreigners to control its petroleum resources.

In foreign affairs, the military over the years have favored close ties with the United States and have maintained an ancient rivalry with Argentina. The armed forces shared with the civilian governments an awareness that the Spanish American nations have never accepted Brazil on the same terms reserved for the Spanish-speaking members of the Organization of American States (OAS) and that the question of international boundaries may once again become a problem. Particularly strong in military nationalist philosophy is the belief in Brazil's manifest destiny, not only in the Western Hemisphere but also through its special role in Africa for security and other reasons. This has led to an active Brazilian role in international organizations, including responsibilities of a military peace-keeping nature.

Relations with the United States military became very close after World War II when all three U.S. service arms had missions in Brazil and while memories of their service with the United States Fifth Army in Italy were still fresh. The *Escola Superior de Guerra* was established on the initial suggestion of the United States. Military doctrine of the United States paralleled Brazilian doctrine in most areas, but U.S. influence, although important, was less than most Brazilians and North Americans believed because the Brazilian army was determined to maintain its freedom of action. The military-assistance program, however, made available the arms and training the Brazilians wanted. For many years the missions were large, totalling over 200, but only occasionally were they headed by outstanding U.S. officers who could effectively communicate with their Brazilian peers, and only a handful of officers at any given time had meaningful relations with their Brazilian colleagues. Probably more important than the missions was the training of Brazilians in the United States and their attendance at U.S. military schools. The close relationships that had been established by officers who had served with the United States forces in Italy declined as these officers retired or died. They were replaced by more nationalistically oriented officers for whom the Brazilian Expeditionary Force did not evoke associations of camaraderie.

The armed forces face an uncertain future. This is not to say that there is any threat to their existence, but rather that uncertainty arises over the character and role of the military in a changing society. The proportion of officers from the north and the northeast continues to be small presumably because of inadequate educational facilities for potential candidates for the Army Academy. On the other hand, São Paulo, with excellent educational facilities, has in the Academy only about one-half the proportion of cadets as its proportion of the total population. The reason is probably the greater availability of attractive civilian opportunities in the south. Moreover, São Paulo has no military tradition comparable to other parts of the country. Heaviest enrollment is from Guanabara, seat of the old capital, and Rio Grande do Sul with its popular military tradition. The expanding economy and growing industrialization was probably also responsible for the general decrease in applications to enter the military academies. In 1967 for the first time there were not enough qualified candidates to bring the Army Academy enrollment up to normal, while students were rioting in universities over lack of room. This decline in interest in a military career might also have been a reflection of disenchantment with the military as political activists.

The Catholic Church

One-third of the world's Roman Catholics live in the southern part of the Western Hemisphere. The Church in Brazil suffers many but by no means all the ills usually ascribed to Catholicism in Spanish American countries. Concern over these problems has grown throughout the Catholic world, as well it might. According to many churchmen a state of spiritual bankruptcy confronts the Church in most of Latin America.[11] Basically it is a matter of the irrelevance of a system still rooted in hierarchic and paternalistic spiritual guardianship among people in transitional societies whose goal is a modern, affluent egalitarianism. In simpler terms, more and more people in Latin America learn about widespread wealth among others, and fewer and fewer believe that their own disadvantages are preordained and can be changed for the better only in the next world. The result is that many have lost interest in the Church altogether, others find comfort in Protestant sects, and still others have found a substitute for spiritual religion in materialistic political movements, usually extremist in nature. The Mother Church has recognized the basic unrest, and, beginning with Pope John XXIII, has taken revolutionary steps to meet it by seeking to identify closer with the poverty stricken masses and to change their condition. This is the reason for the Papal encyclicals *Mater et Magistra* (1961) and *Populorum Progressio* (1967). The many problems facing the Church are of critical importance not only in spiritual matters but also in the modernization process of all developing nations where Roman Catholicism is the principal cultural element in society. Despite widespread awareness of the need for change in Brazil, the Roman Catholic hierarchy and the priests diverge among themselves as to what changes are to be encouraged and how they are to be brought about. The church's changed role has made confrontations with the military governments all but inevitable.

The Brazilian Church, founded on the Portuguese Church, has been more liberal than those of Spanish origin.[12] In colonial days and during the Empire (1822-1889) it was often accused of being too worldly, too closely tied to Brazilian society and the mundane problems of its people, and inattentive to spiritual matters which most concerned Rome. Pedro II kept a firm hand on the national Church. He sometimes quarrelled with Rome and presumably had no objections to conditions described by Father Julio María in 1900, eleven years after the Empire fell, as "Ceremonies that do not edify, devotions that do not refine spirituality; books of novenas that do not reveal fervor; processions that only divert; feasts, finally, that do not profit souls nor give glory to God—behold to what the great and majestic Catholic cult is generally reduced in Brazilian parishes." [13]

But what the Church lacked in spirituality, it gained in closeness to its flock, as became evident when the papacy established firmer control over the Brazilian hierarchy. The spiritual level of the Church's pastoral work was elevated, but it lost the interest of many of its flock and found it increasingly difficult to recruit priests. By the Church's own estimate, only about 15 percent of over 100 million Brazilians today are practicing Catholics, although 90 percent claim Catholicism as their religion.

In 1960, 40 percent of the 10,000 priests were foreign born.[14] As in other Latin American countries, the situation of the Church in Brazil was reaching crisis proportions.

To better understand recent developments, it is necessary to review developments among the elites in the universal Church. These elites, as identified by Ivan Vallier, consist of 1) the traditional, politically oriented hierarchy who seek to preserve the Church's position as based on alliances with the power structure, 2) the papists, 3) the pastors, and 4) the pluralists. The goals of the last three groups are less well known than the first.

In simplest terms, the papists seek to establish a militant, modern Catholicism which will contribute to religious renewal through a Church that builds on its own resources and is less beholden to either government or elite groups than it has been in the past. It seeks to penetrate the social milieu and to establish closer ties with rising status groups, particularly the urban proletariat. Direct political involvement with political parties is usually forbidden, although individuals may be politically active under the laws of the country. The papists believe in strong leadership from Rome.

The pastors are a growing group of bishops and priests who seek to create a spiritual body of priests, people, and the sacraments. Less importance is attached to personal piety than to a more active role for laymen within homogeneous communities. Although this view of Catholicism has been common during the past decade or more in the United States and other parts of the world, in Latin America it has been exceptional until very recently.

The pluralists form the third important new group. They are the most revolutionary in outlook and activity. They believe, contrary to conventional wisdom, that Catholicism in Latin America is a minority faith and that, in collaboration with other similar minded groups, the Church's principal objective should be to develop activity which will help to institutionalize social justice. Attention tends to concentrate on basic ethical action rather than traditional religious concerns. Whatever furthers economic development and social integration is considered essentially religious in nature. Ecumenical ties and cooperation are encouraged.[15]

David Mutchler in 1965 classified the Brazilian Church hierarchy in four groups: ultraconservatives, conservatives, moderates, and progressives. It is a reflection of the changing positions within the Church that Mutchler's typology would better fit the situation in 1970 if the ultraconservative classification were removed and one somewhat more to the left of the progressive were added. Ultraconservatives no longer exist in sufficient numbers or have sufficient power to warrant a separate classification. Mutchler also noted the existence of a small group of priests who believed that violence was necessary to achieve Church goals, but he did not consider it large enough or important enough to include in his classification. The government today does. Yet another classification is that of Father Godofredo Deelen, a sociologist in the Brazilian Church-sponsored social research organization called CERIS, who classifies the priests as conservative (the politicians), moderate (the papists), pastoral (the pastors), and progressive (the pluralists).[16]

Until little more than a decade ago, the hierarchy was under the control of the politicians. Sebastião Cardinal Leme and Jaime Cardinal Camara, who succeeded him were probably the most effective of these leaders. There is a community of interest between them and the *latifundistas* (large landowners), the less progressive minded industrialists and commercial leaders, and the more intransigent military who believe that Communism is at the root of all problems.

To judge by the character of pronouncements by the *Conferencia Nacional dos Bispos do Brasil* (CNBB)—National Conference of Brazilian Bishops—the weight of opinion among the hierarchy rests somewhere between the moderates and the progressives, that is, the papists and pluralists as described by Villier. Because of conditions among the flock in the endemically poverty-stricken Northeast, bishops from that part of Brazil exercise an influence in the CNBB beyond their weight in numbers. Leaders among the moderates are Cardinal Sherer of Porto Alegre and Eugenio Cardinal Sales who was named Archbishop of Rio de Janerio on the death of Cardinal Camara. Cardinal Sales is a leader of the pastors. He gained considerable fame for his work in Natal where he was chief coordinator of the "Natal Movement," which fostered radio schools, labor unions, cooperatives, health clinics, agricultural clubs, and other community projects.

Dom Helder Pessoa Camara, Archbishop of Recife and Olinda, has long been recognized as the leader of the progressives, or pluralists. He is perhaps the best known internationally of Brazilian churchmen as a result of his work as auxiliary bishop of Rio de Janeiro and his out-

spoken criticism of the existing order. His extreme political and social
position—he is a strong critic of capitalism and refuses to blame Communism for all his country's problems—has made him a principal target
of the *latifundistas* of the Northeast and the military. His unrelenting
fight for radical social change has generated so much animosity that his
life has been threatened and one of his aides was murdered in 1969.

Dom Helder Camara does not preach violence. In fact, he has specifically foresworn violence as a means for achieving Church goals. He has
labeled his methods as "Liberating Moral Pressure" designed to force
the government to make social reforms. Nevertheless, his pronouncements leave no doubt that his goals will be hard to achieve without resort to extreme pressure. Writing in the July-August 1969 *Catholic
Worker* of Milwaukee, after observing that superficial revisions of the
underdeveloped world are inadequate, he noted: "It will take a structural
revolution" to break away from "a sort of internal colonialism, in which
the wealth of a small number of priviliged people is bought with the
misery of millions of their fellow citizens." Dom Helder Camara would
doubtless have been silenced a long time ago were he not a personal
friend of Pope Paul VI, as he was of Pope John XXIII when he took a
leading role among the progressives at Vatican II.

Less adept than Dom Helder Camara at gaining public attention—or
less interested in working in the glare of publicity—is Dom Avelar
Brandão Vilela, Archbishop of Teresinha, who has been secretary general of the CNBB and president of the Latin American Episcopal
Conference. Dom Avelar is a convinced pluralist, with a firm belief in
the need to give national Churches more autonmy than Rome seems
prepared to grant. He was made a cardinal in 1973.

It would be well here briefly to review some events that have signaled
the changing temper of the Brazilian Church, irrespective of the divergent
views held by individual bishops and priests. Discontent in and out of
the Church with its sternly conservative role during the 1940's, concerned largely with a decline in morality and the threat of Communism,
coincided with a growing concern in the Vatican over its declining position. Changes were made among the hierarchy and liberal papal nuncios
were assigned. In the 1950's, Pope Paul VI, then Giovanni Cardinal
Montini, took a leading part in bringing these changes about. Archbishop
Helder Camara, then Bishop, was made secretary-general of the newly
formed National Conference of Bishops. In 1962, "at the request of

Pope John XXIII, and conscious of the very special position in which the Church in Brazil finds itself, [the CNBB] undertook . . . an intensive effort at pastoral renewal based on the Emergency Plan." The Emergency Plan was replaced several years later with the Joint Pastoral Plan (1966-1970).[17]

How far the Church had moved by early 1963 can be seen in the statement of bishops made April 30 of that year, reluctantly approved even by the conservative Cardinal Camara who apparently signed only after certain expressions were changed and an injunction against birth control added.[18] Of particular importance in this document, entitled *Pacem in Terris and the Brazilian Reality,* is a section devoted to the expropriation of land, a subject on which conservative churchmen had long been adamant in support of the *latifundistas.* Noting that the social system is "still debased by the heavy weight of the capitalist tradition . . ." it states that the "majority . . . is deprived of the exercise of many of the fundamental and natural rights which are mentioned in the encyclical *Pacem in Terris:* the right of existence and to a decent standard of living, the right of human liberty and dignity, the right to participate in the benefits of culture; in other words the right to live as a man in society . . . No one can ignore the situation of millions of our brothers living in the rural areas who cannot share in the development of our nation, who live in conditions of misery which are an affront to human dignity . . . [Let it be known] that the expropriation of land in such a situation is in no way contrary to the social doctrine of the Church."

The liberal press published the document under headlines of approval; some conservative papers either refused to print it or strongly condemned it. However, conservative reaction then, and subsequently even sharper reaction, failed to sidetrack the new programs first stirred to life at Vatican II. The Joint Pastoral Plan institutionalized and activated changes hitherto often limited to statements of aspirations. The Pastoral Plan envisions the creation of "means and conditions for the Church in Brazil to adjust as rapidly and fully as possible to the spirit of Vatican II." It calls for the Church to assume "a fully civilizing role" in areas of the country where patriarchal structural and subsistence economies persist. Its role is established as "animating the people to a leavening role for the construction of a better world." In other words, it will urge upon communicants an active role in seeking a better life— itself a revolutionary concept. This has been called "concientization," or the transformation of members of a passive lower class into individuals who are aware of their condition and also aware that they can have a role in determining their future. This concept, endorsed by the Latin American Episcopal Conference in August 1968, has been explained as education that liberates as opposed to education that "domesticates." In the words of the Brazilian educator Dr. Paulo Freire: "The result of a liberating education is that it moves the student to act on or transform his world." [19]

"Concientization" in the sense used by Paulo Friere has been employed by a relatively small number of priests and bishops. These are the pluralists, the strong progressives, and those on the far left among the priests. Their orientation has been revealed at such meetings as the VII General Assembly of the Conference of Religious Orders of Brazil held in Rio de Janeiro in July 1968. The basic document of that conference was approved by a vote of 387 to 6. It reveals a political, social, and economic sophistication that differs sharply from traditional ecclesiastical thought. "Vast rural estates little cultivated or not cultivated at all, deterioration of the terms of international trade; lack of savings and capital; inequality of opportunity and income as between regions and classes; economic and political colonialism masking pressures and domination under the appearance of independence and autonomy; obsolete educational systems and methods," are held to be responsible for retarding economic growth and social progress. "The unity of a whole fraternal and dynamic people is destroyed," the document goes on to say, "by the interests of minorities, by the wealth of a small number contrasted to the marginalization of the majority of the population."

The document takes to task those who "seek a solution [to outdated capitalism] through the simple installation of a Communism equally contrary to Christianity," but ends with the charge that anti-Communism often blinds people to the need for "indispensable and radical reforms of structures and mentalities." [20]

The temper of many even more radical priests is evident from one of several statements issued by 102 priests of Rio de Janeiro during the VII General Assembly, which denounced the capitalist system and the profit motive, holding them and private property to be responsible for Brazil's "hunger, misery, sickness, promiscuity . . . [and] exploitation and hemorrhage of our resources." This statement was repudiated by twelve bishops, led by the Bishop of Diamantina, in a letter to President

Costa e Silva contending that the progressives in the Church, although a noisy group, were a minority.

The conservatives and the moderates probably outnumber the progressives by a wide margin, particularly among the diocesan bishops, but it should also be observed that the ideas accepted by the conservatives today would have made them the radicals or progressives of yesterday.

The Laity

Paralleling developments within the Church a new militant and socially conscious movement grew in the lay organizations. This movement had its base among the middle and upper classes and exerted a profound influence on the Church itself, forcing it to change more quickly than if it had been subjected to pressures only from the lower class.

Unlike the strong Christian Democratic political parties of several other Latin American countries, which have been channels for Catholic lay political activities, the Brazilian Christian Democratic Party was slow to develop and never became popular. This can be laid to the success of the Family Electoral Alliances and Catholic Electoral Leagues founded during the Vargas dictatorship. These Church-guided groups were successful in electing candidates who met their criteria and in defeating leftist candidates.[21] It also suited Vargas's interests to incorporate the demands of these lay groups, based on papal encyclicals *Rerum Novarum* (1891) and *Quadregesimo Anno* (1931), into the 1934 Constitution. These successes seemed to make a strong Christian Democratic Party unnecessary, and in any event Cardinal Leme discouraged Catholic lay political activities. That this judgment was wrong can be deduced from the fact that in countries where a Christian Democratic Party has prospered, social reform has moved far more rapidly and politics have been more stable than in Brazil. Such a political party provided an effective channel for Catholic lay leaders to work within the system. There are exceptions, but in countries where political parties like the CDP have been weak or nonexistent, such as Brazil, Ecuador, Peru, Argentina, Paraguay, and Guatemala, the governments have often been repressive and reformers and reform movements have moved into illegal channels to carry on what they would call effective activities.

The period of great economic development beginning in the 1930's and reaching peaks in the late forties and late fifties, led many Brazilians to the conclusion that the conservative churchmen were derelict in their responsibility to adjust to the spiritual and material needs of hundreds of thousands moving from semifeudal rural Brazil to urban centers unprepared to receive them. A Catholic Left—including professional politicians, scholars, students, journalists, and clergy strongly motivated by concepts of nationalism and development as well as social justice—began to take shape.

Some of the newly arrived foreign priests named to strategic posts, such as the young Dominicans placed in charge of Catholic Action, a socially oriented lay group, brought radical ideas from other countries. The relative conservatism of Jacques Maritain, who had inspired the youth of midcentury and earlier, was replaced by the ideas of the existentialist, Emmanuel Mounier, who saw capitalistic institutions as the "principal agents of oppression of the human person." The French Dominican, Father Lebret, an economist, developed a concept of a world made up of the northern hemisphere of developed nations which were indifferent to the southern hemisphere of undeveloped nations. This concept had a profound influence not only on the Catholic Left but on national policy in all Latin America. Herbert Marcuse has also influenced Latin American youth, as he has influenced youth in the United States and elsewhere.

The most extreme group in the Catholic Left arose from the old *Juventude Católica Universitaria* (JUC), Catholic University Youth, the university branch of Catholic Action. The JUC developed close ties with the *União Nacional de Estudantes* (UNE), National Student Union, the major university student organization in the country. Believing that their objectives could be reached more quickly and effectively by alliances with the Left rather than the Right, some of the JUC leaders gained control of the UNE with open support from young Communists. Another, even more radical, group formed *Ação Popular* (AP), People's Action, in 1962 as a nonconfessional political-ideological organization. By 1964 it had a membership of about 3,000, largely university students. One of its basic precepts was that the tide of history gives the underveloped world the role of a revolutionary to further international socialism that seeks human betterment. Many in AP sought to work with independent labor groups or worked with the Communists, convinced at that time (1963-1964) that President Goulart, who claimed to be fighting for basic reforms, was no more than an opportunist seeking to perpetuate himself in office.[22] The Church hastened to disassociate itself from AP when the group took a strongly leftist tack. How representative the AP was (or is) of the Catholic Left is not clear, but most of the evidence indicates that both the AP and the UNE are small minorities. Nevertheless, their capacity for creating large problems cannot be ignored, particularly as excessive repression brings them sympathy and support from moderate groups.

More moderate members of the laity have been active politically as well as in community or educational work that has led them to see the need for social change if Brazil is to become a modern nation. These include men and women in all branches of society, particularly professors in the social sciences, journalists, writers, and even high-ranking military officers.

The extreme Catholic Left was instrumental in polarizing the opposing views of Church and State. The AP and other Catholic youth were the leaders of student demonstrations that began by promoting student grievances and ended by calling for the overthrow of the military dictatorship. Some of the more progressive churchmen were swept up in the reaction against police and military authorities and directly defied state authority, as when they allowed the outlawed UNE to hold clandestine meetings in seminaries. Moreover the government claimed to have established direct links between members of religious orders and terrorist or guerilla groups.

The AP was outlawed early in the days of the Castello Branco Government (1964-1967) and the UNE was shorn of its semiofficial status as university student representatives. In their zeal to uncover Communists, some regional military commanders questioned or jailed priests. A number were forced by the government to leave the country. Many radical Christian Democrats fled the country when Goulart was overthrown by the military. At the beginning of Castello Branco's efforts to get back to democratic procedures and to promote economic stabilization and a number of important economic and social reforms, political calm was the general rule. Later, in 1966, after the government reinstituted "revolutionary" (read dictatorial) rule in consequence of pressure from hard-line colonels and lower ranking officers, terrorist activity began. Increasingly repressive measures to meet terrorist and nascent guerilla activity, coupled with the government's failure to move on the educational front, soon brought mounting protests from the students.

The phenomenon has a dynamic of its own. On the one hand urban terrorism on the part of students and dedicated revolutionaries often leads to mindless police action that turns thousands against the government at home and abroad. An extreme but accurate example is that noted in a laconic Reuters dispatch from Rio de Janeiro dated November 14, 1969, which reported that the Archbishop of Riberão Preto, in the State of São Paulo, had excommunicated the Chief of Police for "using electric shock tortures on an imprisoned convent mother superior," because she allegedly "allowed her convent to be used as a cell for a leftist guerilla movement."

Relations between Church and State promised to improve after President Emílio Garrastazú Médici assumed office late in 1969. Subsequent events, however, showed how difficult it is to regain control of powerful forces like militant priests and overzealous police and military officers once they have escaped the restraining hand of central authority. A case in point is that of seven Dominican priests arrested on charges of aiding terrorists. Ignoring the more moderate policies of the Brazilian hierarchy and the even more accommodating policies of the Holy See, they openly urged revolutionary tactics. As quoted by Father McCabe, a British Dominican editor of the Blackfriars magazine, from a document smuggled out of their São Paulo prison, the priests declared that "Christian love must have a political dimension or be nothing." The Christian response to the Brazilian situation, the priests wrote, would have to be extreme: "The only way a violent dictatorship has left to us is the way of revolution. This is the rightful self-defense of a people desperate under oppression—the right to fight for its life." [22a]

On the other hand the proliferation of security agencies which sprouted when it became apparent that the regular police were fighting a losing battle against the urban terrorists, made it all but impossible for the government to control them. Not only do police and military security officers often act virtually autonomously—particularly in areas far from the capital or the large urban areas—but work under varying criteria depending on the local military commander. Some police and military see all opposition, whether politically or religiously inspired, as Communist. Even President Médici's resolutions and promises often proved ineffective. In early 1970, the President said there would be no mistreatment, and certainly no torture of prisoners. Shortly thereafter a prominent, democratic labor leader of São Paulo died after detention and questioning by the police. The government also promised not to arrest priests without prior notice to the Church hierarchy. Nevertheless, arrests continued. Father José Antonio de Magalhaes Monteiro was arrested August 3 in Maranhão by local authorities and, according to a carefully documented report prepared by churchmen, tortured.[22b] Father José Antonio and a French priest, arrested at the same time, were cleared of charges of subversion by a military court early in October, but local authorities, as they always do, denied charges of torture.

In all these cases the President seemed reluctant to take any action against comrades-in-arms except in absolutely clear cases of defiance of authority which are rare. Exceeding authority is far from rare. More difficult to cope with were the activities of the air force security group under a hardline Air Minister. Only after he had been eased out in late 1971 were effective measures taken to circumscribe its activities.

An uneasy truce between the government and the hierarchy had been reached when the National Conference of Bishops early in 1970 adopted a resolution deploring violence of any kind, meant to apply to both Church and State. The government for its part promised to speed up trials of all political prisoners and to move more cautiously when churchmen were involved. Nevertheless, the situation soon deteriorated, as has been noted, to the point that the government was being charged with persecuting the Church. A study of torture and repression was publicly noted by Pope Paul and the Vatican organ *L'Osservatore Romano,* in late October 1970, denounced "arbitrary repression" and "interference by the State in Church affairs in Brazil." [22c] This latter charge was based in part on continued harassment of Archbishop Helder Camara. The charges, drawn up by the CNBB, were detailed in a letter from Cardinal Sales to President Médici which was delivered personally to the President by the conservative Jaime Cardinal Camara. Many Church authorities had come to the conclusion that the government was using the Archbishop of Recife to justify anti-clerical policies.

In an effort to heal the widening breech between Church and State, Pope Paul instructed Cardinal Rossi of São Paulo to issue a statement to the press denying a campaign against the Church in Brazil. The note, dated October 20, appeared in the Latin American press on November 1. After noting some "Christian efforts" on the part of President Médici, and acknowledging that difficulties had arisen by reason of arbitrariness and injustice on the part of some authorities, the statement said that "the Pope knows that these problems do not constitute religious persecution as has been held, with evident exaggeration, in the press and on radio and television in Europe, the United States, and Canada." The note concluded with the somewhat opaque observation that the Pope is not unware that darnel and wheat are to be found together wherever there are men, in whatever position they may hold." [22d] This statement seemed to be saying that good men and evil men can be found on both sides of the dispute.

That the Brazilian hierarchy and the Vatican at this time were working at cross purposes was apparent from the action of the Central Committee of the CNBB at an emergency meeting four days before the publication of Cardinal Rossi's note. The Committee condemned the abuse of human rights and called on the authorities "to take the most effective and earliest measures to assure a climate of solidarity, justice, and liberty, indispensable for the realization of the great destiny of the nation and for the projection of its true image in the community of peoples." [22e]

Beclouding the issue even more, Cardinal Rossi, who had been chairman of the Central Committee of the CNBB, shortly after was transferred to the Vatican as Prefect of the Congregation for propagation of the faith. The transfer raised many questions and brought conflicting allegations. Protests were so insistent that the Pope took the unprecedented step in modern times to publicly deny that the transfer had any other motive than to put an able churchman at the head of an activity held by the Pope to be of the highest importance. He added that any suggestions that the Cardinal's removal had some relationship "with certain aspects of the political situation in Brazil" were entirely without foundation.[23]

Inextricably linked to the matter of Church vs. State is that of

national vs. universal Church. How far can the Vatican tolerate or—
perhaps more pertinent—control activity within national churches
which may damage the mother Church? And how far can the national
Church let itself be restricted in fighting for principles and social justice
involving its suffering and wavering flock?

It is apparent that the Church is gaining new strength and prestige
through closer identification with the Brazilian masses. The percentage
of foreign clergy had dropped from 40 percent in 1960 to 35 percent
in 1968.[24] The change has probably brought the Church closer to its
early colonial position of independence, when it was concerned more
with the realities of Brazilian life than with purely spiritual values
of the then universal Church. On the other hand, an increasing number
of commissions, national and regional secretariats, and Vatican Councils bring the word and policies of Rome and other national episcopates
to the Brazilian Church. Foreign priests and bishops, many of papist
persuasion, do the same. The establishment of the National Conference
of Brazilian Bishops as well as its social program resulted from Papal
initiative. Nevertheless, the pluralist progressives and some others believe that too close control from Rome will inhibit the effectiveness of
national Churches. The decision of Rome in 1969 to accede to pressure from the Brazilian Government by 1) transfering a liberal papal
nuncio alleged to be encouraging revolutionary attitudes among the
hierarchy and 2) restricting pronouncements by Archbishop Helder
Camara to his own diocese are illustrative of such inhibitory actions.[25]
The papacy must also deal with reality, and the Pope is advised by,
among others, sage, politically minded but very old cardinals who
probably find it hard to overlook some of the aberrations of emerging
societies. On the other hand, many pluralist and even moderate
Brazilian churchmen are more concerned with solving the people's
problems than in accepting a slow pace of reform.

These problems are directly related to issues debated at the Extraordinary Synod of Bishops held in the fall of 1969 in Rome. They
concern the degree of local autonomy to be exercised by the national
Churches and the degree of ultramontane influence to be allowed in
decisions at the Vatican. During the Extraordinary Synod, Dom Avelar
Brandão Vilela, Archbishop of Teresinha, criticized "the rigid control
exercised by the Roman Curia over the Church," suggesting that
it should take into account "the native culture of each region," adopt-

ing pluralism as the way most "capable of concretely expressing the dynamic and local contribution of the local Churches within the universal Church." [26] But the Vatican can well ask itself, if the national Churches are given too great latitude will some become so radical as to destroy themselves and, in the process, the universal Church?

The Church and Modernization

A thesis has been developed that the pace and ultimate success of programs of modernization and development in underdeveloped Latin America will rest on the ability of the Church to adopt to the changing order in the world and to exert its cultural and religious influence to hasten social change.[27] This thesis accepts the premise, which most developmental economists and political scientists are not yet prepared to agree to, that the Church in Latin America is probably the only agency with sufficient moral authority to bring about the kind of social change necessary for modernization without using revolutionary means.

It is apparent that the Church in Brazil has embarked on a course aimed at achieving social justice and integrating the poverty-stricken part of the population into the developmental process. It is not yet clear that it set out to do this. Rather, the liberal Pope John XXIII saw that the Brazilians, like many others, faced the fate of the Church in Cuba and other Communist countries if it did not exert itself to become more relevant to the masses in their problems of day-to-day living. The Church is now consciously an agent of change, seeking to promote and reinforce changes which were first sought by no more than a handful of priests and a few bishops who had been born in poverty. Another spur to renewal, along with the Communist inroads among the masses, is the effective work of evangelical sects who do outstanding social work among the newly arrived urban poor, work which many Catholic churchmen believed could not be done.[28] Not only has the Church been moved by an increasingly popular existential theology that insists it must adapt to the changing order in the world if it is to survive in its diminishingly dominant role, but Catholic lay leaders have also joined with activist Church leaders to fortify the pastoral and pluralistic role of the Church. It is also clear that the moderate and progressive elements within the Church in Brazil, influenced by the more extreme progressives, effectively make the principal decisions.

The question then remains how effective will the Church be in forcing change in a society still dominated by entrenched elites buttressed by the conservatives in the armed forces? The succession of confrontations which began in 1964 threatened an open break between Church and State, but by 1970 efforts were being made on both sides to bring about an acceptable *modus vivendi*. Nevertheless, the priests and nuns who march with and protect students and workers and the bishops who have accepted Archbishop Helder Camara's "Liberating Moral Pressure" methods, will bring on more confrontations unless the government adopts measures to further social justice. These differences will be difficult to deal with even under military-controlled government because of the clergy's high prestige in Brazilian society. After a succession of serious confrontations with students in which the administration appeared more reactionary than it liked, the Costa e Silva administration seemed to become aware of the danger to its stability. It then took important steps toward educational reform and moved with spectacular success in the area of housing.

But the Church will have to change the mentality not only of the industrial and rural elites but also that of many military leaders in order to ease the way to reform. The military as a group may or may not favor social change but many high-ranking generals and active hard-line colonels do not understand social ferment except as a present danger to national security.

More important than the serious and not so serious confrontations are the basic documents issued by the Brazilian Church which, for the first time, have put a stamp of legitimacy on radical social reform. The long-run effects of these documents are almost certain to force on conservative elites a clearer understanding of the need for social change, and they may require the government to hasten the present slow pace of improving living standards for millions of poverty-stricken Brazilians.

Organized Labor

Brazil's labor force is about 32 percent of the total population. In 1970, 42.08 percent of this number worked in agriculture; 26.86 percent in trade, services and similar; 16.83 percent in manufacturing; 7.39 percent in social services and public administration; and 2.68 percent in primary industries.[29]

Although organized labor is usually considered an independent associational group, in Brazil it is tied so closely to the government, and control is usually so tight, that it can best be understood as an institutional interest group. Urban labor is widely organized in the large industrial centers, but the unions have relatively little influence either economically or politically, considering the size of their membership. Rarely have the unions been able to force minimum wages to keep pace with inflation. This paradox arises from the fact that the modern unions were organized under the Vargas dictatorship as a political instrument to support the *Estado Novo,* and, regardless of radical changes in governments since that time, the unions are still controlled through the Ministry of Labor and Social Welfare.

Despite lack of true independence the unions act as pressure groups, sometimes effectively; more often they are given little autonomy and, because they are dependent on the government for financial support and patronage, seldom attempt to go beyond the limits set for them by the government in power. After the 1964 revolution, following a period of partial manipulation with undisciplined action under Goulart, the unions reverted to a more docile role.

Through connections in the bureaucracy and through representatives in the congress, usually Brazilian Labor Party (PTB) deputies and senators, labor leaders have had important influence in formulating policy. They participate in political campaigns, usually those linked to strongly nationalistic movements affecting domestic and foreign policies. Presidents Quadros and Goulart chose to justify changes in Brazilian foreign policy by claiming to be bowing to demands from urban labor. Toward the end of the Goulart period, unions often acted independently when they struck over political issues without official approval. These strikes usually developed under Communist leadership that did not always respond as Goulart would have liked.

Government control is maintained through a system based on the Italian corporate state. The syndical tax of one day's wages per annum for social welfare is the primary source of union funds, and control over disbursement of these funds serves to strengthen the position of the Ministry of Labor. The system of patronage serves a similar purpose. Labor and management representatives are appointed to the social security institutes, the special labor courts, and the management-labor councils established in the numerous government-owned agencies or corporations. Almost all high-level labor leaders hold such appointments, which in most cases are a principal source of their income.

Democratic collective bargaining has been discouraged or, at times, even prohibited; changes in wages are usually controlled by the government. The Castello Branco government, which had promised to reform labor practices, in fact would not permit collective bargaining, maintaining that it was incompatible with economic stabilization. Its wage policies left workers worse off than they were under Goulart or earlier, when governments generally made at least token obeisance to labor's needs.

Communists made important inroads into labor leadership before and during the Goulart period. Goulart allowed them to capture control of the agricultural labor confederation, most confederations of urban workers, and a large number of state confederations. He also permitted them to organize the powerful, though illegal, General Labor Command.

Authoritative figures on the size of the Brazilian labor force and union membership are not available. The 1966 industrial census indicated that 2,148,310 workers were engaged in industrial enterprises, a jump from 1,425,886 in 1960. However, the trade unions claimed a much larger membership. According to "Labor Law and Practice in Brazil," a publication of the U. S. Department of Labor released in 1967, all Brazilian trade unions claimed a total membership of 12 million as of late 1966, including members who paid no dues other than the syndical tax. These were unions affiliated with federations which in turn were organized into eight national confederations covering the major economic sectors recognized by the government: agriculture; industry; commerce; ocean, river, and air transportation; land transportation; communications and public information; credit institutions; and education and culture.

An in-depth study of labor prepared by the pragmatic business weekly *Boletim Cambial Semanal* shortly after President Costa e Silva took office in 1967, gave the figure for urban workers as between 5 and 5.5 million, of whom 2 million were said to be working in the industrial sector. It estimated that only 1.5 million of the total were unionized, that is, were dues-paying members. By union reckoning, however, 5 million members were in industry alone, 3.5 million in commerce, and 1 million in transportation.

Reflecting general opinion, *Boletim Cambial* noted that at times labor unions seemed to be a powerful force capable of changing the directions of the country, as during the Goulart administration when many feared that Brazil would become a syndicalist republic. In fact, union leadership was weak, the membership was only lightly involved with the the leadership, and whether from helplessness or lack of identification with the leadership, hardly a murmur was raised by the rank and file in defense of their leaders or their patron, President Goulart, when he was overthrown in March 1964. This basic weakness can be ascribed principally to the system instituted by Vargas that imposed leadership from the top, partly through the use of so-called *"pelegos"* (political henchman), representatives of the Ministry of Labor within the confederations. As in other areas of government, the system was paternalistic.

The Castello Branco government used intervention procedures to clean out elements considered corrupt or subversive by government authorities. In several speeches the President promised to peg salaries to the cost of living and to give the unions more autonomy. On both counts, he failed to carry out his promises. Some long-term measures to increase worker independence were taken but, since this took a number of short-term advantages from the workers, they were not welcomed.

The short-lived Costa e Silva administration failed to put into effect promises of "a free labor movement without interference from the government." It did, however, free all but a handful of unions from the direct control imposed in April 1964, and made some wage adjustments. Even so it still had to contend with several illegal strikes.

Other labor groups outside the official trade union structure operated as pressure groups with varying effectiveness. Federal and state public servants belonged to the National Association of Public Employees. Catholic Workers' Circles with a claimed membership of 450,000 formed the *Confederação Brasileira de Trabalhadores Cristianos,* (CBTC), Brazilian Confederation of Christian Workers. The CBTC was not legally recognized and was dedicated primarily to welfare and educational activities among its members.

In modern times, rural labor as a body has probably been the worst off of all Brazilian labor. Some attention began to be paid to the lot of the *campesino* during the early 1960's when Francisco Julião, an undisciplined Marxist, was organizing the *Ligas Camponesas* (Peasant Leagues) in the Northeast. Although rural workers were repressed and prevented from organizing—even the organizing and social work of Catholic priests like Padre Melo and and Padre Cicero was beset with difficulties created by landowners and officials alike—the *Estatuto do Trabalhador Rural* (Statute of the Rural Laborer) became law in 1963. The statute gave the rural workers recognition and established the *Confederação Nacional dos Trabalhadores na Agricultura* (CONTAG), National Confederation of Agricultural Workers, as the organization through which they were to be organized. The law of 1963 put the rural worker on an equal basis with the urban worker, but the legal act was largely worthless since implementing legislation was not passed until six years later. A number of important measures became law in 1969, including one instituting the *carteira de trabalho* (the work book) and social security. The day of the rural worker had by no means come since it would take time to force many landowners to obey the letter and spirit of the laws, but the corner had been turned.

Until 1968 AFL-CIO labor unions, through membership in the Inter-American Regional Labor Organization, and the international trade secretariats maintained relations with the principal Brazilian confederations. The foreign unions gave assistance through trade union education and leadership training. The Brazilian confederations were also formally tied to the democratic International Confederation of Free Trade Unions (ICFTU). In 1968 this relationship came under concentrated attack by ultranationalist legislators, labor leaders, and others —including the military who looked on such association as a potential disturbance to the *status quo*. The Castello Branco administration threatened to expel representatives of the international organizations resident in Brazil when criticism was leveled against the government's labor policies in 1966. It did not carry out the threat, but a congressional investigating committee in 1968 claimed to have uncovered illegal and unwarranted interference by the international labor organizations in Brazilian unions and recommended regulations restricting the activities of all foreign labor organizations. The recommendations were carried out.

Paternalistic control by the government over the trade union movement has retarded its democratic development. Control has been maintained in order to hold labor support for the government in power and to keep the movement out of the hands of the Communists. Paradoxically, however, the system has favored Communist labor leaders who are usually better trained than the non-Communists. Since the government keeps the unions under close scrutiny and limits their resources, their leaders sometimes find there is less available to them than to the Communists. The result is that the Communists often have controlled large sectors of the movement. This pattern of Communist control has helped create a vicious circle, and all labor initiatives are viewed with suspicion by the Brazilian middle class and the armed forces. The use of corruptible *pelegos* by the government to control labor action also serves to discredit the unions.

Despite the fact that it has been the largest politically oriented organized group in Brazil since 1964, labor has effectively been excluded from the political process. Labor thus seems to be a powerless, politically malleable giant emasculated by a system that usually meets its material claims sufficiently to ward off uncontrollable explosions. Labor leaders organize demonstrations and campaigns on instructions from government officials seeking to influence public opinion for administration objectives. Labor was an important factor in demands for nationalistic solutions to economic problems, as in the establishment of the petroleum monopoly, PETROBRAS, the power monopoly ELECTROBRAS, and the passage by congress of the profits remittance bill in 1962.

The steady growth of the Brazilian Labor Party from the time of its founding in the 1940's to its pinnacle of power under Goulart served to bring many ambitious politicians to high places of power. The brilliant corporation lawyer, former Integralist (Fascist) leader, San Tiago Dantas, chose the PTB as a vehicle to political power and became the party ideologist under Goulart, whom he served as Minister of Finance and Minister of Foreign Affairs. Goulart himself, one of the wealthiest landowners of Brazil, rose to the presidency as a PTB leader. This leadership was not won but rather was inherited from the party's spiritual founder, Getúlio Vargas. By maintaining tight control over the labor leaders, the political leaders are able to use the strength of labor for political campaign purposes without making corresponding contributions to institutionalizing and strengthening the labor movement or to democratize it so that genuine labor leaders can become important political leaders. Some idealistic leaders like Alberto Pasqualini, a founder of the PTB, his spiritual heir, Francisco Ferrari, and Hugo

Faria were forced to compromise with principles to get even token political concessions for labor, and none wielded decisive power. As in other parts of Brazilian society, the government, whether labor oriented or conservative, has chosen to adopt a paternalistic role by giving its members substantially improved social and economic conditions, but at the expense of making them politically impotent.

Thus, organized labor has been less a political force in the interests of the laboring class than a force used by political leaders for personal political ambitions.

Organized Special Interest Groups

The quasi-corporate state created by Getúlio Vargas set up not only employer and labor organizations but also a number of associations of the liberal professions. Associations of lawyers, engineers, and doctors were among them, and although they were created by the government, most have maintained autonomy and from time to time operate as pressure groups. The government occasionally consults the *Instituto dos Advogados* (Lawyers' Institute) for opinions on proposed legislation, and that body occasionally researches and expresses opinions on cases or issues in which important principles of law or questions of the constitutionality of laws or procedures are raised. Under Castello Branco, the engineers' association took a strongly nationalistic stand against the employment of foreign engineers in supervisory roles on United States Agency for International Development (AID) and World Bank projects. They succeeded in forcing a relaxation of regulations that had made it difficult to employ Brazilian professionals. The press is their principal channel of communications when they try to influence public opinion. Their most effective efforts of this nature are by direct influence or pressure through personal contacts. As members of the elite, they find it relatively easy to establish communications with decision-making centers.

University students make up one of the most unruly groups in Brazil, as they do in most Latin American countries. The influence of major university groups has been much greater than that of students in the United States—at least until the late 1960's—because in Latin America university students occupy an almost unique position in society. Not only are most of them from the upper class and thus lead highly privileged lives, but they themselves comprise a small elite and are recognized as the future leaders of the nation.[30] Harm to a student quickly becomes a *cause célèbre,* and therefore civil and military authorities exercise great caution in dealing with student problems.

For many years Brazilian university students were represented by the *União Nacional de Estudantes* (UNE), National Student Union. It was recognized and subsidized by the government. The UNE was never a completely cohesive organization because opposing groups within it fought for control. As in most such organizations, activists were a small minority. One poll indicated that even among Brazilian law students, the most politically active, only 36 percent claimed to participate in student politics.[31] Most students, particularly those outside the larger capitals, usually go about their studies with little attention to political problems.

The principal groups which vied for influence in or control over the UNE until 1962 were the *Juventude Universitario Católico* (JUC), far and away the largest; the *Partido Comunista Brasileiro* (PCB), Brazilian Communist Party; and some smaller leftist groups such as the Trotskyite *Politica Operária* (POLOP), Workers' Politics. In 1962 a new group call *Ação Poplar* (AP), People's Action, was established as an offshoot of JUC, whose political activities had been restricted by the Catholic Church hierarchy. The UNE was outlawed in 1966 after the revolutionary government that came into power in 1964 was unsuccessful in bringing about its demise by withdrawing the government's subsidy. Coincident with the rise of the new Catholic Left before the revolution, the leadership of UNE had become increasingly radical. Thus in 1959 João Manoel Conrado, President of the JUC, was elected President of the UNE with Communist support. The young radicals became convinced that they had more in common with the Left than with the Right and that, to be effective, students would have to form a united front with the political Left.[32] Simultaneously the same intellectual influences that were helping form the Catholic Left were making a deep impression on university students. This influence was far less Communist than it was Catholic leftist, much of it brought to Brazil by visiting European notables like the French Dominican, Thomas Cardonnel. The influence was indeed heavily weighted toward Marxian thought but was by no means sympathetic to the Soviet Union. Nevertheless, this circumstance probably explains the ease with which

JUC leaders could work with Communist Youth without adopting Communism as a system to cure Brazilian ills. In 1961, Aldo Arantes, who espoused the new Catholic Left outlook, was elected president of the UNE in an open coalition with Communists and other leftists. Leaders from the Catholic Left retained the presidency until the 1964 revolution.

During this prerevolutionary period the young Communists not only exerted considerable influence in the selection of UNE leaders but without doubt they also influenced political action. There is little question that this influence was brought to bear less through the number of Communist students than through their organizational sophistication, as often happened in labor unions. The activities of other extreme leftist groups in the student movement were marginal.

With the founding of the *Ação Popular* in 1962, however, a major new element was injected into the student movement. Its organization, on a cell basis, became highly sophisticated. The AP had arisen out of dissatisfaction with the restricted role of formal Catholic lay organizations in politics. Because of the AP's extremist position, the Church soon disavowed its support of the group, although some priests maintained connections with the students. By the mid-1960's, the objectives of the AP had become so extremist that even the Moscow-oriented Brazilian Communist Party (PCB) severed the ties between them. In mid-1968, the AP in a public manifesto threw in its lot with the small unorthodox mainland China-oriented Communist Party of Brazil, publicly adopting violence as an instrument for change. The Castello Branco government outlawed the AP even before it outlawed the UNE.

In 1968 the AP was still controlled by students, but it sought support from labor and peasants in an effort to broaden its base and become a truly revolutionary force. Justly or unjustly it was credited with a large part of the terrorist activity which began in earnest in 1968, including bank robberies, bombings, and even participation in the kidnapping of the American Ambassador, C. Burke Elbrick, in September 1969. The AP ceased to be a student movement when it went underground and sought general support for revolutionary goals. Although the same might be said of the UNE, as it also was forced to operate underground, the membership of the UNE was confined to students and its chief concern was with educational problems. It tried to preserve its status as primarily a representative student body, and it doubtless expected to be reinstated as the official student organization when the political restrictions of the revolutionary government were lifted.

In an effort to replace the UNE with an organization it could control, or at least that would not have ties with the Communists, the Castello Branco government helped establish the *Direitorio Nacional de Estudantes* (DNE), National Student Directorate. Student leaders of the DNE, however, were soon complaining about lack of government financial support and their inability to win over students without adequate financial resources. It is not clear whether the Government failed to meet commitments with the DNE because of a need to economize or because it concluded that DNE leaders, many of whom were rightist, had too little appeal to win over significant numbers of students.

The political action of student groups is inextricably linked with educational problems, because any group that confined itself principally to political problems, like the AP, would soon lose its character and thereby the authority that student groups enjoy. Political action usually grows out of some connection, however remote, with educational problems. When student groups decide to move, the issue first raised almost invariably has relevance to special student interests. Political action usually develops later when demands are escalated, usually after suppressive measures have been taken by the authorities to quell protests. This was the pattern in 1968 when the military police suppressed the forbidden student protest marches so brutally that students gained not only popular sympathy but also nearly 100,000 more marchers in a later parade that condemned the "military dictatorship." Most of the marchers were from middle-class families, mostly the upper segment, many protesting violence to their sons, daughters, sisters, or brothers. Priests and nuns joined the marchers. Among other consequences, this particular episode resulted in the formation of a number of women's groups dedicated to pressuring the government not only for educational reform but also for other social and political improvements. Many were conservative, middle-class mothers who were shocked at the treatment of their children.

Leonard Therry notes that students claimed "decisive" roles in a number of political crises, including the seating of Vice President Goulart in 1961, the plebescite of 1963 which restored full powers to Goulart, and opposition to Goulart's request for a state of siege in October that same year. He writes that it is more likely that the students themselves were not so influential but that they were influenced by the politicians, some extreme Communists who were mobilizing students as a "maneuver mass" to support goals they and not the students had set. This is probably an accurate assumption, but it fails to take account of student objectives. In Brazil, student goals and goals of politicians often run parallel. Students will work for what they believe to be democratic processes and basic reforms whether or not the politicians themselves are entirely sincere in their objectives. In fact, students are likely to be more sincere in these activities than most politicians. Students in the Catholic Left consciously worked with far leftist political leaders because, mistakenly or not, they saw such collaboration as a means, perhaps the only means, of reaching their own objectives. That they thereby may have served Communist purposes is undeniable, but it is also undeniable that at the same time they were serving their own.

The educational problems that most affect and most concern university students are lack of room in the system for many who pass entrance examinations; poor instruction from part-time professors who enjoy full tenure and cannot be removed; and repressive action initiated under Castello Branco by Ministry of Education officials. The 1968 protests eventually led to a real beginning in educational reform, but one of the prices was a decree-law that established a penalty of expulsion for students and dismissal for faculty members who engaged in unsanctioned protest activities.

Most important among the economic groups are those related to industry, commerce, and agriculture. They include not only representatives of private enterprise but also the *autarquías*,[33] industrial "executive groups," and foreign companies. Private interests in these areas are almost all formally organized, still in the pattern originally set by Vargas during the *Estado Novo*. Most continue to receive financial support from the government. Relatively weak during the Quadros and Goulart period, their influence did not increase appreciably during the Castello Branco government, which often took measures as displeasing to business as to labor in its effort to achieve economic stability. Under Costa e Silva the influence of the "captains of industry" and *latifundistas* began slowly to rise again. These groups all act as pressure groups using political as well as mass media channels to influence government and private opinion.

An organization that does not fit into this pattern and thus is difficult to classify, is the *Instituto de Pesquisas e Estudos Socials* (IPES), Institute of Research and Social Studies. This organization, most of whose members are businessmen of São Paulo and Rio de Janeiro as well as some professionals, was organized shortly after Goulart took office with help from unusually competent specialists in the social sciences. One of the IPES's principal objectives was to alert the public to the potential threat of Goulart as head of government and to thereby limit his freedom of action. Some of its officers claimed a role in educating military opinion, as well as organizing the women who took part in the massive marches before and after Goulart was removed from office in March 1964. IPES has been studied in some depth but it would be a mistake to draw too many conclusions from its activities since it was a group largely organized for a specific, defensive purpose and has been in relative eclipse since the 1964 revolution.[34]

The National Confederation of Industries and the National Confederation of Commerce, made up of similar state federations, are dominated by economic enterprises, most of them controlled by family groups such as the Matarazzo family. This generalization is less valid of the Confederation of Commerce, whose members are more numerous and tend to be less powerful than the industrialists. The interests of the two confederations are not always parallel, but they work together when the principle of private versus state enterprise is involved. The National Confederation of Industries is by far the more nationalistic of the two, since the interests of its members are most affected by competition from enterprises based on foreign capital. The organization had a leading, though unpublicized, role in the passage of a profits-remittance bill in 1962, which strained relations between the United States and Brazil because it adversely affected large business interests using U. S. capital. Communists and vocally extreme nationalists were given credit for forcing the bill through Congress. In fact, more credit was due Brazilian capitalists who have been known to finance the campaigns of extreme, politically active groups, including the Communists, when their interests coincide as they did on the profits remittance issue. As in the United States, contributions to individuals and political party campaigns are common.

These two confederations, along with the politically weakening

Brazilian Rural Confederation, are the most powerful special interest groups in Brazil. Their power is enormous on specific issues when they can mobilize public opinion in their behalf, but since private enterprise is held in high esteem in Brazil and national policy favors industrial and commercial development, conflict is rare. It should be noted, nonetheless, that the national confederations have been notably unsuccessful in influencing many important decisions on economic policy when their interests were narrow and could not be shown to be for the common developmental good. Such decisions, usually made by the technocrats, have often damaged the direct interests of industry.[35]

Most activities of the confederations are more orthodox than the foregoing would indicate. They publish useful economic reports, sponsor institutional advertising designed to educate the public on the virtues of private enterprise or other issues, conduct seminars and undertake extensive economic studies which may be made available to key personnel in the government and congress.

Although the activities of the confederations are chiefly aimed at protecting the interests of their larger and more powerful members, they do not neglect the interests of their weaker members. It is a remarkable fact that Brazilian industrialists as a class and as individuals have been virtually free from attack by politicians and political activists, even the most extreme. This can probably be ascribed not only to able public relations, but also to the importance of the industrialist in the developmental ideology of the country. Most Brazilians are aware of the high profit margin on which most Brazilian industry operates, but this is considered legitimate, whereas profits of foreign enterprises are constantly questioned.

Private enterprise has a voice in *autarquías* such as the *Instituto Brasileiro do Café,* Brazilian Coffee Institute; the *Instituto Brasileiro de Açucar e do Alcool,* Sugar and Alcohol Institute; and others dealing in commodities such as cacao and maté.

The principal officers of these organizations, which set prices, standards, and export quotas for industries, are government officials, but many have been recruited from private industry, and industry representatives are on the boards of directors. The *autarquías* bypass legislative power. They are seldom criticized for favoring the industries under their control since their function is to promote them. Little attention is given to possible conflict of interest. The *autarquías* make recommendations in matters of national policy but they do not make policy. Their importance lies more in making rules in connection with the execution of policy. However, as is the case of the export to the United States of soluble coffee under regulations which U.S. coffee interests call discriminatory to their business, the influence of some of the *autarquías* can be important. These regulations led to acrimonious conflict between the United States and Brazil which in 1970 threatened the existence of the International Coffee Agreement.

Business has an even more direct impact on government policy through the industry executive groups that were established to control and guide the automobile, construction materials, electronics, chemicals, metallurgical, food products and other industries. The industry executive groups are made up of government and business representatives, their principal responsibility being to establish standards, quotas when necessary, and often to protect national producers against foreign competition through tariffs and industry regulations. The industry executive groups (twelve in all in 1967) compete for funds which the Commission for Industrial Development, an agency of the Ministry of Industry and Commerce, makes available for Brazilian industrial enterprise. The commission may grant or deny benefits, but it does not regulate or otherwise control its clients. This is left to the executive groups.

As for the nature of the influence exercised by private industrial and commercial groups, it is noteworthy that family groups are tending to break up, and public participation is now encouraged by active stock markets. Most of these family groups have been strongly self-centered in the past, but the near-chaos to which Goulart led the country made them more amenable to change and to reforms sponsored by the revolutionary governments after 1964. Less acceptable were some of the Castello Branco government's economic stabilization policies which led to great numbers of bankruptcies. Business was powerless to change the decisions based on these policies, and even some of the largest national private enterprises were hurt.

Foreign businesses, many multinational in character, are not usually treated separately as an interest group, but in Brazil their influence is sometimes powerful as a result of their size, number, and importance in the economy. This influence, nevertheless, is far less than that of Brazilian enterprises because of strong nationalistic sentiment. Thus, the latter have no hesitation in complaining publicly about treatment from the government, but a foreign-controlled industry is not likely to make its dissatisfactions public, because it would lay itself open to attacks in congress and by ultranationalists elsewhere. This is particularly true of business controlled by U.S. capital, and many new U.S. firms entering the Brazilian market have taken in Brazilian partners who prove far more able to defend themselves and the firm than do foreigners. One of the most telling campaigns against the United States during the Castello Branco administration was waged over the issue of "denationalization" of Brazilian business, when foreign companies—mostly those with U.S. backing—bought up some Brazilian firms that had gone bankrupt as a result of deflationary measures taken to slow down inflation. In fact, only 5 percent of the country's industries is foreign owned.

Foreign companies usually deal directly with appropriate agencies of the executive branch. On large questions involving a number of companies, a chamber of commerce may represent the views of its members. Most of the approximately 450 U. S.-owned or U.S.-operated businesses are members of the American Chamber of Commerce for Brazil, which has branches in Rio de Janeiro, São Paulo, Porto Alegre, and Recife. Germans, British, French, and others have also established chambers of commerce. The ability of any foreign company to influence events in Brazil often depends on the willingness of its embassy to add its representations to those of the commercial enterprise. The embassy often acts as an honest broker in smoothing out disputes. Its position becomes far more delicate when expropriation is concerned. Thus, after Rio Grande do Sul under Governor Brizola expropriated a subsidiary of the International Telephone and Telegraph Company and offered a meager sum in compensation, the United States embassy pressed the case with Brazilian officials for years until it was finally settled to the satisfaction of the company. United States embassy interest in the profits-remittance law in 1962 and 1963 was the basis for a nationalistic campaign directed against "American imperialism." Even Presidents Kennedy and Goulart became involved in the agreement of the Brazilian government to buy out the properties of the American and Foreign Power Company. Castello Branco honored the agreement less because he liked it than because the United States was persistent in its efforts to secure a settlement.

The influence of foreign companies is not limited simply to matters of policy but ranges far more widely. Foreign companies are usually modern and well managed, and they pay higher salaries than do most national companies, thus becoming a disrupting element in the economy. Their influence is toward modernization, but less efficient national companies or ones with less capital are not likely to look upon such efforts as entirely beneficial to the nation. Nevertheless, foreign businessmen, like their Brazilian colleagues, tend otherwise to be conservative; and they are well aware that their success in the country often depends on the goodwill of the entrenched elites. They usually seek accommodation with them whenever they can.

Other important interest groups are those connected with mining and petroleum activities. The state petroleum monopoly, PETROBRAS, has become a symbol of national liberation from "colonial imperialism" and dependence on foreign capital. Both management and labor have worked together to extend PETROBRAS' operations and to ward off attempts of private national and foreign enterprises to enter the field.

The Brazilian Rural Society with 20,000 members, established in 1897, and the Brazilian Rural Confederation with 250,000, established in 1945, were once highly influential in establishing national policy in Brazil. Their influence has weakened as the industrial and commercial sectors have assumed greater importance in the economy, but they are far from being unimportant, as was made clear by the effective role the spokesmen for coffee interests played in the establishment of support prices for coffee in 1967. The Brazilian Government was under heavy pressure from the International Monetary Fund, the Committee for the Alliance for Progress, and the United States government to continue a policy to deflate coffee earnings, a principal source of inflationary pressure, as well as to encourage agricultural diversification. Coffee interests were successful in convincing the Brazilian government that a substantial part of the economy depended on higher support prices and that economic growth, then bogged down, would be stimulated with the infusion of more money through the coffee sector. It is nonetheless significant that the decision was concurred in by industry-oriented technocrats who believed that economic stimulation was more important at that time than the longer range policy of escaping over-dependence on one crop.

The Brazilian Rural Society is made up of landowners with large holdings. It carries out educational functions. The much larger Rural Confederation has affiliates in all twenty-two states and territories, the largest being that in São Paulo which has some 100,000 members. Its subsidy from the government is sizable, and it carries on extensive technical services and exchanges of information. An important function of the confederation until 1962 was to give guidance to the Rural Social Service, an agency of the government. By moving the Rural Social Service to the Brazilian Institute for Agrarian Reform, the government reduced control by private landowners over rual workers.

Rural interests often exercise more influence on commodity pricing through semiautonomous agencies like the Brazilian Coffee Institute than through their formal associations. Efforts to stall meaningful agrarian reform, obviously a principal preoccupation of any group of large landowners, have been extraordinarily successful.

Women's Groups

Because the Brazilian woman, particularly in the center of the country and in the south, has for years been more emanicipated than women in most Latin American countries, she has always been a force to be reckoned with, and on occasion, an important political force. Vargas first gave women the vote. Women of the upper-middle class were active in the Family Electoral Alliances sponsored by the Catholic Church during the 1950's. In 1967 a state deputy, Mrs. Conceição da Costa Neves, several times vice president of the legislative assembly of São Paulo, pointed out that many politicians underestimate the power of a woman in politics, even when she is not active in politics herself. She based her contention on the thesis that a man's attitude toward his situation is largely set by his wife's degree of satisfaction or dissatisfaction with their status. As for politically active women, she gave high importance to the growing number of politically oriented women's groups at the local level, some modeled after the League of Women Voters in the United States.

The most impressive example of the power of women in Brazilian politics since the era of the Family Electoral Alliances is the part they played in the downfall of Goulart. The *União Civica Feminina,* Women's Civic Union, was the principal organizer of a "March of the Family with God for Liberty," held in São Paulo on March 19, 1964, to protest the general leftist drift of the Goulart government and specifically the mass meeting held in Rio de Janeiro six days before when Goulart had expounded radical proposals which signified a definitive break with his moderate supporters. The São Paulo march was important in convincing wavering Brazilians all over the country that so-called responsible public opinion had turned actively against Goulart. It measurably strengthened the hand of the military and civilians who were already plotting to remove Goulart, particularly those in the key São Paulo Second Army. It weakened the resistence of General Amaury Kruel, the commander of the Second Army and until then one of Goulart's trusted military collaborators, to blandishments from the revolutionaries.

Marches were organized in other cities. The largest, held in Rio de Janeiro three days after the revolution, attracted nearly a million marchers. It was organized by the *Campanha da Mulher pela Democrácia* (CAMDE), Women's Campaign for Democracy, whose membership was largely from the upper and upper-middle classes. The Rio de Janeiro march and others which were held in the crucial days before the post-revolutionary government was established strengthened the military leaders who were maneuvering to keep power in their hands and to block the civilian leaders of the revolution from taking control. CAMDE was strongly conservative; its emphasis was on combatting Communism.

Credit for organizing the "Marches of the Family with God for Liberty"—a clumsy name but who can gainsay the motivating force of the key words "Family," "God," and "Liberty"—has been claimed by several individuals and organizations including IPES, which furnished ideas and considerable support.[36] Such assistance raises the question often asked about student organizations: Are they autonomous or are they being used as a "maneuver mass" by other political interests, in this case rightist business and military groups? Whatever the answer to that question, the objectives of the women were similar to those of the revolutionaries and the marches were highly effective. Whether any of the women's groups can yet be called important political organizations with an independent existence is questionable.

Informal Interest Groups

The behavior of nonassociational or informal interest groups in Brazil, like that of associational interest groups, generally varies substantially from the behavior of pressure groups in more developed countries. The principal reasons for the differences are to be found in the need to conform to the patterns of a hierarchic system at variance with those of developed nations. That system is likely to prevail even when Brazil reaches higher levels of economic and social development, since traditional values and cultural patterns are not likely to change as rapidly as economic. At least one developed nation, Japan, has shown that some traditional cultural patterns usually associated only with traditional societies can be retained in a modern society.

Although the political system in Brazil, as in the United States, offers multiple points of access—including the president, the congress, the bureaucracy, political parties, and the courts—all interest groups in Brazil use the executive and administrative structure more often than the legislative branch and political parties, as is common in the United States. These procedures reflect a pragmatic awareness of the centers of power and conform to a more personal basis of social interrelationships. In other words, it serves no useful purpose to seek relief in congress or in the legislative assemblies if under the prevailing system they are not equipped to deal with the problems at hand. In addition, the continued importance of the extended kinship relationship in all sectors of Brazilian society encourages personal rather than impersonal handling of problems, and this situation is not likely to change substantially in the near future. An uncommon aspect of all interest groups in Brazil is their relative weakness compared to those of more developed countries, in part because they are either directly or indirectly dependent on the government. Nathaniel Leff has pointed out that the political culture of Brazil, unlike that of the United States and Great Britain where the activities of pressure groups are accepted as part of political participation, holds that private efforts to influence public policy are inherently corrupt.[37]

Despite differences, the operations of interest groups in the United States and Brazil are often similar, as would be expected because of the similarity of their political structures. Principal differences arise from the more prominent role of the president in Brazil, the relative weakness of the congress, and the relative autonomy of the vast bureaucracy. The system then—that is, the way pressure groups operate and the way the Brazilian bureaucracy reacts to such activities—is more like the Italian system than that of the United States.[38]

Important among nonassociational interest groups are the powerful family businesses of the industrial and commercial centers. The largest of the family companies, similar in power and influence to U. S. corporations, have their seats in São Paulo. The Matarazzo family, which emigrated to Brazil toward the end of the last century with few assets, today owns the largest complex of industries in the country. Information on the financial status of this complex, or of any of the family companies, is difficult to obtain (few sell shares to the public), but in the 1950's the Matarazzos employed 30,000 people in more than 350 plants. The company's 1957 annual report informed its readers that its plants consumed more electric power than was consumed in all Peru. Other family empires rival that of the Matarazzos, having assets equal to as much as a quarter of a billion dollars. Their influence and importance in the economy is so great that when they have run into financial difficulties, as the Matarazzo interests often have, the government has bailed them out with large loans and made special concessions to keep them afloat. This unstable condition was close to being chronic during the severe disinflationary period of the Castello Branco government between 1964 and 1967 when thousands of large and small enterprises went under, but no one questioned the assumption that the government would support the Matarazzo and similar empires, should the need arise.

As interest groups, these family companies are active at all levels and branches of government. Most of the larger companies with seats away from Rio de Janeiro, until 1970 still the bureaucratic capital, maintained representatives there. They were run by some of the companies' ablest men whose principal function was to promote their company's major and minor interests. Some companies also have representatives in Brasilia, seat of the legislature, but in 1970 these men were usually lawyers with minimal responsibilities. The implication is clear: relations with the congress are of minimal importance; the authority to make decisions rests principally in the executive bureaucracy which has wide powers of making and applying rules. These family interest groups sometimes have their own representatives running for congress, or they finance the campaigns of lawyers or professional men who are expected to look out for company interests in committees or in the full congress. This practice is less frowned upon in Brazil than it would be in the United States.

Intellectuals, like students, are far more influential than their numbers would indicate. There are no intellectual organizations as such but many intellectuals belong to the Brazilian Press Association, other journalists' and writers' organizations, organizations of popular song writers, and playwright groups. Their influence is important because many have regular access to public communications media. Prominent journalists, radio or television newscasters, historians and other writers on the contemporary scene and the past, almost all of whom are considered to be intellectuals, have important roles in forming public opinion. The character of this unorganized group is highly heterogeneous and the lines separating intellectual from nonintellectual are often unclear. In class distinction, if such can be designated, the intellectual ranks lower in social prestige in Brazil than in other Latin American countries although higher than in the United States. In most of Latin America the word of the poet, the essayist, the philosopher, the playwright, or the painter on political matters is often held in highest esteem, whereas the opinions of the successful industrialist or businessman are of little or no interest. This is not so in Brazil where the pragmatic character of the people sees the successful industrialist as a national leader deserving of high regard. In this respect Brazil is much nearer the United States than the Spanish American countries.

The soldier is not usually classed with intellectuals but the intellectual influences exercised by the military have been substantial since the fall of the Empire and never more so than after the revolution of 1964. The most important of these influences is the Brazilian version of Positivism. The studies of the *Escola Superior de Guerra* have also influenced the course of government.

Most intellectuals tend to be nationalistic. Leftist or reformist in ideology, many are influenced by Marxism but few are members of, or are controlled by, the Brazilian Communist Party. They are often labelled Communists because they may be anti-American and support issues which the Communists have also adopted. They are often in opposition to the national government, or alienated from the establishment. Why this should be so has not been clearly determined, but the tendencies are apparent very early in the development of the intellectual. Studies among university students show that students of law and the humanities are more radically activist than students of engineering, medicine, or other professions. The Brazilian political sociologist, Glaucio Soares, has found that students who identify themselves as intellectuals—the humanistic students—are more likely to be leftist than those who identify themselves as scientists or professionals.[39] This may be true in many cases for the prosaic reason that the humanistic student has a relatively uncertain future as compared to the professional student, who has more confidence in the system's ability to provide security after graduation.

Songs and theater productions are used to influence public and official opinion. Brazil's popular songs have traditionally sung the praises of carnival joys and gaity, beautiful women of varying color, requited and unrequited love, and the beautiful beaches and mountains of Rio de Janeiro. One popular carnival song with the words *"Me da, me da, me da-oi-me da um dinheiro ahi"* (roughly: "Can you spare some money") coincided with President Kubitschek's campaign for U. S. economic assistance and the visit of President Eisenhower to Brazil in 1959. This however, was unusual as most Brazilian popular songs have had little political content. After 1964 songs of folk variety were used as vehicles for social and political protest and achieved a certain degree of success and currency. The government took this innovation so seriously that it encouraged the less thoughtful "e-e-e" variety of music popularized by the Beatles.

The military controlled governments exercised censorship in the theater, radio and television. A number of plays with critical political content were ordered to modify or close down. Several chose to close. Actors and playwrights led public protests against censorship in 1968. The instance of radio and TV censorship that attracted most attention was that of Carlos Lacerda, ex-Governor of Guanabara, a strongly pro-military supporter of the revolution who had turned on Castello Branco. Lacerda was permitted for several years to criticize the Castello Branco government freely through the written word and in public addresses but was denied the use of radio or TV to prevent him from reaching a wider audience.

The influence of intellectuals on larger issues is illustrated by the part played by political scientists, economists, and sociologists in creating and cultivating a national ideology for economic and social development. This *tomada de conciencia,* as it was called—loosely translated as awareness of the Brazilian reality plus the need to build a modern nation—had an important part in developing a sense of nationalism among Brazilians. The vast majority of Brazilians, who were born and raised and expected to die in poverty and ignorance (particularly in the North and Northeast but in other parts of Brazil as well) had little interest in the welfare of the country. By creating an ideology of national development on which an imaginative president like Juscelino Kubitschek could base his government, Brazil was launched on the road to developed status supported by a people many of whom for the first time were motivated by euphoria which comes with patriotic nationalism. These intellectuals are credited with constructing the consensus that Brazilians favor planned action toward a productive economy of self-sustained growth, controlled by Brazilians, giving higher standards of living for all.[40]

The institution that perhaps did most to propagate the ideology of national development was the *Instituto Superior de Estudos Brasileiros* (ISEB), a graduate school established in 1955 by the Ministry of Education as an independent unit to apply the social sciencies to "the analysis and critical understanding of the Brazilian reality with a view to the elaboration of theoretical instruments that will permit the stimulation and promotion of national development." ISEB had its beginnings in the ideas developed by a small group of able and dedicated young students and bureaucrats called the Itatiaia Group, named after their regular meeting place in a national park between Rio de Janeiro and São Paulo. An important leader was San Tiago Dantas, who held cabinet posts under Goulart. Others of this group later held high positions in government where they were able to carry out and propagate their ideas for national development.

The ISEB was intended to be a civilian counterpart to the *Escola Superior de Guerra,* but it was short-lived. Starting off with a reputation of being Fascist, it ended its existance in 1964 branded as Communist. Communist influences were indeed strong, but the group generally had a broad base. Early in its existence the ISEB split sharply on the issue of the *realpolitik*-oriented publication *O Nacionalismo na Atualidade Brasilera* by Hélio Jaguaribe, one of the members of the Itatiaia group. His book held that development and bourgeois leadership were not incompatible, a thesis not particularly to the liking of the more leftist ISEB members. But perhaps even more objectionable was the ultrapragmatic/ opportunistic character of the book.[41] When generals at the *Escola Superior de Guerra* in 1960 were openly referring to the ISEB as a watermelon—green outside but red inside—its demise was only a question of time if it could not control the extremists on its staff. One of the first acts of the 1964 revolution was to close down the school. Yet its contribution to Brazilian thought was recognized even in the armed forces, which adopted many of the nationalistic theses developed at ISEB.

Like many ideas and philosophies that are seldom noted by masses of people but still change the course of their lives, the work of intellectuals in Brazil has contributed to the country's development. Not all the contributions have been constructive, but even some of the negative work of the intellectuals has occasionally had the salutary effect of forcing complacent governments and key individuals to re-examine long-held views.

Communications Media

Considering Brazil's status as a developing nation and its 40 percent illiteracy rate, communications media are relatively highly developed and political communication is generally good except in the sparsely settled rural areas. These areas lack electric power and transportation, which together with high illiteracy rates and the high cost of transistor radios limits all mass media communications. Nevertheless, Brazil ranks high among the Latin American countries in both quality and spread of public information. More than a thousand newspapers are published, of which 250 are dailies. Total circulation of all newspapers late in the 1960's was around 8 million. Although most newspapers defend the viewpoints of their owners—and most of the larger dailies are con-servative—they do publish news from different sources. Varied views are often injected by journalistists and rewrite men. Over 1,000 radio stations are licensed, some of them owned by the leading dailies. By 1967, forty-seven television stations had been licensed. Most were in the state capitals along the east coast, although the larger cities of the interior were installing outlets. This medium reaches the middle class, above all, but TV antennas are to be seen in Rio's *favelas,* and TV's in bars and store windows attract crowds.

As for other media, literate Brazilians read a great deal, but the public library system is still rudimentary. The 1960 census indicated that there were 9,300 libraries, less than 2,000 of which possessed more than 300 volumes. The national library and some of the university libraries as well as the municipal library of São Jaulo have excellent collections and modern operating procedures and the booming publishing business produces more books annually than the combined holdings of all libraries.

Radio has the largest audience in Brazil, as it reaches all social strata.[42] Among the middle and upper class in urban areas, newspapers and magazines are preferred and are more effective as communications media. The literate urban lower class read not only the more conservative dailies but also support sensationalist dailies with larger circulations than the more respected moderate press.

Brazil enjoyed freedom of press and speech with but minor exceptions from 1945 to December 1968. The government has powers to limit such freedom, but traditionally it has been reluctant to use them. Thus it has used its licensing power for radio and television stations with a minimum of favoritism and its power over the distribution of newsprint with a generally even hand. The Castello Branco administration was so conscious of possible public opprobrium on this score that it failed to foreclose on delinquent government-controlled bank loans to the *Tribuna da Imprensa* of Rio de Janeiro though it was attacking the administration daily. Following the suspension of constitutional rights in December 1968, a poorly disguised press censorship was installed for the first time since the Dutra administration (1946-1951).

A further explanation for government reluctance to take repressive measures against mass media is their generally conservative character. Many of the more widely read newspapers are owned by the wealthy old families who may control several important newspapers and radio stations, as well as a television station. Most are conservative in outlook, but few hesitate to attack the government for its administrative failings or encroachments on democratic procedures. Public opinion strongly supports the freedom of the press.

Most political communication reaches Brazilians through press, radio, and television; a great deal, particularly that aimed at the lower classes, comes by word of mouth. Members of political parties, the Church, and others have a part in this process. Surveys in rural areas indicate that such communication is largely through stratified informal channels, with preference given to that received at family gatherings, the market places, and in church.

Another important verbal channel of communication has been identified by Nathaniel Leff. His study of communications in economic and political decision-making led him to the conclusion that the most important element in this process is verbal exchange of information among the technocrats and the various elites. This may well be a Brazilianization of a rather universal phenomenon, perhaps more effective in the Brazilian milieu because of the importance of personal and class relations. Obviously, the mass media still plays an important role in this process since its news coverage helps form the opinions of the elite as much as any class.

Communications media are used not only for the purpose of transmitting information but often serve objectives similar to those sought by interest groups. The press serves as the channel for most of the day-to-day political information reaching the reading public, a good deal of which gets down to the illiterate population. Generally speaking, news and views tend to be presented in terms of the political predilections of the owner of whatever medium is used, and they usually reflect the social views and economic preferences of his class. The conservative press generally exercises a strong influence for maintaining the *status quo;* the liberal and radical press are vehicles for presenting demands for change.

The government relies on the *Agencia Nacional*, its news service, and the radio program *Hora do Brasil* to communicate official news and point of view to the public on peak time daily. To filter out news or points of view considered harmful to government interests, censorship—sometimes heavy, sometimes more subtle—has been exercised since 1968. The political opposition is allowed, with some restrictions, to use various media to propagate its views in electoral campaigns. Few parties use the media systematically, although before the 1964 revolution the Brazilian Labor Party sponsored a daily radio news program to reach the illiterate masses in rural areas.

As Brazil develops economically and socially the number of interest groups will grow, keeping pace with the increased complexity of society. Many of the characteristics of established interest groups suggest a traditional society in which the ruling elite shares the power to make all important decisions only with its peers, seldom influenced by public opinion. Yet many modernizing changes that are made benefit the lower class. The most important of these changes have been made on a paternalistic rather than a participatory basis. They have not been less appreciated by the people for this reason. They probably will be less acceptable as the process of stimulating group self-awareness proceeds and the masses decide they prefer to make the decisions about their welfare to having them made by others. Meanwhile, the important decisions will continue to be made by those in power. Such decisions may be supported by the advice, help, and importuning of those most affected by them, acting as individuals or in groups ranging from the highly sophisticated confederations of industry and commerce to the mutual benefit groups of engineers or physicians. Whatever may be said about the functioning of these groups, it can be argued that they are usually less noxious in Brazil, where the common good is held to be higher than that of individuals or groups, than in other countries, where the activities of lobbyists in behalf of powerful small groups and narrow interests are highly effective and are seldom frowned upon.

VI: Changing Economic and Social Patterns

Change toward modernization may be measured by urbanization, commercialization and industrialization, education, restratification, and secularization.[1] The growth of the cities in Brazil is a major social phenomenon because it reflects a flight from stagnant rural areas where conditions have deteriorated under an archaic social and economic structure. Commercialization and industrialization are almost exclusively urban based and are the proximate goal of modernization in Brazil. Education determines the character and competence of human resources available for the growing number of jobs requiring specialized skills in modernizing societies, but at the same time it can create politically disaffected citizens if their skills are not employed. Profound changes are taking place in the alignment of social classes. It is as yet impossible to analyze these changes fully because available statistics are inadequate. More subjective is secularization; in essence it is an attitude toward society involving the substitution of traditional values by those of modern societies. This involves reducing the kind of religious influence that impairs national unity or obstructs economic and social modernization. It also concerns giving employment on a competitive rather than a kinship basis and making government loans without political or personal favoritism. All these indices are interrelated. An immediate result of industrialization is urbanization which in turn must affect secularization and stratification, and all increase demands for more and better education.

The problems of uneven development of different parts of the country makes analysis difficult. The backwardness of the Northeast has been one of Brazil's most burdensome problems from the time of the abolition of slavery in 1888. Perhaps one way to summarize the story is with population statistics. Whereas in 1872 the nine Northeast states accounted for 46.7 percent of the total population, by 1900 the proportion had fallen to 38.7 percent, and in 1967 to an estimated 29.5 percent.[2] Still the 25 million inhabitants in the Northeast, their greatest number concentrated in the coastal area, are far more than today's economy can support.

The great concentrated efforts of the 1960's to solve the problem of the Northeast had as a principal mechanism its industrialization, concentrated in and around Recife and Salvador, the largest cities. Capital, much of it from São Paulo, was generated under a tax-forgiving arrangement. The rural problem was attacked by sporadic efforts at agrarian reform including an elaborate attempt to modernize the sugar plantations. Although SUDENE, the agency responsible for planning and supervising a good deal of these efforts, was established during the Kubitschek regime, it has been the military governments since 1964 that have taken extraordinary measures to hasten development. This reflects the concern of the military over the negative effects of uneven development on national unity and national security. The problem was far from solved by 1972, but Planning Minister Velloso announced then that growth rates indicated that per capita gross domestic product by 1980 in the Northeast should increase to $400 compared to less than $200 in the 1960's.[3] The growth has been largely industrial, with little change noted in the rural areas, but its more widespread influence will be felt eventually.

Urbanization

In 1850 the Brazilian population amounted to 7,234,000, by 1900 it had risen to 17,984,000.[4] Fifty years later it had grown to 51,976,000, and the last census, taken in 1970, indicated that Brazil had 94,500,000 inhabitants. It passed the 100,000,000 mark in August 1972. An unchanged growth rate would mean that by 2010 Brazil could have a population equal to or over that anticipated for the United States. The rapid growth of the fifties was a spur to modernization in some ways but also a drag on economic growth, because too many of the persons included in the increased population were not in productive enterprises. In 1970 some 42 percent were under 14 years of age. In terms of social and economic problems this means that to avoid increased unemployment Brazil today must create new jobs for only slightly fewer youths than must the United States.

Even more rapid has been the rising rate of urbanization. In 1930 the urban population was 20 percent of the total. By 1950 it had increased to 36 percent, and the 1960 census indicated that 45 percent of the population lived in cities and towns with more than 2,500 persons. Almost 59 percent of the 1972 population was urban. These data represent a two-stage movement. They include urbanization, as generally defined, and also movements from rural areas to small towns.

Unlike smaller Latin American countries, the population of Brazil is not concentrated preponderantly in the capital city. Brasilia, the new capital, had over 250,000 ten years after its founding in 1960 (an additional 200,000 occupied the satellite cities in the Federal District), and the old capital, greater Rio de Janeiro, had just over 7 million that same year. Greater São Paulo, which included the contiguous industrial municipalities, was estimated to have over 8 million inhabitants. Its claim to being the fastest growing city in the world is based on a lethargic beginning. In 1900 São Paulo had less than a quarter of a million people, in 1920 a little more than half a million, but in 1960 it had more than 3.8 million. Without its industrial suburbs, it has nearly 6,000,000 inhabitants. The growth rate of cities with populations of more than 100,000 from 1950 to 1960 was 7 percent, more than double the national rate. The rate of increase from 1960 to 1970 held steady in the two largest cities but tended to decline in the regional capitals.

Only one of the twenty-two state capitals, Cuiabá, capital of Mato Grosso, had less than 100,000 inhabitants. The capitals of the remote territories had over 50,000 each (excluding the Island of Fernando de Noronha and Boa Vista, which had less). Five state capitals had populations of more than a million: São Paulo, Rio de Janeiro, Belo Horizonte (capital of Minas Gerais, which in 1950 had 352,700 and in 1970 had 1,110,000), and Recife (capital of Pernambuco, which had 524,700 in 1950 and 1,050,000 in 1970). More slowly growing Salvador, capital of Bahia, with 651,000 in 1960, did not reach the million mark until 1970. Porto Alegre, capital of Rio Grande do Sul in the extreme south, which had 394,150 in 1950, was expected to reach the million mark by 1975.

In 1965, well over 200 cities had more than 50,000 inhabitants. Much of this growth could be attributed not only to natural factors but also, particularly in the south, to migration from the north. During the booming 1950's, some 200,000 persons left the Northeast each year, with larger numbers leaving when drought conditions became serious. Two-thirds of this number moved away permanently, the rest returned. Migration slowed down as economic development picked up in the late 1960's.

Migration is not just a matter of fleeing hardships. Many are attracted by stories of opportunities that cities offer even uneducated *campesinos*. Kubitschek's widely publicized Target Program played its part in bringing rural workers to the city. The government's efforts to slow down this migration have had little success, but a growing number of people have been encouraged to move to the underpopulated North and West where opportunities are more plentiful. The opening of the new capital was the most important catalyst in this process. New highways leading to and beyond Brasilia have brought new towns and way stations in their wake. This is a pioneering, dynamic growth which relieves pressure in stagnant areas.

Foreign immigration added about 5 million new persons from 1900 to 1968. At first the immigrants settled in rural areas in São Paulo and the southern states, but many of them, and more of their children, soon moved to urban areas.

The rapid growth of Brazil's cities, unprecedented in some cases, has put virtually intolerable strains on public utilities. In some of the less favored locations, water must be brought great distances and electric power has been inadequate to meet the needs of an expanding industrial complex and recreational areas. Inadequate urban transportation results in inefficiency and lowered worker productivity, to say nothing of inconveniences and hardships. Workers spend as much as three hours getting to work. Construction on subways in São Paulo and Rio de Janeiro did not begin until 1969.

The great slums, *favelas*—particularly in Rio de Janeiro, Salvador, Recife and also in modern São Paulo—have received considerable attention from sociologists. In Rio de Janeiro, more than 25 percent of the population in 1967 lived in *favelas*. These communities of wood, tin, canvas, and packing case dwellings are usually without sanitary facilities or electricity. They generally occupy some of the more beautiful hillsides surrounding the city, and are better located climatically than the homes of the more affluent on the lower streets. They have little else to recommend them. The slopes are subject to landslides, and the precariously erected dwellings are subject to collapse. The government is slowly providing low-cost housing and forcing slum dwellers to move.

The *favelas* had their origins in the dislocations caused by urban improvement in city centers, but their continued growth has taken on more the form of a ruralization (Brazilian style) of suburbs as great numbers of migrants come in from the rural areas. The *favelas*, however, are not simply havens for migrants, the unemployed, or vagrants. Since rents here are often free or very low and prohibitive elsewhere, many lower ranking civil service employees remain in *favela* dwellings. In Rio de Janeiro and São Paulo, improvement associations have grown up in the *favelas*. Through them some of the more urgent needs are communicated to the municipal authorities. For the migrant inhabitants the conditions in the slums of the modern cities, bad as they are, seem to be preferable to life in rural areas. Most have schools and the urban atractions keep them from returning to their places of origin.

What little can be said about the efforts to improve *favela* conditions in Rio de Janeiro and São Paulo is even less applicable to conditions in Salvador and Recife. In the former the slums, called *alagados,* are concentrated on dumps that extend into the bay and grow as the dumps move farther out in the water. In Recife, they are built on the infamous mudflats, subject to floods from the landward side and to high tides from the sea. Neither city has so far been able to finance substantial improvements.

The number of urban dwellers who actually work in industry is relatively small. The Brazilian experience has been quite different from that in the United States and Europe, where industry absorbed a good part of the increased urban populations. Industry throughout the world today is more mechanized and less labor intensive than it was formerly. Thus, although industrial output increased 10 percent from 1950 to 1960, employment in industry increased only 2.8 percent. With the use of even more capital intensive technologies since then, the situation has not improved. On the other hand, industrialization did create a larger demand for service labor, which some of the migrants can fill, and increased public expenditures in many fields gave additional employment. The net effect, however, has been to create a large pool of unemployed or underemployed city dwellers who represent one of the most serious social problems the country must face.

The solution to the problems of unmanagable migration to the cities would seem to lie in improving rural conditions. Opening up opportunities in the dynamic developing areas in the North and West will serve a similar purpose. The government's housing program, one of the largest in the world, which began in 1965 had produced 700,000 units in seven years. It will not, however, solve this problem, one of the most serious of urbanization, since better housing attracts more migrants. The housing deficit is estimated at ten times production to date.

Restratification of the Social Order

Stratification of the social classes is changing rapidly, and such statistics as are compiled are inadequate or are outdated soon after they are compiled. Nevertheless, an indication comes from recent sociological studies which, unlike former studies, deal with lower-lower, upper-lower, lower-middle, and upper-middle classes, as well as the upper classes.

Concomitant with urbanization, industrialization, and the commercialization of agriculture, which can be dated from 1930, four new groups have made their appearance in Brazilian society. One is the rural proletariat, comprised of victims of a changing pattern in agricultural economy—changing from a personally owned and paternalistically run *fazenda* to the so-called corporate type of farm where the owner assumes no responsibility for the welfare of the workers he employs. The other new groups are the divided urban lower class, which has grown vastly in size; the expanded middle class; and the new urban elite.

Rural society changed little from the time of the Empire until recently. The appearance of a rural proletariat in the Northeast marks an economic change and a deterioration in relationship between employer and employee. The shape of future change can be seen in the South with its relatively small holdings, many of them run by immigrants from Germany, Italy, Poland, and Japan. São Paulo has become almost a special case of large numbers of commercial farmers with medium-sized holdings, replacing the coffee growers with very large holdings, some of whom are moving south and west. The emergence of a rural middle class, though still small, is identifiable.

In the urban areas, the great change in stratification is the emergence of a middle class. This process begins today at the very bottom with the rural migrant who, as noted above, believes, and there seems no reason to question his own judgment in this respect, that in the main he has risen in the social scale by virtue of having come to the city. Aside from the variety of offerings in city life, the basic attraction seems to be the hope for further improvement in status. Not only does the urban area offer opportunity for economic advancement for the individual himself, but it also provides better health care, opportunities for education and work for his children, an important stabilizing element in a situation much more volatile than that of the passive and hopeless rural worker.

The middle class was estimated in the 1960's to consist of between 15 and 25 percent of the population. As a class it contributed more than any other to the overthrow of the oligarchic Old Republic in 1930, but is was unable to force the establishment of a liberal democracy which most members favored. In the United States the strength of the middle class was based on ownership of independent properties, but in Brazil the power of the middle class was limited by a social and economic base largely dependent on the government or on large landholders. If the economic power of the rural aristocracy could not be broken then neither could its political power, except through authoritarian means such as Vargas used. Although it takes a dominant part in forming public opinion, the middle class has still to find a way to develop its potential to influence national decisions.

Brazilian society since 1930 has become very dynamic; signs of change can be seen even in the North. Industralization demands skilled and unskilled workers, foremen and managers. Commercialization requires more clerical, secretarial, managerial, and sales personnel. Many make their way up from the rural and urban lower classes to fill these newly created jobs. Through education, marriage, or success in business, many move upward into the elite groups of the urban centers. The estimated 3 to 7 percent of the population which makes up the new urban elite includes some members of the traditional rural aristocracy, but, by contrast, the histories of some of the others who have made great industrial fortunes read like Horatio Alger stories of early vintage. Many were immigrants or sons of immigrants; others came up from the Brazilian lower class.

While giving due weight to the upper social mobility symbolized by some of Brazil's wealthiest men today, the wider effects on society of the Brazilian way to industralization cannot be overlooked. Data from the 1970 census indicate that the gap between the wealthy and the poor widened over the preceding decade. The real income of the entire population rose; that of the wealthy went up rapidly, that of the poor hardly at all. In 1960, the poorest 40 percent of the population earned 10 percent of the national income. In 1970, that share had dropped to 8 percent. On the other hand, the richest 5 percent of the population earned 29 percent of the income in 1960 and 38 percent in 1970. These data confirm a poll conducted in the metropolitan area of Rio de Janeiro in 1967, according to which the percentage of families in the highest income brackets increased from 4.1 percent in 1963 to 7.0 in 1966. The percentage in the lowest group, reflecting a fall in real wages, increased from 30.8 to 40 percent over the same period.[5]

Industrialization

Industrialization in Brazil has had a cyclical history of its own. Long discouraged by British preeminence and special privileges, industrialization began to assume some importance during the Empire when the end of the slave trade made capital available for other enterprises. The Viscount of Mauá was the capitalist and industrialist *par excellence,* enobled for his service to the Empire as an entrepreneur who from 1850 to 1875 built railroads, financed industries, established a shipbuilding industry, and through banking and loans, even served some of the imperialistic/defensive objectives of the Empire in neighboring countries. His career came to a premature end when the government failed to give him support during a time of crisis. The restricted national market, which the social structure and the special privileges enjoyed by export agriculture helped maintain, also contributed importantly to his failure and to that of other industrialists of the time. Compared to manufacturing, agriculture was a relatively riskless area for investment.

World War I stimulated industry, but because the government had no policy for protection of the infant industries, most of them died when international trade resumed again after the war. National policy only protected coffee. Vargas's policies encouraged new industries, less actively during his first term than during his second in the early 1950's. Most were import-substitution industries built on a foundation of unavailable and restricted imports and as a spin-off of maintaining coffee prices during the 1929 depression. Industrial development spurted during World War II. Vargas was responsible for the establishment of the national steel industry at Volta Redonda and signed the law creating a national petroleum monopoly.

It was only after World War II that Brazil attained a stage of economic development that gives some grounds for Hélio Jaguaribe's insistence that Brazil had reached the take-off point and is now in a self-sustained process of industrial growth.[6] This thesis was shared by few at the time (1968), but fewer would question it after five years of annual economic growth over nine percent.

The direction and rate of industrial development in Brazil is a two-pronged process. Government economic policy and infrastructural development sets the parameters within which private enterprises makes its contributions toward modernization. Government involvement in production is considerable by U. S. standards, but small by those of socialist countries and is likely to remain so because private enterprise enjoys unusually high acceptance among Brazilians.

Having successfully negotiated the transition to an industrial complex based largely on import substitution, the next step toward self-sustained growth required further expansion through new heavy industries which can compete in foreign markets. These in turn require heavy capital outlays and a high degree of technical competence. Progress is already substantial, although many changes need to be made to improve labor skills and mobilize more capital, to say nothing of broadening the domestic market. Better education, agrarian reforms which intensify land usage, sound monetary policies, industrial restructuring for greater productivity, and wage policies which allow workers to buy more will be required to effect the conversion to a mass consumption economy.

The government's efforts continue to be directed toward transforming the industrial plant, already by far the largest in Latin America, to one that will make Brazil a leading industrial power. As has been noted, this is not the dream of only a few men but rather a national goal shared by almost all Brazilians since it has been so long heralded as the key to Brazil's problems. In pursuit of this goal the government since 1947 has allocated domestic resources and imports to stimulate large-scale industrial development. The same can be said of policies related to foreign capital, although in recent years some restrictions have been added to assure that as much industry as possible remain under the control of Brazilians. Recent economic studies conclude that, except during the Goulart administration, the formulation and execution of economic policy have been unusually sound and consistent, and the results are perhaps unequalled among the developing countries of the world.[7]

Brazil's first large-scale development plan was put into operation under Kubitschek, shortly after he took office in 1956. His slogan "Fifty Years Progress in Five" symbolized his *Programa de Metas* (Target Program). The Target Program was based on several previous plans, mostly on the report of the Joint Brazil-United States Technical Commission which had not been implemented during the Vargas administration because the external financing on which it had been predicated was never forthcoming. Kubitschek also failed to obtain adequate financing from the United States government and international agencies, but he attracted a good deal of foreign private capital. Much of the program was financed through inflationary means, but the results were little short of spectacular—a word that could also describe some of the deleterious effects that continued to plague the country a decade later.

Kubitschek stimulated internal investment by creating a development mystique that had other important consequences, not the least of which was to engage the people in an enthusiastic commitment to his plans. According to political scientists this kind of productive participation is difficult if not impossible to create except in mass democracies or under charismatic leadership. Brazil lacked mass parties, which Robert Scott believes necessary to withstand the concerted pressures that confront developing nations when faced, as all are, by crises inherent in the developmental process. They can be met successfully only by "unity and widely based representation in the political process." [8] Kubitschek's charisma, however, coupled with the people's evident belief in and practice of democracy proved to be a substitute for weak political institutions. The "fluidity and self-adjustment required for voluntaristic human mobilization," for nation building in a democracy referred to by Kalman Silvert, was supplied by a president sensitive to the needs and aspirations of his people.[9]

The president's program set thirty-one targets grouped under six heads: energy, transport, basic industries, education, food, and the construction of the new capital. Although the relationship of the building of Brasilia to industrialization was minor, the President gave it highest priority because of its anticipated influence on change. Not only did Kubitschek plan to draw people and industry toward the vast, unexploited hinterland and to open up new agricultural land, but he also thought that the government would be more efficient away from the distractions of an overcrowded tropical city facing on beautiful beaches. The new capital was inaugurated April 21, 1960, three and a half years after work began, with a population already near 100,000. Its cost and inflationary effects engendered heated discussion as to its wisdom. The Getúlio Vargas Foundation estimated that by 1962 a billion dollars had been spent on it. However, its long-range political and social importance alone seemed to justify the high economic price. Of the total investment for the other five categories 43.4 percent was to go to energy; 29.6 percent to transport; 20.4 percent to basic industries; 3.4 percent to education; and 3.2 percent to food. With minor exceptions, all the targets had been reached or had been surpassed before the end of his term.[10]

Not long after Kubitschek left office virtual disintegration began. The paralysis of governmental functions before and after Quadros resigned, and the inability of Goulart to cope with the country's larger problems precipitated the radical political polarization and economic stagnation that led to the 1964 revolution. Only after three years of painful deflationary measures did the economy begin to revive. Once it started on the upgrade, with first substantial results showing in 1968, growth exceeded even the most optimistic forecasts of Brazilian and international observers. In 1967 AID officials working with Brazilian planners set 7 percent growth in GNP as a goal. Few had hope that it could be reached. In fact, it did not fall below 9 percent from that date to the present (1972).

All governments since 1964 prepared short and long term plans for economic and social development in accordance with Alliance for Progress prescriptions. Varying in minor respects only, their value was to set priorities and national goals. The National Integration Program was established in 1970 by President Médici. One of its principal objectives is the opening up and settlement of the Amazon region through the construction of two roads crossing the basin. One is to run a thousand miles south to north from Cuiabá to Santarem, and the other, the *"Transamazonica"* 1,500 miles east to west from João Pessoa and Recife to the Peruvian border.

Industrial growth through these periods is summarized in the pages that follow.

ELECTRICAL ENERGY
(Installed Generating Capacity)

Year	kw
1950	1,883,000
1956	3,550,000
1960	5,000,000
1965	7,400,000
1969	10,350,000
1971	12,740,000

In 1965 just under a million kilowatts of the total was generated by self-producers, 2 million by private companies, and 4 million by state, other government-owned, and mixed companies. By 1970 state-owned installations were expected to reach a capacity of 6.5 million kilowatts; other sources were expected to remain more or less stationary. The big increase was to come from the Urubupungá plant, moving toward completion in the state of Sao Paulo, its 4.4 million kilowatt capacity will make it the fourth largest in the world, more than double the size of the Grand Coulee Dam on the Columbia River. Brazil's 150 million kilowatt generating potential for hydroelectric power is fourth largest in the world, after the Congo, China, and Soviet Russia; the potential of the still unexplained Guairá Falls on the Paraguayan border is estimated to be 12 million killowatts, the largest of any known source in the world. Brazil and Paraguay have agreed to cooperate in its building by 1984.

As for nuclear energy, no plants had been installed by 1972 but one large one was part of government planning. Only small quantities of uranium had been discovered before 1972, when it was announced that deposits found in Minas Gerais would satisfy any possible needs for the present century.

Petroleum is virtually a government monopoly. All phases of the industry, except refining and distribution, are operated by PETROBRAS. Existing private refineries, owned by Brazilians, have not been permitted to expand their capacities. In 1966 they were limited to some-

PETROLEUM PRODUCTION (BARRELS PER DAY)

Year	Crude	Refined
1955	5,600	108,300
1960	75,000	218,000
1966	116,500	367,700
1968	164,000	400,000
1971 (estimated)	174,200	535,000

(1968 data from PETROBRAS release, *Jornal do Brasil,* June 25, 1969; 1971 date from *Prospectus.*)

what less than 20 percent of the total, while the PETROBRAS share gradually increased as its new refineries came into production. Most of the distributing companies were foreign owned, although PETROBRAS and Brazilian private capital were moving into the field. A small number of Brazilians contend that private exploitation would meet the country's increasing needs better, but they get little attention. Production increased greatly within a decade of the discovery of oil in the large Reconcavo field, but increased requirements of the industrial complex made large imports necessary. New discoveries in Sergipe and Alagoas raised 1967 production by 26.1 percent from that of the year before. At the end of 1969 PETROBRAS estimated its reserves to be about 852 million barrels. Despite rising production, Brazilian petroleum in 1971 supplied only 32.5 percent of requirements.

One of the largest oil-shale deposits in the world, in the states of Paraná, Santa Catarina, and Rio Grande do Sul, promised other sources of energy. Soviet technicians were brought in to advise a private Brazilian company, and PETROBRAS began building a commercial proto-type plant in the area. Coal is found in limited quantities and is generally low grade; production runs over 3 million metric tons per annum. Natural gas is becoming increasingly important; 532 million cubic meters were produced in 1964, 789 millions in 1966, and 1,247,-873 in 1969. At the end of 1969, reserves were estimated to be 25.6 billion cubic meters.

Transportation

The dimensions of Brazil's problem in transportation—that is, moving the people and the goods that sustain them in a territory of 8.5 million square kilometers—are suggested by the fact that during the

1950's and 1960's, when large sums had been spent on improving the highway system, little more than 30,000 kilometers of paved roads had been built throughout the country. This is still somewhat short of the total length of railways.[11] In 1955, when Kubitschek was elected to the presidency, only 2,376 kilometers of federal highways had been paved. The railways with the exception of one or two privately owned companies, were burdened with antiquated rolling stock, inflated payrolls, chronic deficits, and unrealistic freight rates and fares which could not be raised for fear of the reactions of suburban commuters long accustomed to nominal charges and bad service. Coastal shipping, which at one time had been the principal means of transportation between most of the important population centers in Brazil, was a virtual government monopoly inefficiently run because of antiquated ships and deteriorated port equipment, to say nothing of disproportionate sums allowed to personnel rather than to maintenance. Until the early 1960's some shippers preferred to send cargoes by truck from the port of Belem at the mouth of the Amazon to Sao Paulo, rather than entrust them to the coastal shippers. Brazilian ocean shipping was in only little better shape, still not fully recovered from the loss of some 100 merchant vessels during World War II. Little thought was given to using Brazil's vast river systems to carry the growing volume of goods moving within the land. Brazilian ports, in some of the world's best harbors, were reputed to be among the most costly in the world. A traditional shipbuilding industry had fallen into decay.

The Target Program gave high priority to the transport sector of the economy since for decades it had been recognized as a principal obstacle to economic development. Nearly 30 percent of resources were allotted to transportation, second only to electric power; 1,195 kilometers of new track were added to the more than 30,000 already in use, and rolling stock was improved; 12,500 kilometers of new federal roads were built and over 7,000 kilometers were paved. Increased tonnage for coastal cargo ships and tankers fell 10 percent below the target goal, but increase in ocean-going vessels exceeded it by 113 percent. Japanese and Dutch shipbuilding interests were encouraged to establish shipyards capable of building oceangoing vessels. Seventeen large ships aggregating 70,000 deadweight tons, were constructed during the Kubitschek administration. Targets were met for port improvement and fluvial transportation.

The accomplishments of the Kubitschek administration in the area of transportation were in many respect dramatic when compared to the 1955 base, but they did little more than scratch the surface of needs. Much of the work had been performed on the basis of satisfying the noisiest demands among a plethora of high-priority projects. This situation grew worse after Kubischek left office as funds were cut back and public works tended more to satisfy political objectives than national needs. After 1964 this picture changed radically. The performance of the military-controlled governments, all of which give high priority to transportation as a matter of national security and integration has been outstanding.

The Brazilian army has long prided itself on its engineers and its well-built railways (most rail laying is carried on by the army) and highways (most of the uneconomical, strategic roadbuilding to the far western and far northern borders has also been done by the army). The navy for its part has taken a direct interest in merchant shipping as an auxiliary to the fleet, and after 1964 high-ranking naval officers were charged with rehabilitating coastal and ocean-going services. An article on naval policy in the transportation supplement to *Visão* notes that "to think in terms of Brazil as a great power without dominating the sea is to pretend national security without a powerful navy." One conclusion to be drawn from this premise, according to the article, is that it is as important "to assure the survival of our shipbuilding industry . . . as to safeguard military interests." The Brazilian air force, through its dependency the Directorate of Civil Aviation, takes credit for building up commercial aviation from its first days. The air force instituted initially uneconomical airmail and passenger service to remote parts of the country and subsidized the acquisition of equipment by commercial companies. The national air network was so widespread that it was accurate to say, as Charles Wagley did in 1960, that Brazil jumped from the oxcart age to the air age almost overnight. The Brazilian network of airlines is one of the largest in the world, but its relative importance (except for passenger service) has been declining as other transportation services improve in quality and efficiency. In 1968 over 3 million passengers were carried by plane in Brazil, 3.5 million kilos of mail were transported, and 37 million kilos of air freight were discharged.

A second wave of rapid progress in transportation began in 1967, when a politically minded, energetic career army officer with charismatic qualities, Colonel Mario David Andreazza, was made Minister of Transportation. In railway transport since then the emphasis has been on improvement and better utilization of existing equipment. About 28,000 excess employees (nearly 15 percent of employees in 1964) were discharged over a period of several years; the railroad was extended to Brasilia; about 3,000 kilometers of uneconomical runs were eliminated; roadbeds were improved to allow higher speeds; almost all steam engines were replaced with diesel or electric engines; tariffs were raised, and the deficit was decreased gradually from nearly U.S. $40 million in 1963 to less than U.S. $1.5 million in 1968. The increased efficiency in handling cargo is illustrated by comparing the number of trains, the tonnage-kilometers of freight, and the tonnage-kilometers per train from 1962 to 1968. From a base of 100 for the three items in 1962, the 1965 index for number of trains formed dropped to about 92, tonnage-kilometers of freight rose to 112, and tonnage-kilometers per train to 130. In 1968, the indices were 90, 125, and 162, respectively; 300 million passengers and 44 million tons of cargo were carried in that year.

The pace of roadbuilding begun under Kubitschek did not move into high gear again until 1967, during the Costa e Silva administration. In three years 6,122 kilometers were paved. Highways are of greatest importance in the Brazilian economy because of the deficiencies of other means of transport. Railways do not reach many of the new large cities in the interior, and because most run east-west they do not connect the large coastal population centers. Brazil as a result has had to rely heavily on roads. More than 500,000 automobiles and trucks were produced in 1971; over 2.1 million vehicles were registered in 1966, 548,000 of them trucks. Over 4,000 bus and trucking companies were operating in that year; nearly half were engaged in interstate commerce. Traffic over the 392-kilometer stretch of the Rio de Janeiro-São Paulo highway grew so heavy that no sooner had it been made into a double, four-lane highway used by 10,000 vehicles daily than it became necessary to speed up work on an alternate coastal road between the two cities.

Immediate goals for the highway system include connecting all state capitals in the Northeast, the East, and Central-South by paved road. The Brazil-Paraguay highway across Paraná has been completed; the trans-Rio Grande do Sul highway to the Argentine border was due for completion in 1970 as was the transcontinental highway beginning at Victoria and ending at Corumbá near the Bolivian frontier. Other important "links of integration" are under construction. The most ambitious of all the projects is the trans-Amazon highway. With 24,000 kilometers of navigable waterways in the Amazon basin, government planners see the highway as a means of making the areas between the principal tributaries of the Amazon accessible to those waterways.

In 1968 Brazil paid out half a billion dollars to carry its products overseas and bring in necessary imports. In 1966 the Brazilian fleet carried only 12 percent of that trade; in 1968 it was carrying 30 percent. The Brazilians intend before long to be carrying at least 50 percent of the trade. This record of accomplishment was made possible by increasing the size and efficiency of the fleet and through a series of confrontations with the leading maritime powers at which Brazil demanded and won a greater share of the traffic. Private capital was encouraged to get back into the shipping business, long a virtual monopoly of the neglected government owned Lloyd Brasileiro. The shipbuilding companies were given large contracts and additional tonnage was acquired through purchase and barter arrangements with countries which had not bought much coffee from Brazil before. By the end of 1969 the Brazilian merchant marine had reached a little more than 2 million deadweight tons and had set a goal of 4 million tons for 1975, which could make it larger than the combined fleets of all the other Latin American nations.

A beginning has been made toward rational utilization of waterways and possibly some of the most ambitious plans in the world are under study for making Brazilian rivers into principal highways. Modern tugs and barges similar to those that ply the larger rivers of the United States and European waterways are gradually replacing sidewheel and sternwheel equipment still being used on some rivers. The Tiete, which will serve from Sao Paulo west, is being made navigable and the Sao Francisco and other rivers are being dredged and locks are being built to move around cataracts. A French firm is under contract to study the feasibility of joining some of the more important river systems. Plans for connecting the São Francisco with the Paraná and connecting the Amazon with the Paraguay through the Madeira and Araguaia rivers are under study. If these plans eventually turn into reality it will be possible to travel by inland waterways down the middle of the continent from Belem to Buenos Aires, a distance of over 5,000 miles.

Improved transportation is playing an important part in changing the face of Brazil from the lethargic, rural-oriented nation of the first half of the century to the quick-moving, urban-oriented country in which trucks, buses, jeeps, and passenger cars move not only in and between large cities but also in increasing numbers across great open backlands and the Amazon jungle.

Communications

Improvement has been slow in the field of communications, retarded by vast distances and lack of funds to improve mail and telegraph service in areas where needs did not exist a few years ago. Most towns have radio or telegraph communication but much of it is primitive and much still under the control of the armed forces because of lagging civilian efforts. Beginning with the microwave system installed between Brasilia and Rio de Janeiro in 1960, improved systems are gradually connecting all important regions of the country. The inadequacy of the system even in 1967 could be seen by the fact that land lines between Rio de Janeiro and São Paulo were so clogged that businesmen with urgent matters to discuss sometimes routed calls from one city to the other, 250 miles apart, through New York. In mid-1969, however, the new microwave system between these two largest cities opened up nearly 4,000 interurban channels east to west and 3,000 west to east.

The total number of telephones installed in Brazil in 1954 was 752,-374; by 1964 it had risen to 1,282,942. In 1970 about 2 million had been installed, but 500,000 requests in São Paulo and Rio de Janeiro alone were still pending.[12]

Mining

Books written before 1970 that mention Brazilian mineral resources almost invariably dismiss the subject in a few words after mentioning the rich iron deposits in Minas Gerais, the manganese deposits in Amapá, and other minerals found in small quantities throughout the nation. The extent of these resources were simply not known and are still not known because much of the surface and sub-surface has yet to be explored. Today, mineral production is only 1.3 percent of gross domestic product but nevertheless has an important place in the economy as it contributes over 10 percent to the value of total exports. The potential is greater.

Export of high grade iron ore (69 percent Fe concentration) leaped from 15 million tons in 1968 to 34.7 million tons in 1971. Iron ore deposits were believed to be principally confined to the mountains of Minas Gerais but in 1967 vast deposits of 67 percent ore were found in the Serra dos Carajás in the Amazon state of Pará. These deposits are being exploited by the government controlled Cia. Vale de Rio Doce in association with United States Steel. Preliminary surveys indicate reserves of at least 1.6 billion tons and as much as 11 billion tons which would make it the largest reserve in the world. In all, present known reserves are estimated at 40 billion tons.

In two other important areas Brazil claims probable world leadership: uranium and casserite which is used for manufacturing tin. Uranium was believed to exist in only small quantities, whereas thorium was relatively plentiful. In July 1972, the National Commission on Nuclear Energy announced that a large area near Belo Horizonte, capital of Minas Gerais, had been found to contain uranium ore of good grade in quantities which might reach 1 million tons. If this proves to be accurate it would be the largest known deposit in the world. Casserite deposits in Rondonia, in the Amazon basin, are also large. Brazil has become an exporter of tin whereas a few years ago it had to import. Estimates are not yet firm but government officials anticipate that reserves will be larger than all known deposits elsewhere in the world.

Production of other metals has increased rapidly, most of the production going into national industries and decreasing the dependence on foreign sources. Lead is now exported in small quantities from the 40,000 ton level of production in 1972. Copper has been found in sizeable quantities but much of it in association with sulphur which makes industrialization difficult. As a consequence copper has been a heavy drain on foreign exchange ($84 million in 1971). A newly established company has scheduled production at 70,000 tons by 1975, which would bring a substantial savings in foreign exchange.

In value, manganese is the second most important mineral resource, nearly 2 million tons having been exported in 1971. Production has come mostly from Amapá where it is exploited by a Brazilian controlled private enterprise in which Bethlehem Steel has a little less than 50 percent interest. Exports of quartz crystal (about 6,000 tons in 1970). Scheelite (for tungsten, 1,640 tons in 1970), and dolomite (1,088 tons in 1969) are worthy of mention.

Manufacturing

Energy production, transportation, and communications facilities form the infrastructure base on which manufacturing rests. Numerous other factors, such as policies on credit, wages, and exports and imports set other limits. Availability of capital and skilled labor also affects produstion, but the physical limits are determined by the adequacy of power and means to move products to markets. The measure of industrialization is the total of manufactures produced, but the measure of modernization beyond the relatively simple import-substitute manufactures is to be found in the basic industries—often those in the so-called industry-of-scale category. Brazilian industries which may be included in this category are steel, cement, fertilizers, petrochemicals, paper, transport equipment, electric appliances, and electronics. Recent growth in two of these industries is indicated in the following:

STEEL AND CEMENT PRODUCTION (MILLIONS OF METRIC TONS)

Product	1955	1960	1965	1968	1971
Steel ingots	1.2	1.9	2.9	4.4	6.11
Cement	2.7	4.4	5.6	7.0	9.8†

†Data from *Prospectus.*

The *Cia. Siderurgica Nacional,* USIMINAS, and COSIPA, the government-controlled steel plants, produced 57 percent of the national total in 1968. More than 40 private companies produced the remainder. Increasing efficiency is indicated by exports, including steel products amounting to nearly $12 million shipped to the United States in 1967. About $70 million of metallurgical products were exported in 1971.

In a country as large as Brazil with its small railway system the automobile industry holds a key position. Since 1957 when production began under the Kubitschek program, Brazil has risen to eighth place among world producers. It manufactured over a million vehicles in its first decade. Productive capacity continued to rise in the ten manufacturing plants and 2,000 parts factories which produce Volkswagens, Jeeps, Simcas, Chevrolets, Ford Galaxies, and Renaults, among passenger vehicles. Mercedes Benz, Ford, Chevrolet, Scandia-Vabis, and other companies produce trucks and utility wagons. The following table shows the growth of the industry:

AUTOMOBILE INDUSTRY

Type	1955	1961	1965	1968	1971
Heavy trucks & buses	2,500	5,147	4,080	4,280	43,258
Medium trucks		25,352	20,899	42,632	
Small trucks & buses		42,492	46,720	63,281	124,831
Utility vehicles (jeeps)		17,618	10,057	8,289	5,635
Passenger vehicles		55,065	103,437	160,216	342,214
Total	2,500	145,674	185,193	278,698	515,938
			1962	1965	1971
Tractors			7,586	8,123	25,428

(1968 figures from *Jornal do Brasil,* January 9, 1969; 1971 figures from *Prospectus.*)

Early emphasis was on the production of trucks, buses, and jeeps. Attention later turned to passenger automobiles as the middle class and the better paid members of the lower class began to enter the market. The industry, still far from competitive in world markets because of its relatively small production, high taxes, and other factors, has nevertheless managed to bring down its prices gradually and has exported Jeeps and Volkswagens. Other factories are beginning to export. Its contribution to change in the form of improved transportation facilities and the creation of a skilled-labor pool has been large. In 1970 it was the fifth largest industry in the country, producing 9 percent of total manufacturers, with 3.5 percent of the work force directly or indirectly dependent upon it.

Changes in the character of manufacturing are illustrated by changes during the past two decades in the relative importance of capital goods, intermediate goods, and consumer goods industries to total manufactures. In 1949, capital goods industries contributed only 6.2 percent of total manufactures. By 1959, they were producing 15 percent, and by 1967, the contribution had grown to 19.5 percent. Within that category, electrical and communications materials acounted for 1.7 percent in 1949 and 6.2 percent in 1967. Manufactures for transport increased from 2.3 percent in 1949 to 8 percent in 1967. Intermediate manufactures, which contributed 35.5 percent in 1949, 41.8 percent in 1959, and 43.6 percent in 1967, are also illustrative of the changing economy. The traditional rubber, wood, leather, and nonmetallic minerals industries in this category declined in importance while metallurgical and paper industries increased moderately. On the other hand, in terms of value produced, chemicals became the largest single industry in the country, rising from 9.4 percent of the total in 1949 to 13.4 percent in 1959 and 18.8 percent in 1967. This percentage grew larger as large-scale petrochemical, fertilizer, and plastics companies, several of mixed Brazilian-U. S. capital, came into full production after 1967. Brazilians anticipate that the petrochemical industry will replace the automobile industry as the spark igniting industrial expansion in the 1970's.

The contribution of consumer goods to national income increased as the population grew and more Brazilians entered the money economy, but the proportion of the contribution to the whole declined. Thus in 1949, consumer goods represented 58.3 percent of the whole. In 1959 they dropped to 43.2 percent and by 1967 to 36.9 percent.[13]

Another trend beyond growing sophistication and import substitution is the slow but steady spread of industry away from the overwhelming concentration in São Paulo. In 1964, São Paulo's share in total industrial production was 61.9 percent, but it had dropped to 54.9 percent by 1967. Industrial production in São Paulo continued to rise, but that in other parts of the country rose at a higher rate.

Total exports increased almost 100% from 1967 to 1971. The export of industrial products increased at even a higher rate. The value of industrial goods exported in 1967 rose to $364.8 million. By 1971 their value had increased 110 percent and contributed 27.5 percent of total exports. In 1966 more than 50 percent of these exports went to countries in the Latin American Free Trade Area, about double the amount sold to the United States. Argentina took slightly more Brazilian manufactures than did the United States.

Imports of manufactures began to increase in 1967 as the result of liberalized import policies. From that date until 1967, capital goods imports increased from $517.9 millions to $2,253 millions of a total of $3,225 millions. The new policies were intended not only to make available better equipment to expanding Brazilian manufacturers, but also to stimulate greater efficiency through competition and to reduce inflationary pressures resulting from shortages of certain consumer goods. Imports of consumers goods, however, amounted to only 10 percent of the total.

Agriculture

Agriculture is still a greater producer than manufacturing, supporting about 65 percent of the population. However only about 41 percent of the people now live in rural areas. Modern agriculture is largely confined to the South; in the Northeast a hoe agriculture still prevails, although first steps toward modernization are being taken. Credit facilities, cheaper fertilizers, improved seeds, and technology are effecting a change throughout the country from overconcentration on coffee and other exportable commodities such as cacao, rubber, cotton, and sugar.

Basic crops kept pace with the growth of population throughout the Empire period; an interest in crops widely consumed by people of more complex societies came with the immigrants. Thus, food in the far south, where Germans, Italians, and Poles undertook diversified farming, have long been varied. After World War II the Japanese, through their large-scale cooperative at Cotia, changed the eating habits of many, first in São Paulo and then in Rio de Janeiro. From there more diversified food consumption spread to other parts of the country. The Japanese made small-scale agriculture profitable for the first time. Such progress as came about in agriculture was made largely through the efforts of the states and private initiative rather than through the federal government, which concentrated its efforts on encouraging a few export crops. Like many other Latin American countries, Brazil still suffers from the ills of monoculture.

The concentration on industry during the period 1959-1952 changed the economy of Brazil from one predominantly agricultural and export oriented into one much more complex. Thus by 1971 industry contributed 30 percent of gross domestic product, compared to less than 24 percent in 1950. Agriculture remained more or less stationary in this process, contributing 28 percent in earlier years, but by 1970 its contribution had been reduced to 20 percent. Production grew but at a slower pace than industry. Between 1947 and 1961 growth in the agricultural sector averaged 4.6 percent, but the industrial sector grew

9.6 percent during the same period. Not until 1964 did the implementation of planning begin to redress this imbalance. In 1969 agriculture grew 6 percent and in 1970 by 5.6 percent. Even at this rate, as a Brazilian government publication notes, "The agricultural sector's contribution to the domestic product has been far below the potentiality of the sector and not much in line with the volume of resources invested in rural progress." [14] This terse statement says much about the high cost of changing systems rooted in primitive techniques and archaic social orders.[15]

Less than 4 percent of the national territory is devoted to cropland, which produces about two-thirds of the agricultural contribution to the gross domestic product. The other third is contributed by the livestock industry, which occupies about 15 percent of the area of Brazil. The beef herd, with 95 million head, is the third largest in the world.

The following table summarizes the growth of the agricultural sector from 1960, the latest year of the Kubitschek administration, to 1966, when the agricultural credit and other measures initiated by the Castello Branco administration began to take effect:

INDEX OF AGRICULTURAL PRODUCTION
(Base: 1953=100)

Product	1960	1962	1964	1968
Internal Consumption	134.8	155.8	172,9	202.5
Food	138.2	152.3	165.6	184.3
Industry	118.8	176.8	210.4	284.7
Export	148.2	162.8	124.9	144.6
Coffee	146.4	154.0	73.3	90.2
Cacao	119.2	102.5	112.2	128.0
Others	145.2	169.5	172.2	194.8
General total	138.4	157.9	163.8	191.2
Total without coffee	135.8	156.5	172.0	200.8

Subsequent years showed a continuation of the pattern.

The changing character of agriculture can be seen from the above. Peanuts, babaçu nuts, tobacco, and soybeans, all industrial crops, showed greatest growth. Of food crops, rice, corn, tomatoes, eggs, and dairy products increased most. Banana production soared 72 percent from 1966 to 1970. In all, agricultural products accounted for 60 percent of the value of exports in 1970. Coffee, cotton, cacao and sugar accounted for nearly 50 percent of the total.

Coffee continues as one of Brazil's principal problems in adjustment

to a more modern economic system. Diversification efforts to replace
coffee with industrial crops continue, but coffee is still too valuable
a crop to be neglected. In 1971 3 million metric tons were produced—
40 percent of world production. The value of exports totalled 27 percent of the total. In its effort to achieve less dependence on one crop,
Brazil may find its principal collaborator in Nature. The appearance
of coffee rust, *roya,* has made serious inroads on production and is
spreading. Freezes in 1971 and 1972 further reduced the crop.

Land Tenure and Agrarian Reform

A principal cause for the failure of agriculture to contribute as much
as it should to the growth of the country is the antiquated land
usage system in which *latifundios* dominate. Nevertheless, because of
the availability of unused land to enterprising individuals, relatively
little political and economic pressure was generated on the subject of
agrarian reform before 1962. When Goulart assumed the presidency
in 1961, he made agrarian reform one of his principal political banners.
He tried to force a constitutional amendment permitting payment for
expropriated land in government bonds rather than cash, which would
have made it economically feasible to give land to the landless. His
efforts failed, but the revolutionary government, in better control of
the congress, managed to have such an amendment passed in 1964. It
provided, however, that small farms expropriated would continue to
be paid for in cash. In addition, that same year congress passed an
agrarian reform measure that was a first step toward changing an
uneconomic and socially archaic structure. One of the principal instruments given the authorities by this measure was the power to tax
land progressively according to size and regressively in terms of intensity of use. Credit was to be provided to enable small farmers to
buy land from private interests.

The *Instituto Brasileiro de Reforma Agraria* (IBRA), the Brazilian
Agrarian Reform Institute, executive organ of the *Instituto Nacional de
Desenvolvimento Agraria* (INDA), spent its first five years organizing,
but by 1969 it was beginning to exercise some of the authority vested in
it to undertake colonization projects, agricultural extension, marketing
programs, and rural electrification. In 1967 it acquired some $328
million worth of land to be given to peasants. Nevertheless, a general

inability to move forward on the program has plagued its early years
of existence.* Intent on speeding up the slowed down program, Costa
e Silva in 1969 decreed several measures that put aside legal recourses
that were until then open to landowners. Even this measure failed to
produce results in the face of what seemed to be a national conspiracy
on the part of bankers, bureaucrats and others working with landowners to block significant reform. In mid-1971, Médici established his
PROTERRA program under which land is to be distributed to small and
medium farmers in the North and Northeast. Slow progress led him a
year later to order the designation within 180 days of large landholdings
which would be divided and redistributed. That this far from radical
measure intended to create a new middle class of farmers brought fiery
speeches in congress and warnings that landowners would resort to
arms, indicated that the government was at last being taken seriously
and that change might be in the offing.

The main problems the government sought to solve were related to
minifundia and latifundia. The most recent figures, developed from
the 1960 census, indicate that holdings of less than 10 hectares (24.7
acres) represented some 45 percent of total holdings but occupied only
2.2 percent of total area in agriculture. In 1950 such holdings represented 34.5 percent of the total, occupying only 1.3 percent of the total
area. Holdings larger than 1,000 hectares, however, formed only 1
percent of the total in 1960, but they accounted for nearly half of
all land designated as farmland, although much of it was uncultivated.
Data for 1950 showed the same area constituted 1.6 percent of holdings.
The only data available on changes which have taken place since 1960
showed a 5 percent increase in the number of farms and a 16 percent
increase in the total farm area. Areas under cultivation increased by
nearly the same amount. A national cadastral survey begun by the
Agrarian Reform Institute in 1966 indicated that of a total of 851,187,-
500 hectares, 307,250,348 are claimed by private individuals and
543,937,152 (some 64 percent) constitute land belonging to the
states.[16]

A pattern for the future may be that established in the state of

*In July 1970, IBRA and INDA, together with the subsequently formed
Executive Group for the Agrarian Reform (GERA), were abolished and replaced by the National Land Settlement and Agrarian Reform Institute (INCRA),
an autonomous agency in the Ministry of Agriculture.

São Paulo, where an agrarian reform program based on increased taxation with nonintensity of use was inaugurated when Carvalho Pinto was governor in the early 1960's.[17] By 1967, some 80 percent of farms in São Paulo were less than 500 hectares. More than two-thirds of all salaried agricultural workers were employed on these farms which operate at a high rate of commercialization.

Education

Brazil has made enormous strides in improving its educational system over the past few decades, yet many consider it still the problem which deserves highest priority if the nation is to industrialize. Progress has been dramatic quantitatively, measured against the baseline which indicated some 80 or 85 percent of the population to be illiterate in 1930.[18] The growing availability of education is shown in the following table:

NUMBER OF MATRICULATIONS IN PRIMARY, SECONDARY, AND HIGHER COURSES

Level	Enrollment (in thousands)					
	1933	*1950*	*1906*	*1964*	*1967*	*1971**
Primary	2,107	4,352	7,141	10,217[a]	11,613[a]	13,300
Secondary	66	....	....	....	2,700[a]	4,100
First level		540	1,177	1,453[a]	....	....
Second level		50	93	439[a]	....	....
	1940	*1957*	*1963*	*1964*	*1968*	*1972**
Colleges and Universities	20	75	117	137	259	500

*Estimated.
[a]Enrollment at the beginning of the school year. An average of about 14 percent drop out almost immediately after enrollment.

The 1970 census indicated a general literacy rate of 70 percent of the population aged fifteen and over, which was a substantial gain over 1950 when the census reported 49 percent of those over fifteen were literate. The increase in the number of educational institutions has been dramatic, particularly in higher education. Brazil had thirty-eight universities in 1966, of which all but five were founded after 1946. In 1964 other institutions of higher learning—law schools, engineering schools, schools of dentistry or pharmacy, agricultural colleges, and small liberal arts colleges which have an important role in training teachers—numbered more than 500. Between 1968 and 1971 alone, 20 new institutions of this nature were established throughout the country.

The distribution of pupils reflects a number of basic problems. Of 10,695,391 pupils enrolled in primary schools in 1966, 5,208,365 were in first grade, 2,223,048 in second grade, 1,658,027 in third, 1,150,836 in fourth, and 410,596 in fifth.[19] Only 180 per thousand finish primary school and of these only 92 per thousand enter secondary school. The latter consists of two cycles—a four-year *ginásio* course and a three-year *colégio* course. In terms of thousands, 52 of 92 complete the *ginásio* course; 50 continue in the *colégio* course, of whom 34 graduate; 17 of the 34 enter schools of higher education but only 13 graduate.[20]

Because of school and teacher shortages little more than 60 percent of the population of primary-school age attends school. Many of these children are first-grade repeater pupils, a great number of whom fail because of a disadvantaged situation in which their parents are illiterate and cannot help them. In school they must compete with pupils from literate families of the middle class.

Another bottleneck in the Brazilian education system is the secondary school. Here, too, the central government and the states have made considerable porgress, but over two-thirds of the secondary schools, with more than 50 percent of the pupils in this age group attending school, are still privately owned and charge tuition. This means that it is very difficult for children of the lower class to get beyond primary school. Not until 1964 did São Paulo pupils in secondary public schools outnumber those in private secondary schools. It was the first state to cross that threshold.

Aside from problems of giving all children an education, those related to the quality of education also concern many Brazilian educators. Except for the increasing number of vocational schools, most of the educational system is geared to educating the elite. For many years, educational philosophy and pedagogical methods were based on antiquated patterns. Secondary schools are only slowly changing from the French *lycée* system, primarily directed at educating an elite. *Visão* in its March 15, 1968, issue focuses on this problem, presenting it graphically in charts. One chart indicates the flow of students through

the educational system and the effects on the society, producing a total
of only 21,000 graduates a year to add to the country's leaders.

Visão charges that the system is designed to preserve the power
and influence of the elites, noting that according to a sociological study
by Nadia Franco da Cunha, *O vestibular na Guanabara,* it was found
that 53.5 percent of the students in higher education in Guanabara were
from the upper class, 39.2 percent from the middle class ,and only 7.3
percent from the lower class, which represented 70 percent of the population. Although these data indicate a lamentable situation by standards
of industrial nations, they nevertheless show that considerable progress
has been made in Brazil. A decade or two earlier universities were
open only to students from the upper class and a mere sprinkling from
the middle class. Families of the latter had to make financial sacrifices to
give their children a university education.

Nonetheless, there is basis for the charge that a philosophy favoring
the elite guides many decision makers in the field of education even
today. In 1960 this philosophy was expressed as a social and economic
problem to the late Governor Adlai E. Stevenson by a Brazilian,
Tancredo Neves, who had held high office under the Vargas Administration and was subsequently a moderate Prime Minister under
Goulart during the short-lived parliamentary period 1961-1963. When
Governor Stevenson, during a discussion of problems of development,
referred to the importance of education, the future Prime Minister
agreed but with the reservation that education should be broadened
only as economic development progressed. Any other course, would inevitably lead to social unrest as educated persons came into an economy
unable to absorb their skills and give them employment. Unemployed
intellectuals, he observed, would do little good to Brazil or to themselves. The philosophy reflects a pragmatic and paternalistic view of
society at the base of political and social processes in Brazil. It helps
explain the Brazilian system, which permits and even welcomes social
change of an evolutionary nature so long as it does not threaten the
basic fabric of the elite society. It does permit, however, "making room
at the top" for new recruits to the "establishment" or the directing
elites of the country, and it may be one reason why Brazilian society as
generally nonviolent.

Although applicable but a few years ago, this elitist philosophy may
already be the victim of changing times, swept away by the need for

all manner of skills to run the nation. Part of the acrimonious discussion over income distribution centers on the government's emphasis on turning out more university graduates at the expense of primary school students. Real earnings of university graduates rose on the average over 50 percent during the 1960's, whereas the earnings of those who did not finish primary school rose only 14 percent in ten years. The income of unskilled, presumably illiterate workers, did not rise at all.

Substantial efforts are being made to help unskilled workers to raise their level of skills. The importance of vocational education has been recognized for years, but much of it was carried out under private auspices (with government assistance) through the National Industrial Apprenticeship Service (SENAIC) and the National Business Apprenticeship Service (SENAC). In 1965 about 65,000 students were enrolled in 115 establishments in the former and some 55,000 in eighty centers in the latter. Nearly 800,000 students were enrolled in state and federal technical, agricultural, industrial, and normal school programs in 1966. The government also sponsored a National Coordination Service for the Training of High Level Personnel (CAPES) to provide professionals for research and other similar high-level needs in science and technology. Increasing emphasis on vocational education in secondary schools is changing outdated patterns.

By 1972 it was still not clear how the educational pattern would eventually be set. Reform has been decreed but it is slow in being implemented and questions have been raised as to its adequacy. Student unrest and protest, with demands for meaningful educational reform, led to violence and organized protests in the student cause by normally passive citizens. These protests were put down with force. Whether the now dormant pressures will flare up again at the failure to push through satisfactory reform remains to be seen, but the pressures are real was indicated in general public opinion polls which in 1969 showed education as the area given highest priority by all classes of society.

VII: Foreign Affairs and Manifest Destiny

Brazilian foreign policy has been remarkably consistent through the years. This can be ascribed to several circumstances, not the least of which are a number of outstanding foreign ministers and a career diplomatic service with its roots in the Empire period. Until the middle of the twentieth century, whether from lack of popular interest in foreign affairs or in deference to patently successful professionals, Brazilian governments almost always enjoyed a free hand in policy formation without interference from the public or the congress.[1] In no other field have the Brazilians so successfully exercised their talent for pragmatic negotiations with clear goals. Policy formulation and diplomatic practice have generally been successful in maintaining national interests in relations with other countries. Except for the border with Paraguay, which was set after the Paraguayan War (1865-1870), the country's farflung boundaries were won peacefully through negotiation.

Geopolitical Background

Brazil's national policy has conformed closely to Brazilian geopolitical interests. Although its foreign policy can be traced without reference to geopolitical factors, the past and present logic of policy decisions, to say nothing of the probable future trends, becomes clearer when the bases on which such decisions were made are understood. These geopolitical interests can be traced in several treatises which have influenced modern decision makers no less than Admiral Mahan's *Manifest Destiny* influenced political leaders in the United States.[2] During the 1930's Mario Travassos, Brazil's most influential writer on foreign relations, saw Brazil's heartland, the land most suited for development, as an area between São Paulo, Rio de Janeiro, Victoria, and Belo Horizonte. In the first phase of historical development beginning in the colonial period, according to his concept, this base had to be joined to the Northeast and the Far South, which jut out from the heartland like two peninsulas. This was done by building highways, and railways and by utilizing waterways. The second phase required that the Center-West be incorporated into the base, chiefly through advanced nucleii, usually army posts that would establish the frontier along the great river arteries. This phase was completed in its most important aspects, the nucleii serving as points of concentration from which wider settlement could take place. The third phase was what Travassos called the "cultural," or what we would call the political, dominance of the Amazon basin by the central government. This was done principally through the establishment of frontier military posts during the period of the rubber boom at the turn of the century, when national governments gave considerable attention to the area. When these stages of territorial expansion and consolidation had been effected, Brazil's boundaries were stabilized.

The next step was to consider Brazil's neighbors to the west. Of the four, Colombia and Peru are Pacific powers, but Bolivia and Paraguay are landlocked republics which are dependent on foreign neighbors to move goods in and out of the countries. Both Bolivia and Paraguay faced the advanced Brazilian military posts in Guaporé and those on the upper Paraguay river; their capitals were already linked to Argentina by rail and, in the case of Asuncion, by waterway. Diplomatic action, then, had to be based on geopolitics. Brazilian-Argentine rivalry in Bolivia and Paraguay is still strong, and this rivalry is reflected in all phases of diplomtic activity, including political, economic, and cultural.

Argentina, Brazil's only important rival in South America, has an even more prominent place in geopolitical factors bearing on the formulation of foreign policy. During the Empire and under the Old Republic in Brazil, Argentina's power and relatively more advanced stage of development overshadowed Brazil, then a widespread, strongly regional, and therefore weakly organized nation. A possible resurrection of the old Vice Royalty of the Río de la Plata, composed of Argentina, Uruguay, Bolivia, and Paraguay, was a constant threat as were secessionist currents in Rio Grande do Sul that had to be kept under control. Access to the Brazilian West through the Paraná and Paraguay rivers, the lower reaches of which were controlled by Argentina, was also a vital policy consideration.

These factors explain why Brazil's relations with the rest of the hemisphre have diverged widely from those of its neighbors. The rivalry between Argentina and Brazil contributed to keeping Brazil isolated from the Spanish-American countries. Other factors of divergence have been differences of national and racial origin and, in the nineteenth century, Brazil's status as an Empire among many republics.[3]

Although in recent years new national and international developments have changed the bases of Argentine-Brazilian rivalry, as late as 1951, a leading Brazilian diplomat, Ambassador Lyra, then Chief of the Political Department in the foreign office, outlined the three cardinal principles of Brazilian foreign policy as: (1) Maintenance of boundaries against the territorial pretensions of neighboring republics, based on the ambitions of the Kings of Spain. (2) Defense of Brazil's territorial supremacy in South America against the threat of a reconstruction of the old Spanish Vice Royalties, particularly of the Río de la Plata. (3) Maintenance of internal political stability against Spanish *caudilhismo*.[4]

These three basic national interests, defensive in nature, have dictated Brazil's overseas alliances. From its early years of independence to the end of the nineteenth century, the alliance with Great Britain was maintained because, as a great naval power, it could not only protect Brazil from extra-continental threats but through its influence in South America could maintain the territorial *status quo*. Early in the twentieth century Brazil selected the United States as its principal ally. By this time the nation to the north had become strong enough to enforce the Monroe Doctrine with more than words alone and, moreover, had become Brazil's best customer for its principal export, coffee.

Diplomacy based on these concepts served more than adequately to protect Brazil's interests until after World War II, but many changes have taken place since then. Many of the bases for suspicion between Argentina and Brazil have disappeared; relations with the United States have deteriorated. A principal new factor in Brazilian foreign policy has been an extension of world-wide commitments as the nation's internal strength increased and as it acquired interests parallel to those of other developing nations. Some of these interests have clashed with those of the United States.

Latin American Policy

It is impossible to understand the motivation behind most of Brazil's diplomatic activity without understanding its place in the hemisphere.

As has been noted, Brazil cannot be considered just another part of Latin America. Most historians divide the hemisphere into Anglo-Saxon America and Latin America. The Brazilians have always divided it into three parts: Anglo-Saxon America, Spanish America, and Brazil.[5] To some extent this was inevitable because of Brazil's imperial past and cultural differences that led the Spanish American nations to distrust their giant neighbor, which had spread like an irresistible tide across the face of South America during the expansion period. The "colossus of the South" still suffers a degree of exclusion from the inner councils of the eighteen Spanish American nations [6] just as does the United States, the "colossus of the North."

The first two of the three basic principles of Brazilian foreign policy, as outlined by Ambassador Lyra, are mainly of historical interest, since the nation no longer has great concern about the permanence of its boundaries or the reconstitution of any of the old Spanish Vice Royalties. But even if they are no longer of primary concern, neither are they entirely forgotten, as attested by Brazil's steadfast insistence on the sanctity of treaties and its coolness to regional agreements among other Latin American nations. Brazil still maintains almost half its standing army in the South, where Argentina is on or near the other side of the border.

The third principle, the maintenance of internal political stability against foreign influences, is very much alive, but it is directed less against Spanish *caudilhismo* than against Communist or other subversive infiltration. This problem assumed more serious proportions after the 1964 revolution as opposition to military control increased. Some of the terrorist activity which developed after 1967 was charged to political refugees who reentered the country clandestinely from exile abroad. Only some were Communists, but all constituted a threat to political, if not social, stability.

Brazil suffered far more from the effects of the five-year Paraguayan War that ended in 1870 than did Argentina, which not only recovered much sooner but moved on to become the leading industrial and commercial nation in all Latin America. Until the middle of the twentieth century, Brazil was forced to pursue the defensive policy established by Baron Rio Branco, Foreign Minister from 1902 to 1912. More than once relations between the two countries became tense enough to cause the usually optimistic and pacific Rio Branco to say: "We must be prepared for the worst." He had an important voice in the decision under President Rodrigues Alves to rebuild and strengthen the armed forces, which had been neglected since the early 1890's.

Rio Branco's diplomacy and Brazil's economic growth, together with its alliance with the United States (which found relations with Argentina almost as difficult as did Brazil), served to stabilize relations with Argentina. They became difficult again under Peron who either dominated or directed the country from 1943 to 1955. Not only did Peron exercise considerable pressure on Chile and Paraguay, both friendly to Brazil, in pursuit of hegemony in South America, but he also encouraged dissident elements in Uruguay and Rio Grande do Sul. Several factors have subsequently improved relations with Argentina, principally that Argentina fell behind economically under Peron whereas Brazil has developed rapidly over the past fifteen years. An equilibrium was restored for a time, and the balance has now shifted in Brazil's favor.

Another factor, perhaps of less durable nature, is that the two countries have been ruled by military men who found their common interests to be greater than their differences. What Meira Penna calls a Brasilia-Buenos Aires axis apparently has been a Brazilian objective for a number of years. Ambassador Lyra, in his 1951 talk, noted that he was "always convinced that the day Brazil undertakes to be the channel for close understanding between the United States and Argentina, and bases its American policy on an intimate relationship between the three countries, things in the hemisphere will be much better . . ., and the position of Brazil and Argentina in the international field will gain considerable status." Although it was perhaps not so apparent in 1951, today it is evident that leadership in the south will rest with Brazil.

The Buffer States

Even in 1970, when personal relations between leaders of Brazil and Argentina were on the best of planes, interests of the two countries diverged. This was nowhere clearer than in the continued competitive dealings with the buffer nations.

Travassos believed Brazil could strengthen its ties with Bolivia and Paraguay by offering both countries outlets to the Atlantic via producer and consumer markets. Foreign Minister Rio Branco in 1902 explained the Brazilian rationale regarding Bolivia in a memorandum to

President Rodrigues Alves: "Argentina and Chile, inspired by wise economic concerns, are constructing railways in Bolivian territory destined to channel commerce their way. Yet neither Chile nor Argentina has contact with Bolivia through territory so rich as Beni and Madre de Dois, where access to Europe and North America can only be made through the Madeira and the Amazon. We will be deprived of great profits which our greater promixity to European and American markets would give us if we do not enter into honorable competition, also seeking the benefits of Bolivian transit commerce." Rio Branco could claim credit for the important Treaty of Petropolis in 1903, which provided for improved channels of trade and gave a number of other attractive concessions to Bolivia. But all the words about helping Bolivia and about "honorable competition" could not hide the import of another part of the treaty by which Bolivia was forced to give up all claims to the valuable territory of Acre.

Other agreements over the years culminated in 1958 in the Act of Roboré, a comprehensive series of agreements relative to communications, technical cooperation, free ports, navigation, cultural exchange, the right to exploit certain oil lands, and the establishment of a branch of the Bank of Brazil in La Paz. As communications improve, it may well be that Brazil will become the principal outlet for products of the rich eastern zone of Bolivia, including the oil fields, making a reality of Rio Branco's improbable prophecies.[8]

Relations with Paraguay have been more important politically than those with Bolivia, but more attention has concentrated on Bolivia because of its petroleum reserves which could become important to Brazil. Negotiating with Paraguay is also more difficult because Argentina's position in that country is considerably stronger than it is in Bolivia, since usual access to and egress from Paraguay is through Argentine terirtory. In addition, Brazil's part in the Paraguayan War has left a residue of distrust, as has its refusal to countenance Paraguayan claims to part of the Guaira Falls with their enormous potential for electric power. However, Brazil's interest and economic concessions in Paraguay are a welcome balance to Argentine preeminence.

Brazil maintains military missions, economic cooperation missions, and cultural missions in Paraguay and has helped build bridges across the Parana river linking Brazil and Paraguay and giving access to roads leading to the Atlantic, where free ports have been established to handle

Paraguayan products. As yet, these routes cannot compete with river or even railway traffic moving south. They do, however, make it less likely that Argentina, as it sometimes has done in the past, will apply burdensome obstacles on the movement of goods between the two countries or to and from Paraguayan overseas markets. A Brazilian company has prospected for oil in the Paraguayan Chaco near the Bolivian border, but it has been as unsuccessful as several international companies. Agreement to exploit the Guairá hydroelectric potential jointly was reached in 1972.

Uruguay has been a bloody battlefield for Brazilian *caudilhos* and Argentine *caudillos,* and has at times been occupied by both of its neighbors. In 1828, the two powers agreed that Uruguay would remain independent, a buffer state that would keep Argentina away from Brazil's southernmost border and Brazil away from the eastern shores of the Río de la Plata. The Uruguayans, racially distinct from the mixtures in Argentina and Brazil, have generally treasured and fought for their independence. In modern times their nation has been a Latin American model of democracy in a sea of variations on democracy. Because of a more viable economy which remained strong until the 1960's, Uruguay had much less need for Argentine or Brazilian assistance than either Paraguay or Bolivia, but it might be said to exist by the sufferance of both rival states.

Since the advent of military governments in both neighboring countries, along with serious internal problems, Uruguay has had to walk a dangerous tightrope. Any hint of the ascendence of leftists in Uruguay brings rumblings from the security-conscious military governments of its giant neighbors. How real is Uruguay's concern is evident from a discussion of the subject in Ambassador Meira Penna's treatise on foreign affairs. When discussing the Inter-American Defense Force (IADF), first proposed by the United States but subsequently rejected by most of the Latin American countries, he observes that an IADF would have great value in meeting extra-continental threats and internal subversions inspired from abroad. He then poses the question: would the majority of the countries "held back by fear, egoism, hesitation, ineptness, and latent resentment against the United States allow it?" The United States, he prophecies, will guard the Caribbean, but, he asks, will it respond to grave crises in some state near the Río de la Plata? "Our interests and security are directly affected even to a greater degree than the United

States. . . . We can conceive of a situation in which the old foreign policy of the Empire, seeking to maintain order and tranquility in South America, if necesary through armed intervention, will have renewed application in a reversal of the modern principle of collective security . . ." [9] A return to civilian government in either country would doubtlessly forestall the possibility of such intervention.

Brazil and the Inter-American System

Apart from concerns arising over the Río de Plata and boundaries, the new nation showed little interest in the Latin American side of inter-American affairs until Baron Rio Branco took charge of Itamaraty, the Foreign Office, in 1902. Brazil was invited but did not attend the Panama Congress of 1826, called by Simón Bolívar. Brazilian attendance at other inter-American meetings for the rest of the century was spotty. Consonant with his move to change the base of Brazilian foreign policy to a Rio de Janeiro-Washington axis, Rio Branco determined to expand Brazil's relations among the other Latin American countries. Close relations with the United States, however, stood in the way of improved relations with many of the Latin American countries, particularly Argentina. Support of the Monroe Doctrine during the height of President Theodore Roosevelt's "big stick" period led him to recognize Brazil as the Doctrine's joint guardian. He sent Elihu Root, the first Secretary of State of the United States, to travel abroad, to the Third Pan American Conference held in Rio de Janeiro in 1906 as a symbol of his appreciation. Most other Latin American nations were less appreciative.

Brazil opened diplomatic missions in Latin American countries where it had not been previously represented, but its best effort was Rio Branco's proposal for a "Treaty of cordial understanding and arbitration between the United States of Brazil, the Republic of Chile and the Argentine Republic." He gave the Chilean Minister in Rio de Janeiro a draft of such a treaty in January 1909 in the hope that Chile would take the initiative in seeking its acceptance; and he told a special Argentine envoy his reasoning behind the proposal, which was that having "already constructed the map of Brazil," he wished to contribute to unity and friendship among the South American nations.[10] Nothing came of the proposal because of Argentine suspicions of Brazil's long-term objectives, which Brazil's sponsorship of the Monroe Doctrine did nothing to overcome.

Pan Americanism

Inter-Americanism has at least three well-defined aspects. The Bolivarian goal has often been called the romantic aspect, which has concentrated on political development, one of its ultimate objectives being a widely American or more exclusive Latin American union or community of nations. Another aspect is economic development which can also be viewed as a phase toward gaining the objective of a community of nations. The third aspect, the Monroevian view, has concentrated on security. The first pronouncement of the Monroe Doctrine had as its purpose the discouragement of outside interference in any part of the Western Hemisphere.

The so-called romantic side of Pan-Americanism has to do with Bolívar's belief, shared by some statesmen in the early days of the republic in the United States, in a special relationship among the republican nations of America which set them off from the rest of the world. This has been called the Pan-American Ideal by some and the Western Hemisphere Idea by others. Brazil has had a special interest in this concept because many of its leaders foresaw that their nation would have a dominant role in the southern part of the hemisphere. More than just supporting initatives of the United States in this field, Brazil went farther than the more cautious United States by seeking to institutionalize the concept. At the 9th Inter-American Conference held in Bogota in 1948, Brazil proposed that the new inter-American organization to succeed the Pan American Union be called the "Union of American Nations." Because of Argentine objections, however, it was called the "Organization of American States." The Brazilian Foreign Minister, João Neves de Fontoura, later expressed regret for the "resistance that prevented us from following the universal movement toward the federalist ideal of abolishing the limitations of an extreme nationalism" with its dangerous consequences for peace among nations.[11]

Collective and National Security

The question of the Monroe Doctrine and inter-American security has as long and a more controversial history than the Bolivarian idea of an American community of nations. The Brazilian decision in the early 1900's to adopt the United States as a principal ally was based largely on security considerations. In the face of a good deal of resistance to U. S. policies and activities in the hemisphere, Brazil cast its lot with the United States as between Spanish-America and Anglo-America. However, like most of the rest of Latin America, it too was soon seeking inter-American agreements providing for collective security that eventually could make the Monroe Doctrine unnecessary. Brazil's support did not necessarily mean that it approved all U. S. actions. While publicly supporting the United States in Latin American councils, it often argued the errors of its ways in private. As Meira Penna notes, "the principal objective of the OAS can be defined as that of reducing unilateral action to a minimum . . ."[12] Unilateral action usually refers to action by the United States.

The first steps to multilateralize the Monroe Doctrine came under Franklin D. Roosevelt's Good Neighbor Policy. The principle of collective security was reaffirmed and broadened at the Pan American Conference of Lima in 1938, in a document called the Declaration of Lima, just before war broke out in Europe. Efforts at Lima by the United States and Brazil to found a common defense system were blocked by Argentina, which at the time was strongly influenced by totalitarian ideas. Argentina countered Brazil's efforts to promote collective security with proposals for Spanish-American hemisphere commitments "generously including Brazil," notes the sardonic Delgado de Carvalho in reporting the event, but excluding the United States.

Not until ten years later was a binding collective security treaty agreed upon. This Treaty of Reciprocal Assistance was signed at Rio de Janeiro on September 2, 1947, becoming effective the following year. It condemns war and provides peaceful procedures for the settlement of all disputes among the American nations. The treaty establishes the principle that an attack against one American state will be considered an attack against all, and that each will undertake to assist the attacked state, either individually or collectively, until the United Nations can take appropriate measures. The treaty provides for consultation when the peace in the hemisphere is threatened, and it also provides for sanctions ranging from suspension of diplomatic relations to the use of force. It was the culmination of efforts of half a century to establish a mechanism for mutual defense, and it was welcomed equally by the United States and some Latin American nations which had long sought ways to restrain unilateral intervention by the United States as well as pressures from their larger Latin American neighbors.

Since the advent of military governments in 1964, "security" has assumed high priority in Brazil. However, security usually refers to internal problems, since few responsible political or military leaders believe in the danger of external aggression. Brazil today sees no aggressors on its borders; threats against national security would take the form of subversive infiltration.[13]

In response to the alleged threat of Communist takeover in the Dominican Republic in 1965, Brazil proved to be the staunchest ally of the United States in the joint intervention in that Latin American country. It sent over a thousand soldiers during the occupation and the command was given to a Brazilian general, with an American acting as his deputy. There was a minimum of public protest in Brazil to this novel role for Brazilian forces since it was justified as a common inter-American initiative. The fact that a Brazilian was placed in command of all forces was a matter of national pride. The U. S. proposal at the time of the Dominican crisis to create an Inter-American Peace Force (IAPF) to be used to maintain peace and to meet such problems as that which arose in the Dominican Republic was welcomed by Brazil but by few others. As one foreign minister is reported to have observed, an IAPF would never be used against the United States. Brazil, on the other hand, believed that the existence of an IAPF under joint command would restrain unilateral U.S. action, but it was unable to convert many Latin Americans to its point of view, and by 1970 the idea was a moribund, if not a dead, issue.

Brazil's policy toward Africa will be considered later in another context, but it should be recalled here that West Africa is considered by many Brazilians as part of "Fortress America." Meira Penna quotes with approval the words of Col. Meira Mattos that "considering that the Atlantic has its strait in the so-called strategic bridge, Natal-Dakar, it is of very particular interest to Brazil to have the assurance that the Atlantic side of Africa always be in friendly hands." He goes on to say: "We are, in other words, an interested party in an African Monroe Doctrine which constitutes the strategic base by virtue of which we can insist on . . . respect for the principle of non-intervention and self-determination." [14] Elsewhere, Meira Mattos is somewhat more blunt in saying that strategically (as of c. 1955) Africa interests Brazil more than any other area of the world. He continues: "It will be there that we will have to protect our own territory from the horrors of war. If the Atlantic side of Africa should be lost, there would no longer be a security mission to perform; it would be war at home." [15]

As supersonic planes and guided missiles make distances less relevant, it is doubtful if Brazilian military strategists entertain views so strong as those of Meira Mattos about the importance of Africa to Brazilian security. Nonetheless, the relative proximity of Africa to Brazil, as well as other ties, will always make it an area of interest to the Brazilian military.

Economic Aspects of Inter-American Relations

In today's world one of the principal elements of disruption is the "revolution" of rising expectations. This "revolution" has made economics and economic development of highest importance in relations among the American nations. It would not be wrong to say that economic relations are often more important than political, but it would be more accurate to say that the two have become inseparable. The Brazilian Ambassador in La Paz, Bolivia, Alvaro Teixeira Soares, made the point in a justification for new policy directions in a report to his government in 1958. Commenting on the growing population in South America, Teixeira Soares concluded that "the countries of this continent should strengthen Pan-Americanism principally in politico-economic and social terms because the academic or juridical phase of Pan-America has already passed." [16]

Spanish-American political leaders would be less inclined than their more pragmatic Brazilian peers to jettison the "academic or juridical" phase of Pan-Americanism called the "romantic" phase by others, but like President Juscelino Kubitschek, for whose pragmatic eyes Soares was probably writing, many Brazilians saw the handwriting on the wall long before many of their colleagues in other countries. That Brazil hoped to be a principal recipient of aid from the United States for modernizing its out-dated economic and social structure did not make the Teixeira Soares thesis less valid.

Patterns of assistance had been set principally in the areas of public health and agriculture during and after World War II by the Rockefeller Office of the Coordinator of Inter-American Affairs and President Truman's Point Four program. During the Eisenhower Administration the level of cooperation receded sharply until the threat from Castro Cuba moved the United States government to initiate new efforts to undercut Communist promises and other, more tangible, subversions.

Brazil's greatest contribution in the area of economic developmentalism was Operation Pan America (OPA). OPA was drawn up by several of Brazil's younger and more brilliant diplomats, particularly Ambassador Sette Camara, and was given weighty support within the Kubitschek administration by presidential adviser Augusto Frederico Schmidt. It was launched in an exchange of letters between Presidents Kubitschek and Eisenhower, but it failed to acquire substance because of lack of U.S. interest. Nevertheless, it served as the core idea behind President Kennedy's Alliance for Progress and is so acknowledged in the Preamble to the Charter of Punta del Este. It was also a principal effort on Brazil's part to integrate fully into the Latin American bloc, thus, as one of its creators has noted, "ending the proud isolation we had always attempted to maintain." Rejected by the United States and treated either gingerly or with suspicion by most of the Spanish American countries, OPA showed how far Brazil still had to go to achieve integration in the hemisphere.

More gradual approaches to integration among the Latin American nations are being sought through common markets and free trade. The Latin American Free Trade Association (LAFTA) was established in 1960 when Argentina, Brazil, Chile, Mexico, Peru, and Uruguay signed the Treaty of Montevideo. Paraguay, Colombia, Ecuador, Venezuela, and Bolivia subsequently signed, making all South American nations (except Guyana) plus Mexico adherents to the treaty. In ten years of existence LAFTA (ALALC in Spanish and Portuguese) has taken halting but real steps toward economic integration. Brazil was at first reluctant to commit itself to major concessions, doubtful of the effect on trade and industrial growth. When its trade with the signatory nations showed major increases, particularly in national manufactures, Brazil's participation became more enthusiastic.

Despite real progress under LAFTA, the halting and difficult steps toward free trade led the Latin American presidents at the Summit Meeting of American Presidents, held in Punta del Este in April 1967, to agree progressively to establish the Latin American Common Market (LACM) within a period of not more than fifteen years, beginning in 1970. Brazil was again reluctant to commit itself to a Common Market, uncertain how its range of interests would be affected. Brazilian insistence led to changing the original U.S. proposal for a ten-year limitation on the creation of LACM to one of fifteen years. Progress has been slow in this area.

More recent developments in inter-American integration and its effect on Brazil's relations with the United States are better described within the context of its relations with other countries in the past and its own view of its expanded role in the world today.

The United States and Brazil

Close relations between the United States and Brazil were an objective of statesmen of the two countries even prior to Brazilian independence. When in 1787 a Brazilian student in Paris approached Thomas Jefferson, the Minister to France, seeking the support of the United States for a republican group plotting independence from Portugal, Jefferson gave him considerable encouragement, if he failed to pledge material support. The United States was the first country to recognize the new nation in 1824, despite the reluctance of some officials within the United States to give encouragement to a monarchy. The first Brazilian Chargé d'Affaires in the United States proposed an alliance between the two nations to resist interference in Brazil "in case Portugal called a partner to her assistance." The reference to "a partner" was to England, which, Brazil feared, could be prevailed upon to help suffocate the new monarchy.

The United States was not then interested in alliances that might become entangling, but in 1857 it made a similar proposal. In presenting his credentials to Pedro II, Washington's envoy suggested that "such an alliance will ensure unity of action and feeling that will prove invincible in the future for mutual defense." At this time Brazil was no longer interested—at least nothing came of the proposal—probably because relations with Great Britain had measurably improved with more or less satisfactory status of the slave-trade issue.

After the Spanish-American War, when the United States had amply demonstrated its capability to enforce its hemisphere decrees, Brazil shifted the northern end of its diplomatic axis from London to Washington, raising its mission in Washington to embassy level.[17] By 1914 the United States was taking more than 80 percent of Brazilian exports, mostly coffee and rubber.

A Brazilian military mission was stationed in the United States during World War I to acquire military equipment and work out military cooperation procedures. In 1922, the two countries signed a naval agreement providing for a U.S. naval mission in Brazil. One of its objectives was to help reorganize the Brazilian navy. Argentina protested this agreement on the grounds that it would obstruct action on arms limitation among the ABC powers (Argentina, Brazil, and Chile), but Brazil disavowed any intention to increase the size of the navy. The first U.S. army mission to Brazil was provided for in a 1936 agreement, but cooperation did not reach high levels until the departure from Brazil a few years later of the large French army mission.

United States economic assistance to Brazil before and during World War II was instrumental in stimulating production of raw materials of great importance to the war effort. Franklin D. Roosevelt made possible the establishment of a capital-goods industry by helping finance the construction of the Volta Redonda steel mill. But the postwar period was less felicitous for relations than the war years. This was surprising, because the President of the United States under whom relations worsened was former General Dwight D. Eisenhower, a popular hero in Brazil. He had both affection and sympathy for Brazil, which he visited once as ex-Commander-in-Chief of Allied Forces (and therefore of the Brazilian Expeditionary Force) and again as President of the United States. However, his strong-minded Secretary of State, John Foster Dulles, devoted little time to shoring up relations in the Western Hemisphere. Since there seemed to be little threat from Communism in Latin America at that time, he gave the area little attention. The result was an era of neglect that had adverse consequences for U.S. national interests.[18]

Shortly after the new administration came into power it announced that it would no longer consider financing a series of projects drawn up by a Joint Brazil-United States Economic Development Commission while Truman and Vargas were still Chiefs of State. Brazil believed that the United States Government had committed itself to this aid; but the Eisenhower administration, emphasizing the role of private over public capital, denied the commitment. Relations became increasingly strained.

The Kubitschek administration coincided with Eisenhower's last five years in office. Some cautious gestures of economic aid were made by the U.S. but Brazil's proposed Operation Pan America (OPA), was allowed to die aborning. Only when Castro triumphed in Cuba, did the Eisenhower administration decide to give attention and increased aid to Latin America. By this time, however, much harm had already been done and, as President Kennedy pointed out when the Alliance for Progress was established, the aid given was less effective than it would have been had it been worked out earlier.

When the United States under Kennedy was prepared to cooperate, Brazil was ineffective in making the most of the aid. The unstable Jânio Quadros soon adapted a more independent (from the United States) policy calling for renewed relations with the Soviet Bloc and close relations with Argentina. Both Quadros and his successor Goulart preferred to play on anti-American sentiment than to take full advantage of the Alliance for Progress to further economic development.

After Goulart was overthrown by the military in 1964, Brazilian policy was reversed under General Castello Branco. Traditional policies of closest cooperation with U. S. were reinstated. Cooperative economic efforts that followed were never closer or more effective, but so much ground had to be recovered from the deterioration under Goulart that the effects of the mammoth efforts did not become apparent until after Castello Branco left office in 1967. Castello Branco had to resort to economic restraints and deflationary policies which made it one of the most unpopular administrations in recent Brazilian history. Because the United States was then working closely with Brazil, an unwanted side effect was an upsurge of anti-American feeling that reached alarming proportions. Not only was the United States Government held responsible for the restrictive economic measures which drastically limited credit and resulted in a high number of bankruptcies, lowered standards of living for workers, and increased income taxes for the wealthy, but U.S. business interests also came under increased attack, accused of taking advantage of the bankruptcies to buy up Brazilian businesses at liquidation prices.

A gradual reduction of the "American presence" in Brazil, which at its height saw 1,600 North Americans and 1,000 Brazilians on United States government payrolls throughout the country and U.S. citizens in virtually every department of the Brazilian government, began during the last year of the Johnson administration and was continued under the Nixon administration. The early Nixon "low-profile" policy seemed to fit the mood of Brazilians. It also proved advantageous to the United States to decrease its presence at a time when the Brazilian government was increasingly repressive in political affairs.

Most diplomatic problems, which before 1960 were with little difficulty kept below the boiling point, must today be considered in a different context. Brazil has changed. Those changes which most affect United States-Brazil relations are:

• Brazil no longer believes, as it once did, that it is virtually dependent on the United States for security protection. Collective security in the hemisphere has given all Latin American countries more confidence in their ability to meet most foreseeable threats. Whether or not U.S. nuclear power is in fact essential for ultimate defense, the presence of the United States is no longer considered necessary.

• In choosing to break with its traditional policy of "splendid isolation" and to seek to integrate within the Latin American community, Brazil leaves behind its mediating role between the United States and the Spanish-American nations. It aligns itself with the majority, which is always less inclined to accept the U.S. view of problems. Even if Brazil assumes leadership in the southern part of the hemisphere, it will still have to support or make concessions to majority views.

• Since early 1964, Brazil has been controlled by military governments of varying degrees of nationalistic fervor. The military view of the national interests is less susceptible to influence than that of civilian politicians whose experience has taught them that national and international politics must be the art of the possible.

• Brazil's view of itself as a nascent major power whose interests may or may not coincide with those of the United States demands that problems be discussed on a different plane from times past. As a self-professed spokesman for the developing world, Brazil must inevitably take positions that will not be to the liking of the developing nations, including, or perhaps particularly, the United States.

On the other hand, certain factors will work to keep debate on issues at acceptable levels. The most important are:

• The United States buys between 30 and 50 percent of Brazilian exports and usually takes about 80 percent of the Brazilian coffee crop, the most important export.

• Although the ultranationalistic sectors of the military often force nationalistic decisions, the majority of the military favors continuing close ties with the United States and its armed forces.

• So long as military control of the government continues, it will be strongly influenced by the fact that the United States continues to be the leader of the anti-Communist world. The need for equipment and training against guerrilla and other internal subversion will also counsel moderation in dealing with matters affecting the United States.

• Brazil still sorely needs economic assistance whether under the Alliance for Progress program or in the form of trade preferences.

• Although their number and influence is decreasing, a body of traditionalists in Brazilian society holds that close ties between the United States and Brazil are necessary for the well-being of Brazil and a strong, united hemisphere. Public opinion polls have shown that these traditionalists have considerable support among the elites and also among the masses.

Among the most important issues are terms of trade, Alliance for Progress aid, Brazil's position in the hemisphere and in the world, and the identification of the United States with Brazilian military governments since 1964. A new issue is Brazil's recent claim to offshore jurisdiction to a 200-mile limit, a policy reversal from the old 3-mile limit. This now aligns Brazil with other Latin American countries against the U.S. position on offshore rights.

Terms of Trade and Economic Assistance

In 1963 President Goulart dramatized differences between the United States and Brazil on the question of terms of trade by giving support to the often repeated charge that if the United States would pay a few pennies more for the coffee it bought, benefits to Brazil would outweigh all the economic aid it was then receiving. The statement is not true, but it does have enough truth in it to give it plausibility. Goulart did not want to stop foreign aid, any more than he wanted to further enrich the coffee growers. He was, however, protesting not only the terms of trade, but possibly more importantly, the close control by the United States over allocations by the U.S. Agency for International Development (AID).

Economic and social development in underdeveloped countries requires large loans from international agencies and developed nations. These loans can only be repaid through exports unless a country is fortunate enough to attract large numbers of tourists or can provide other services on a large scale. The more economic assistance Brazil receives from the United States and other countries, the higher become the debt repayment charges against the balance of payments. Paradoxically, the nations helping Brazil the most with development loans, and whose technicians encourage manufactures for exports, are often the ones that limit or shut off foreign trade. The United States restricts imports of certain cotton goods, soluble coffee, meat, and other products from Brazil under pressure from domestic interests. Some of Brazil's former best customers in Europe have shut off trade as a result of European Common Market restrictions and others because of concessions to former colonies. This is one of the explanations for the growing gap between the developed and the underdeveloped nations.

A number of internal political problems in the United States have made administration of the Alliance for Progress or similar programs increasingly difficult. The difficulties grew as isolated examples of mismangement came to light and when it became difficult to show quick results. Strong nationalists in the United States demanded not only more and more bureaucratic hobbles but also direct evidence that the programs were benefitting the economy of the United States as well as that of the recipients. This was a far cry from the altruistic and idealistic language with which John Kennedy had launched the Alliance for Progress and with which Harry Truman before him had initiated the Point Four program. Political wranglings in the United States inevitably increased Brazilian cynicism about U.S. objectives in promoting the Alliance and made it more difficult for the United States to speak with authority when Brazil failed to follow guidelines set by the United States and international agencies.

Efforts in Washington to continue and enlarge the assistance program were not helped by poor performance of some of the recipients. Brazil was no exception. The developmental nationalist policy constructed during the second Vargas administration and the Kubitschek administration accepted inflation as a concomitant of development. This clashed with the orthodox fiscal policy of the United States and also its philosophy of development, even in the highly tolerant Kennedy administration. The International Monetary Fund (IMF), which for years treated the problems of developing nations almost exclusively in terms of policies best serving already developed nations, was even more negative. In these circumstances, the failure of Vargas, Café Filho, and Kubitschek to apply certain deflationary policies was considered by the IMF to be grounds for withholding aid. Brazilian official and private attitudes toward the United States and the lending agencies became increasingly negative, preparing the ground for Kubitschek's succesor, Jânio Quadros, whose anti-American policies would have been unacceptable to the Brazilian people before then. Meaningful cooperation during the Goulart regime was all but precluded.

The period of massive U.S. economic assistance began with the installation of Castello Branco in 1964. The President believed not only that Brazil's security ultimately rested in the hands of the United States, but also that its troubled economy could only be saved with help from the United States. The resulting intimate relationship proved effective in bringing unprecedented cooperation and assistance, but it damaged the U.S. position in Brazil. Many critics of the Brazilian government saw this close cooperation as interference in the nation's internal economic affairs. The government accepted it, not willingly, but as part of the ritual which goes with economic assistance. Technically, agreement to accept such interference is contained in so-called "conditions precedent" to granting aid, and the United States, often on orders from congress, is usually more demanding in those conditions than other countries and the international lending agencies. In Brazil this interference may take the form of minute audits of government accounts; a close watch over its budgetary expenditures; supervision over project engineers; and insistence on government action often highly unpopular politically. As in all underdeveloped countries granted U.S. aid, the United States ambassador exercises the power of life and death over the selection of projects, and his criteria and priorities are often not those of the government to which he is accredited.

It is apparent that the nature of diplomacy has changed radically, coincident with the massive effort to help developing nations. Some of this change was inevitable but the role of the tutelary power granting economic assistance is a controversial one and inevitably causes friction. As a nation develops, supervision becomes less acceptable, but the aiding nation cannot ignore its responsibilities to its own people and even to the people of the aided nation if its leaders cannot satisfactorily make use of the aid. The dimensions of the responsibility in Brazil are apparent from the fact that from August 1961 to July 1968, $3 billion in foreign credits in which the United States shared were granted to Brazil. Of this total, $1 billion 715 million were from the United States Agency for International Development, and its allocation and use had to be a responsibility of the donor nation as well as the recipient. If the United States exercises this responsibility unreasonably, demands for an "independent foreign policy in the national interest" will increase. This can embarrass the government and create political problems.

Brazil's Position in the Hemisphere

Brazil's growing power and population place it in a towering position over most of its hemisphere neighbors. The Organization of American States considers its members equally important and must so treat them. The United States deals with all as equals except in matters of economic and military assistance, where different criteria prevail. Brazil is as aware as the United States of the importance of holding equal respect for and giving recognition of prestige equally to all the American nations. Nevertheless, as Brazil continues to grow and sees itself nearing developed, major statehood, it resents being dealt with on the same level as the smallest and poorest of the Latin American republics. Brazil has often expressed disappintment that the United States gives as much attention and aid to nations which have either been uncooperative in matters of importance to the United States or have worked against the interests of the United States and the United Nations, as Argentina did during World War II. When the United States, in an effort to discourage using for armaments resources which could be allocated to economic development, proposed a ban on supersonic military aircraft in 1967, some Brazilian officials took serious umbrage to the proposal. Not only did the military and some civilians object to having restrictions of this nature placed on their country's sovereignty and freedom of action, but they also raised objections to any blanket limitation that did not take into acount the country's size and defense requirements. Data on allocation of military assistance are not made public, but it is no secret that more than half the funds available in recent years for Latin America have gone to the program in Brazil. The Brazilians welcome these demonstrations of U.S. good intentions, but they also seek recognition of their status as a nascent major power.

None of the instances cited above and others like them singly have created serious tension between the two countries. Cumulatively, however, they have prepared the ground in which anti-American Brazilians, ultranationalists, Communists, or simply demagogues could work without censure. The gradual erosion of cordial relations through some minor and some major disagreements and misunderstandings inevitably have resulted in serious long-term damage, some of it irreparable.

United States Identification with Military Governments

The issue of how closely the United States lets itself become identified with dictatorial, undemocratic, or simply military governments is one that has been debated too often to require review here. Only the dimensions of the problem need be outlined. As already noted, the U.S. economic aid to Brazil after March 1964 entailed a degree of cooperation that made it virtually impossible to say where U.S. influence began or ended. The Castello Branco government relentlessly carried out necessary but unpopular economic measures, a procedure which the United States could only applaud. During Castello Branco's last year and a half in office, his economic measures were increasingly criticized by almost all sectors of society; and in carrying them out he moved Brazil sharply from a relatively bland policy in transition toward democratic procedures to an authoritarian regime. The United States was ambivalent in its public posture, because it could not and did not want to disassociate itself from the salutary economic program, but at the same time is had no desire to be held responsible for or to seem to be indifferent to the setback for democracy.

During this period the United States embassy took cautious steps to disengage itself from its posture of firm commitment, but anything short of open disavowal of the government in office could have only limited effect. The problem increased as successor governments adopted more repressive political measures against the political opposition and against a large number of intellectuals, including university professors, composers of music, playwrights, and journalists. It also instituted censorship. More than simply a matter of public posture is involved since the United States not only continued its military assistance program but also financed a large public safety program (costing nearly half a million dollars annually) under which authoritarian police were given training to make them more effective. This increased effectiveness was applied not only to normal problems of law and order but to repressive activities as well. The true dimensions of the problem extend beyond those arising from repression. Even before such extreme measures were adopted, many Brazilians had protested against the extent of U.S. military influence in Brazil.

The United States was held responsible for the 1964 military coup, and its military establishment was blamed for adversely influencing the Brazilian military. Some held the influence exerted by the U.S. military missions and components of the Military Assistance Advisory Group (MAAG) as principally responsible for transferring U.S. postwar concerns to the Brazilian military. This attitude surfaced only when the armed forces took political control in 1964. José Honório Rodrigues, a well-known historian and spokesman for the intellectual opposition, at one time observed that "the present and catastrophic disintegration of the Brazilian democratic system and of individual liberties and guarantees is a result of military vitality. It is the fruit of the infiltration of ideas disseminated by the Pentagon among the military elite of the underdeveloped or developing nations. The primacy of ideas on [national] security, the great subversion [by the Communist Bloc], internal aggression, transformed the thinking of certain military groups." [19] Rodrigues uses Arthur Schlesinger, Jr. to support his thesis. He cites Schlesinger's comment on Truman's 1946 proposal "under Pentagon pressure" to standardize military organization, training methods, and equipment throughout the hemisphere with the evident hope of ultimately producing an inter-American army under United States generalship. Later he quotes Schlesinger's observations on the "incestuous relations" between the Pentagon and the military of Latin America, which by 1961 threatened "to distort United States policy much as the special interests of business had distorted policy thirty-five years earlier." [20]

This view underestimates the independence of thought of the Brazilian military in general and the Brazilian *Escola Superior de Guerra* in particular. The ESG was not unique in adopting a "Pentagon view" of world problems, as most of the nations outside the Communist Bloc after World War II, rightly or wrongly, held the same view. That Rodrigues seriously overestimated the influence of the U.S. military on the Latin American military is as patent as the error that the United States fostered the coup that upset the Goulart government. This is not to say that it did not welcome it, but the military in Brazil had the support of public opinion in removing Goulart from Office and did not need U.S. sponsorship.

Nonetheless, the importance of the issue of identification of the United States government with the military in Brazil, which only a few years before enjoyed the reputation of being one of the least politically active and most professional in the hemisphere, is difficult to overestimate. Attitudes being formed today about the responsibility of the United States for repression in Brazil, or at least for an indifference to it, can well haunt policy makers of the future who may wonder why Brazilians seem to act irrationally and fail to understand U.S. motives. In hindsight it can be seen that the altruistic aspects of the Kennedy policies toward Latin America failed to convince many opinion makers in Brazil, including President Goulart, of professed U.S. intentions, because policies of the previous U.S. administration had damaged attitudes beyond easy repair.

Early in 1970 the Brazilian government announced that henceforth it would consider its offshore jurisdiction in certain matters to extend 200 miles out to sea. This was a reversal of policy which until then had supported the traditional 3-mile limit for which the United States has fought strenuously for many years. Less than three years before, Brazil had protested when a southern neighbor adopted the 200-mile limit, but in 1970 it joined a growing number of Latin American nations which claim resources beyond even the continental shelf as well as the right to regulate activities such as fishing beyond the traditional limits. The 200-mile limit, first adopted unilaterally by Chile and Peru, had led to acrimonious confrontations with the United States when its fishing boats have been fined or fired on well beyond the 3-mile limit.

The adoption by Brazil of the 200-mile limit signified its decision to abandon its policy of nearly seventy years of closest relations with the United States in favor of a policy of integration with Latin America. One of the effects of this new outlook would be the exclusion of the United States from Latin American councils on matters of great consequence to the interests of the United States. As for the 200-mile limit, its importance lay in the fact that it was the most serious breach to date of an international rule (the 3-mile limit or somewhat larger ones) on which U.S. world-wide security plans are based.

The two nations reached agreement in 1972 on means to avoid confrontations over excercise of sovereignty in the 200-mile limit in which U.S. fishing vessels often work. The agreement was facilitated by an improved climate engendered by the official visit of President Médici to the United States, invited by President Nixon late in 1971.

Médici's visit had other important consequences at a time when relations had reached a low point after World War II. President Nixon had planned his 1972 visit to Communist China without informing some of the closest allies of the United States, even those with greatest interests. Brazil's interests were not direct but no country was angrier at the slight since it expected to be consulted or at least informed about all important U.S. policy moves. The Communist China issue was especially delicate as the United States for years had exercised pressure on friends and neutrals alike to keep mainland China from displacing Taiwan in the United Nations, and the reversal of policy caught many friends off balance. Thus the Médici visit, during which China was discussed, had profound psychological repercussions in Brazil, the more so because Nixon consulted with less than a handful of other allies before the Chinese talks. The "colossus of the South" was given the boost it sought on the world scene as attention was drawn to its status as an "important" if not yet "major" nation. It remains to be seen if the gain can be sustained given the endemic nature of neglect that has characterized the attitudes of Republican administrations toward Latin America in the past. In any event it is unlikely that Brazilian determination to seek integration with Latin America, at the expense of the traditional relationship with the United States, will change.

Portugal vs. Africa: A Foreign Policy Dilemma

Brazilian-Portuguese relations are increasingly affected by diverging interests in Africa, despite the fact that good relations with the mother country have been more constant than with any other country. Although Brazilians have an unlimited fund of jokes at the expense of the slow and steady Portuguese imimgrant, who is very unlike the quick and bright Brazilian, the Portuguese colony is an influential force with many of the characteristics of an interest group. In recent years, Portugal has tried to raise the special relationship between the two nations to a community or federal level. The Brazilian constitution grants Portuguese all rights enjoyed by Brazilians, rights granted to no other people. Even President Kubitschek, who emphasized development of the interior and de-emphasized overseas influence, strengthened this two-nation community concept. Many others have written on the subject, Gilberto Freyre being one of the most effective advocates of the concept. He sees Brazil as the eventual leader of a Luso-tropical system that would include all Portuguese communities and Portuguese colonies in Africa.[21] Portugal would be the European leader, but he anticipates that Brazil would become the literary, intellectual, and scientific leader.

Despite this strong body of Lusophile sentiment, by 1960 the proponents of a close relationship with Portugal had to contend with a growing body of opinion that Brazil's character and increasing potential in the world counseled a far more ambitious role than unity with the mother country which was under constant attack by black Africa because of its colonial policy.[22] This opinion had its roots in the desire to move from a peripheral to a direct participant role in world affairs, and the belief that the move could be made more effectively by working with the developing nations of Africa and Asia than with Portugal. This rationale was espoused by Brazilian nationalist intellectuals, but it was shared to a degree by many military men who believed Africa to be more important than Portugal for national security reasons. They saw Brazil's destiny as linked to the South Atlantic and were particularly sensitive to the exposed north and northeast coastlines. The military hierarchy, however, despite a palpable desire to play a larger international role, had little taste for jettisoning Portugal and would have liked to maintain good relations with both if that were possible.

The most articulate proponent of a Brazilian role of influence in Africa is the historian José Honório Rodrigues, who argues that a Luso-Brazilian community no longer exists, because it has no economic base and because the national interests of the two countries have not coincided internationally since 1822. He holds that from the seventeenth to the nineteenth century Brazil had more contacts and greater bonds with Angola, Dahomy, and parts of the coast of Mina (Gold Coast) and Guinea than did Portugal, and that this relationship was stopped by the British, who were seeking domination of the black continent.[23]

Closer relations with black Africa, and downgrading of the relationship with Portugal, became an important element of Brazilian foreign policy under Jânio Quadros and was continued under the Goulart administration. Relations with Portugal were severely strained as a consequence, particularly when Brazil voted with Africa against Portugal in the United Nations. Influenced by intellectuals who favored an "independent" foreign policy, that is, a more ambivalent one than that which placed the United States and Portugal at the top of the list of Brazilian friends, Quadros stated that he had changed Brazil's foreign policy priorities because Africa "today represents a new dimension in Brazilian policy. We are linked to that continent by our ethnic and cultural roots . . . Our country should become the link, the bridge, between Africa and the West . . ." That Quadros was conscious of all the implications of his new policies is evident from his statement: "For many years Brazil made the mistake of supporting European colonialism in the United Nations. This attitude—which is only now fading—gave rise to a justified mistrust of Brazilian policy." [24]

Not only were diplomatic missions established in some African countries, but an Institute of Brazilian-African Affairs was created in the Foreign Office and scholarships were made available to African students. One hundred were granted in 1965. To make his point about mistakes that "gave rise to a justified mistrust of Brazilian policy," Quadros financed the early scholarships with half the savings from reductions in the salaries of Brazilian diplomats abroad.

The return to traditional foreign policies after the 1964 revolution put an end to the African and Portuguese policies inaugurated by Quadros in 1961. The importance of Africa to Brazil was not discounted, but many traditionalists in the Foreign Office, some of whom once again held key positions, believed that Brazil's ties to Africa should be through Portugal. These diplomats believed that relations with Portugal should have a higher priority than new "adventures" or allies in Africa. More realistic than their adventurous colleagues, they believed, not without some justification, that Africa neither sought nor welcomed Brazil as an interpreter to the developed world.

On the other hand, Brazil cannot long support Portugal's colonial position in Africa because of the damage to its relations with the anticolonialist nations—virtually the rest of the world. It is impossible to seek better relations and leadership among the developing nations around the world and at the same time support Portugal's colonial policies. These facts augur either for a change in Portuguese colonial policy or an inevitable cooling in relations between the mother country and her increasingly mature daughter.

Relations with the Communist Nations

Brazil has never broken relations with Poland, Czechoslovakia, and Yugoslavia, but it has never recognized Communist China. Relations with the Soviet Union were maintained briefly after World War II but were suspended in 1947 when the Soviet press attacked the Brazilian government, with insulating references to President Dutra. Relations were renewed in 1961 after Jânio Quadros, during a presidential race, promised to maintain relations with all nations of the world, a stand applauded by espousers of "an independent foreign policy." Although the military government of 1964 reversed many other policies of the Quadros-Goulart governments, it decided to leave those affecting the Soviet Bloc unchanged. The justification was increased trade, which amounted to nearly $100 million each way during the first four years of renewed interchange. Meira Penna explains pragmatically that a concrete interest in trade for Brazil compensates to a certain degree for the propaganda and espionage of the Soviets, a review presumably shared by the military.

Throughout the late 1960's few Brazilians had grounds to complain about their relationship with the Soviet Union. In 1964 the Communists went deep underground and caused no further political problems. Communists who diverged from the Moscow line left the party and joined small dissident groups that looked either to Communist China or to Castro Cuba for inspiration and material assistance. If the maintenance of diplomatic relations had advantages for both countries—largely commercial for Brazil and largely political for the Soviet Union—those advantages seemed likely to remain limited for years to come. The Soviet Union could take only a relatively small amount of Brazilian products (it prefers tea to coffee), and Brazil found that it could generally do as well if not better by importing from other markets.

The New Diplomacy

The government in power in 1972 was probably as conservative and traditionalist as any Brazilian government is likely to be in the foreseeable future. Its foreign policies in most respects were very near those of Castello Branco, who led the first government that followed the 1964 revolution. Despite these circumstances, a profound shift has taken place in Brazilian diplomacy, one which is likely to become more pronounced as time passes. As suggested earlier, this shift is based principally on Brazil's changing transitional role as it moves toward more developed status and increases its national power and interest in world affairs. The shift has been hastened by the work of strong nationalists among intellectuals in civilian life and in the armed forces. Trends toward extreme nationalism have been facilitated by the failure of the United States to maintain leadership adequate to preserving, or improving, the unique relationship that began at the time of independence and was advantageous to both Brazil and the United States.

The foreign policies pursued by Presidents Quadros and Goulart were not abberations. They obeyed a growing demand among Brazilians for policies under which Brazil would not be so closely, sometimes involuntarily, tied to the United States. This was apparent from the general approval given to policy changes made by Quadros which were viewed by many Brazilian conservatives, to say nothing of the United States, as highly radical.[25] This new public attitude had begun to develop first under Vargas, whose second term was a failure partly because the United States would not grant economic assistance to the extent Brazil believed had been agreed upon under President Truman. These beginnings were nurtured in the public domain by President Kubitschek when he broke off negotiations with the International Monetary Fund in June 1959 with a blast against those whom he charged with obstructing Brazil's progress. Behind these public demands for better treatment by foreign countries and international agencies was the work of many Brazilian economists, political scientists, sociologists, and other intellectuals, a few of them Communists, but most simply nationalistic, who developed the thesis that Brazil must pursue "an independent foreign policy." Considerable work had been done in this area before the establishment of the *Istituto Superior de Estudos Brasileiros* (ISEB), under the aegis of the Ministry of Education. The institute became an established center for research and publication for what had formerly been haphazard enterprises.

The growth of nationalism is basically responsible for an ambivalence (perhaps more truly a "trivalence") in Brazilian policy. The traditional policy based on proximity to the United States and Portugal is balanced against closer integration within a Latin American community (with the U.S. presence lessened) or against closer relations with African and other developing nations. Some see a possible combination of the three policies. One facet of the ambivalence is the question of national identity, which appeals to the nationalistic intellectuals; another is the concept of Brazil's "manifest destiny," which appeals to the military.

The dilemma of identity can be capsulized into the question that has occupied many intellectuals: What is Brazil? Is it the usually accepted white-dominated offspring of a European mother country whose ideals and goals continue to be closely associated with those of the more conservative nations of the Western democracies? Or is it, as José Rodrigues holds, "a mestizo republic, neither European nor Latin American—a Tupi [Indian], African, Occidental and Oriental synthesis—a unique and original creation." [26] If Brazil is, as its traditionalists and elites insist, a Western democracy, or at least is slowly but steadily evolving to that ideal, then its present and future foreign policies should reflect that identity and work to maintain close association with other Western democracies. If it is a mestizo republic whose destiny makes it naturally the kin of the developing nations of Africa and Asia, then it should adopt policies which will make it a leader of the developing world, even if some of those policies affront the great powers.

Rodrigues's thesis of close ties with Africa and Asia is set forth in *Interesse Nacional e Política Externa;* the most modern statement of the traditionalist view has been made by Meira Penna in *Política Externa, Segurança e Desenvolvimento.* A more pragmatic approach to the Rodrigues thesis has been constructed by other Brazilian writers, among them a number of brilliant but nonconformist Brazilian diplomats most of whom were forced out of their jobs after the 1964 revolution. Two leaders of this group, Antonio Houaiss and Jayme Rodrigues, were editors of a short-lived foreign affairs periodical the first issue of which appeared in May 1965. The rationale behind the need for "an independent foreign policy" is set forth in this periodical.[27]

The case for "reality" and the "national interest" (or for playing "international blackmail," as Meira Penna calls it) is based on the premise that "at any given moment Brazil's destiny is being decided in the foreign offices of the great powers, in the financial and commercial centers of the rich nations, in the universities of the developed nations. . . . In truth, the life of millions of Brazilians is conditioned, manipulated every minute in Washington, London, Paris, Bonn or Moscow . . ." [28]

The other part of the nationalists' premise is that the great problem of our time is not only the great discrepancy in wealth among the nations of the world, but above all the fact that the gap between developed and underdeveloped countries continues to widen. The final result, according to *Política Externa Independente,* will be the pauperization of the underdeveloped areas of the world, among which Brazil is included. Under present circumstances therefore, Brazil's foreign policy should have development as its objective, and diplomatic action should be motivated principally to secure the external means and resources necessary to an accelerated expansion of the Brazilian economy.

According to *Política Externa Independente,* any other major objective in Brazil's international conduct "would imply the acceptance of values and interests foreign, if not actually antagonistic, to Brazilian development. The formula now imposed on us of 'cultural and political fidelity to the Western democratic system,' is a good example of what should be stigmatized and denounced very simply as incapable of characterizing the national interest. . . We cannot be so ingenuous as to suppose that a great power would not seek to convince us to pursue a determined national or international course in the name of its specific interests." Such efforts are actually directed at "restricting the diplomatic freedom of action of countries like Brazil, obliging them to fall into the rigid political and military regimentation of the cold war imposed by the supposed imminence of world conflict. This occurs just at a time when the bi-polar system is disintegrating and the protagonists of the East-West conflict, contained by the nuclear impasse, are seeking mutually advantageous forms of peaceful coexistence." [29]

These nationalists hold that Brazil is one of the protagonists, with a large burden of responsibility, in the North-South conflict between the rich and poor nations of the world. Thus the underdeveloped nations of Latin America become natural allies of Brazil in the formulation and execution of a developmental foreign policy. This natural alliance should not content itself solely with seeking common aspirations but, in addition, should seek "to establish ways and means of coexistence that would make possible progressive integration of the economies of Latin American countries exclusively." Development would have the highest priority among nations with their own "peculiarities and historical exigencies—which would require a reconsideration of the validity of institutions such as the Organization of American States, the Rio Treaty or such programs as the Alliance for Progress." The true alliance of the underdeveloped nations of Latin America is that which places them with the other underdeveloped nations of Africa and Asia "in search of a new international order capable of bringing to the immense populations of those countries just and dignified living conditions." The thesis concluded with the contention that the Final Act of the United Nations Conference on Trade and Development (UNCTAD) of June 15, 1964, reflects the basic antagonism between the North-South nations in which the rich, "with the United States of America noticeably in the van," refused to accept the "validity of the economic postulates of the poor nations."

Many of the foregoing premises and recommendations, made in 1965 by radical extremists including diplomats removed from the service because of leftist views, have since been adopted. Since 1967, foreign policy pronouncements have emphasized "security and development," as the basis of Brazil's foreign relations. Although *Política Externa Independente* gave relatively little importance to the security aspect, particularly as it reflected concern with the cold war concept, it proposed development as the basic concern of foreign policy. Downgrading of relations with the U.S. in favor of closer relations with the Latin American countries and the nations of Africa and Asia has also become a reality, begun under Costa e Silva and intensified under Garrastazú Médici. A good part of this policy shift can be ascribed to the inclination of the military to work toward realization of Brazil's "manifest destiny," a thesis as patent among the leftist nationalists as among the military.[30]

Brazilian governments since 1967 have been less concerned with the African and Asian objectives outlined by the leftist nationalists than were governments of the earlier 1960's, but even their position has been ambivalent. In pressing for more economic assistance in international forums, Brazil has advanced the thesis of the existence of conflict between the developed nations of the northern part of the hemisphere and the underdeveloped nations of the southern part. Yet the traditionalist military would prefer to see Brazil as one of the democratic nations of the West, and they so consider it. This attitude will probably change if it becomes apparent that the present high rate of economic growth is only temporary and that Brazil is doomed to remain a "pauperized" nation, while the developed nations continue to grow even wealthier.

Latin American integration at the expense of cooperation with the United States has progressed far beyond what the leftist nationalists could have dared to anticipate. The present Brazilian government has no intention of dismantling the OAS, as demanded by *Política Externa Independente,* because the OAS holds too many advantages for Brazil and the rest of Latin America, but that it is casting its lot with Latin America even when U. S. interests are adversely affected is very apparent. Latin American economic integration as seen by some Latin Americans could have disastrous effects. The abandonment of Brazil's traditional role as intermediary between the Spanish-American nations and the United States has long been an objective not only of Brazilian ultranationalists but also Argentine policy, which is aimed at decreasing U. S. influence in the hemisphere.

The first important manifestation of Brazil's new policy direction came out of the meeting of the Presidents of Brazil and Chile in September 1968. The communiqué issued after the meeting was a strong plea for Latin American unity and solidarity in which by inference, at least, the United States was relegated to a secondary role. This trend was furthered by the Comisión Especial de Coordinatión Latinoamericana (CECLA), Special Latin American Coordinating Committee, which met at Viña del Mar, Chile, early in 1969, to draw up a common list of Latin American financial and other needs for development in the area. The meeting was held with the encouragement of the Unitd States despite the fact that CECLA was a highly useful instrument for implementing the policy recommended by *Política Externa Independente* to "seek to establish ways and means of coexistence that would make possible progressive integration of the economies of the Latin American countries exclusively." This trend toward Latin American integration is by no means directed consciously against the United States as some of the nationalists would have it; integration has long been a principle of Brazilian policy. Its anti-American character is in the exclusion of the United States, a new element injected by the strong nationalists. Such meetings as CECLA, wittingly or not, encourage this trend.

It would be a mistake to assume that radical shifts in Brazilian policy are the product of far rightist military or far leftist civilian pressures.

Their roots run far deeper and respond to nationalistic considerations based in considerable measure on estimates of U. S. intentions and how they affect Brazilian long-term and short-term interests. This could be seen during the Castello Branco administration. Even though he reversed the foreign policies of the Quadros and Goulart governments, returning them to their traditional channels, Castello Branco did not hesitate to oppose the United States (or, in fact, virtually all Latin America except Argentina) during the 1966 negotiations for a Latin American nuclear-free zone, originally proposed in 1962 by Brazil. Brazil refused to commit itself to any agreement in any way limiting the development of a nuclear capability. This principle was later extended to negotiations for the world-wide Non-Proliferation Treaty. Brazil refused to sign the treaty, despite pressures from both the United States and the Soviet Union because it was unwilling to depend on the "nuclear club" powers for materials given under supervision. Its position was that it would use nuclear power for peaceful purposes only. The nuclear powers, however, remained unconvinced that this assurance precluded the manufacture of nuclear weapons at some future time should world events so dictate.

At this time, Brazil also objected to the attempt by the United States to prevent the acquisition of supersonic military planes by all Latin American nations. Brazil did not disagree with the premise that the smaller nations of Latin America had no need for supersonic planes, but it insisted that a nation as large as Brazil, and one with as many responsibilities for national security as Brazil, should not be cut off from what had become a common weapon throughout the world.

The two instances cited—disagreements about nuclear power and supersonic planes—were kept out of the public domain because Castello Branco had no wish to appear to be quarreling with the United States. His successor, General Costa e Silva, had fewer qualms; in fact, he considered that public differences with the United States would be politically advantageous because of widespread criticism of his predecessor's close ties to the United States. In any event, the Nuclear Non-Proliferation treaty issue was brought into the open with public debate stimulated by the Foreign Office.

Reviewing Brazil's new diplomacy in perspective, it is apparent that Brazilian foreign policy has changed as the nation has developed economically. Its economic position influences its relations not only with the U.S. and other hemisphere partners but also with the Communist powers and the developing world. Its sense of growing power has produced general changes in world attitudes; as Brazil industrializes and attempts to export such manufactured products as soluble coffee and textiles, which meet obstacles to normal entry in the United States and other developed nations, conflicts arise. The commercial basis for close relations, complementary economies, becomes more fragile. Increasing power has given Brazil's leaders grounds to aspire to its manifest destiny on the international scene. The once intimate relationship between Brazil and the United States may have changed irrevocably, but this change need not necessarily work to the detriment of either nation if the old idea of an American community of nations is preserved.

Brazil's future role in world affairs will be an expanding one, because its leaders are conscious of the nation's potential as well as its tradition as a peace-loving country. It has solved most of its own international problems peacefully and has worked effectively to reconcile conflicting points of view among other nations. Many are convinced that Brazil has a special role to play in the world. Although this conviction has not been fully articulated, it rests firmly on the nation's peaceful international history, its tradition of pragmatic adjustments to world realities, and the negotiating skill of its diplomats.

Brazilians like to think of themselves as a pacific, reasonable people who have made valuable contributions to the maintenance of peace among other countries. This is a legitimate analysis. Some among them, however, see this attitude as romantic and have more prosaic views of the Brazilian temperament. Ambassador Meira Penna explains this point of view as follows: "The way in which we have settled international problems indicates a large dose of good juridical sense and political sagacity. There is nevertheless much poetic license in these allegations. Various aggressive wars on our southern borders are an example. If we didn't conquer Uruguay it was because we were defeated in battle. More recently, when rubber interests were involved, we obtained Acre, Bolivian territory, through means juridical in form but at bottom coercive, which the talent of Baron Rio Branco ably camouflaged. If boundaries have been settled peacefully by arbitration, it is because far away lands covered by impenetrable forests were concerned. Just let rubber, hydroelectric, and uranium interests make an appearance and disputes will arise! The Brazilian is no better or worse than anybody else." [31]

The picture drawn by Meira Penna shows a healthy awareness of the importance of means other than the use of power to obtain foreign policy objectives, but at the same time it admits that when important objectives are involved, Brazil has not hesitated to persuade with a degree of muscle-flexing. Perhaps this is inevitable in any nation that arrogates a manifest destiny to itself, at least within the context of the rules of international behavior as they have been interpreted during the past century. The relevance of his analysis to the contemporary scene lies in the assumption that Brazil's development and rise to major nationhood is not likely to be delayed by pusillanimity.

VIII: Prospect: Great Power or Tropical Slum?

If history has any meaning, or human progress any order, it would be mandatory to say that Brazil will become a major power by the time the century ends. Yet the capacity of man for mischief is so great as to make unqualified predictions little more than expressions of subjective goodwill with inadequate basis in reality. It would have been almost an expression of illwill to state at the end of 1960, that Brazil was not on a cleared road to economic and social well-being. Yet in less than a year a miscalculation by a president seeking dictatorial powers was to set in motion a series of events from which a decade later the country had not yet recovered. If "God is a Brazilian," as many Brazilians with irreverent humor insist, and protects the nation from bungling political leaders, it has to be said that He has a larger and longer view than is apparent to a good many Brazilians as well as foreigners. They fear that the human element in Brazil is too uncertain and institutions too weak for the nation to rise above the level of an underdeveloped tropical backwater in the foreseeable future. A large one, yes, but India is large and so is Indonesia. Even accelerated economic growth from 1968 to 1972 failed to remove all the contradictions many observers see.

Certainly, by size, quantity and quality of population, natural resources, and geopolitical situation, Brazilians have every justification for claiming a large role for their country in the present and future centuries. Gilberto Freyre's characterization of Brazil as a tropical civilization that will offer new frontiers of human relations in a world long dominated by the temperate powers of the northern hemisphere may well have acquired immediacy sooner than anticipated.

In any consideration of the potential of Brazil, high on the list of assets would be that it is a nation-state of considerable depth and unity. This adds substance to the fact that in size alone only China, the Soviet Union, and Canada have larger contiguous landmasses. On the other hand, distance and poor communications, along with isolated political and social development arising from a bequeathed system of private, familial land-grant administration, have made strong regional development inevitable. Regional diversity, nonetheless, poses no threat to national unity in Brazil any more than it does in the United States. In fact a study of the similarities of national unity and loyalty in the two countries as well as pride based on unique regional and cultural characteristics in both is rewarding.

The Brazil whose national attention had perforce to be focused on Rio de Janeiro as the political and cultural capital is, for all practical purposes, a thing of the past. President Juscelino Kubitschek, the builder of the new inland capital, saw that the Rio-centered civilization, organized by and for an agrarian aristocracy that ruled a land in which some 85 percent of its population and even more of its wealth were concentrated along a narrow 3,462-mile coastal strip, would have to change. By forcing the nation to look inward toward Brasilia, a modern, spectacular capital, he laid the psychological groundwork which would make it easier to escape the straightjacket of a society that had looked outward, more concerned with what transpired abroad and affected it commercially and culturally than with developing its potential for a new world in the tropics.

This is not to say that the Brazilian who was more oriented to the old than the modern Brazil was not an ambitious, hard worker, but rather that Kubitschek was able to transmit his vision of "a new dawn" in terms that stimulated commitment and participation in individual and national achievement. In sociological terms a change in the order of values took place, or, perhaps more accurately, dormant values were awakened. It is probable that the Portuguese early gave higher importance to achievement than did the Spaniards, to judge by their generally greater interest in things material. This approach ran counter to the ideal of the more mystical Spaniard, and by inheritance to that of the Spanish-American whose literature extols the virtues of traditional society and "spiritual" values, deploring those of industrialized society, particularly as manifested in the "materialistic" United States.[1] Brazilians always understood this aspect of U. S. civilization better than the Spanish American did. The wide acceptance of the "ideology of national development" formulated by Brazilian technocrats and intellectuals takes this early predisposition several steps forward. It is, in effect, a commitment to those achievements associated with modern societies and is a rejection of Brazilian writers with the "gentleman complex," the litterateurs of the agrarian aristocracy, and some of the more modern middle-class conservative Catholic writers, who have lost most of their relevance and are heeded by few today. Without doubt, the importance of achievement values, in part at least, accounts for Brazil's successful developmental experience.

A changeover is already underway, and the likelihood of turning back is remote. The final goal, however, is still a long way from realization. It will become a reality only when the country approaches developed-nation status. The time element in this process must remain indeterminate because it is dependent upon many factors, not the least being the wisdom of leaders who may spur or slow down the awakening process of the stirring giant.

Problems

No infallible formula has yet been discovered to assure transition, to say nothing of tranquil transition, from underdeveloped to developed status for any nation. Brazilian growth for the thirty years before 1960 was unprecedented. But problems of economic development and many problems of transition from an archaic to a modern social structure, while preserving those characteristics that make it a more humane society than many developed nations of the northern hemisphere must yet be solved.

To evaluate the Brazilian potential it is just as well to begin at the roots. Some observers—including not a few Brazilians suffering from *mazombismo,* a mental attitude which denigrates things Brazilian —believe that the country can never become a great nation so long as the mestizo element remains dominant in society. Evaluating the importance of race and social structure on national potential is an uncertain and highly speculative exercise that has fallen into disrepute in recent years. Nevertheless, some facts should be reviewed to dispel existing negative stereotypes. Two extreme views on the influence of racial composition on national potential can be outlined. The *mazombistas* maintain that the small contribution to material development made by Negroes is clear evidence that progress can come only under white leadership and that more white immigrants are needed. The other view is that the racial composition is already set beyond change as a mestizo nation of whites, Negroes, Indians, and Japanese, and that this mestizo people, favored with a wealthy land and high motivation, will build a great nation without need for further immigration.

There is no question that highly important contributions to progress toward modern status, as defined in Western terms, have been made by recent immigrants of Portuguese, Italian, Spanish, Japanese, German, and Near Eastern origin. The industrial and agricultural developments in the South testify to the fact. Most of these immigrants live on the more temperate plateau beyond the coastal plain or in the cooler lowlands of the Far South, whereas the mestizo population predominates in the tropical coastal areas where progress has been slowest.

Nevertheless, to maintain that the white population is the only group that can contribute significantly toward achieving major nationhood is patently misleading. Negroes in Brazil have been afforded far less educational and economic opportunities than those in the United States, and despite this fact, a number of Negroes and mulattos have made important contributions to national life. There is no reason to doubt that contributions by black people and white people would be similar if opportunities were similar. In fact, with less racial tension between Negroes and whites in Brazil than in the United States, true integration will be far easier. The native Indian component is so small as to be negligible as either stimulus or deterrent.

Evaluating the influence of social structure on national development presents more of a challenge. As noted, some Brazilian leaders, several among the military, believe that Brazil can reach great-nation status with only minor social disturbances so long as the traditional structure remains basic. These leaders know that urban society and the growing middle class (already breaking down into subclasses) cannot easily be fitted into a traditional pattern but they hope to preserve the old paternalistic two-class system in the rural areas. They also hope to hold the urban lower class in a traditional pattern of deference to the upper class, permitting only a minimum of upward social mobility. The basis for this concept is the traditional society of the Empire. It is thus not surprising that a growing number of such leaders point to modern Japan, which has managed to retain many of the features of an old society while growing into a great industrial nation. As for the relationship to the English two-caste social system, it is worth noting that upper-class Brazilians chose the British Empire as a model for the constitutional monarch that governed Brazil from 1823 to 1889.

The majority of Brazilians see the futility of trying to preserve, under democratic government, social structures that worked satisfactorily under a monarchy. The once traditionalist Catholic Church saw that anomaly more than a decade ago and now seeks faster change. Although semifeudalism still exists in some parts of the country, Brazil was never a feudal nation, as was Japan, and traditional loyalties have either ceased to exist or have been weakened. It is not likely that the traditionalists can for long sustain their thesis. Brazil will develop socially in the pattern of most Western nations, and it is likely to do so under relatively peaceful conditions since social animosities do not run deep.

As for the more concrete side of the developmental equation, few of the indices used to demonstrate national development—except economic growth—had reached satisfactory levels by 1972, yet progress has continued even under intermittent internal disorder. Urbanization, industrialization, and restratification continued, sometimes falteringly but also with evident progress in meeting concomitant problems these changes created. Even education seemed on the way to modernizing under perhaps the most sustained and wide-based pressure the government had ever felt from Brazilians of all classes and from the Roman Catholic Church. A rise in college and university enrollment from about 10,000 (1942) to almost 500,000 (1972) illustrates both problem and progress. Yet 500,000 seeking higher education in a total of 100 million is grossly inadequate, as persistent student discontent suggests.

The changes brought about by Vargas during the 1930's and early 1940's responded to the need to open up a political system in which power had been concentrated on a narrow base controlled by the rural elite, the dominant element in Brazilian society of that day. After World War II and the fall of Vargas, an expanding urban electorate and more honest elections broadened political participation. Social changes also came as the urban population grew. Democracy became more representative, although vestiges of the coronel system, in a modified and more clientelistic form, still leave rural politics largely unchanged, with competing families disputing power. The backward rural North and Northeast not only needed economic and social progress but political reform as well to correct their over-representation in the congress, which gave them the power to block legislation of national interest. Even today in the urban areas, democracy retains clientelistic aspects of personalistic government grounded in the old patriarchal system. The migration from country to city has had relatively little effect on this cultural pattern. Informal family ties and the *patrão* relationship are still highly important in politics, in employment and in satisfying other personal and official needs. This helps explain the failure of political parties to perform their role. Since no modern political system has yet been invented which does not require a strong party system to remain stable, their failure contributed to the breakdown of the system in 1964. It also accounts for the cynicism of most politically educated Brazilians toward politics, and explains the importance of a strong executive in Brazil's political culture and the low level of political socialization.

The Castello Branco and Costa e Silva administrations effected too long delayed structural economic changes; they also sought to correct weaknesses in political institutions, including the party system. Despite their arbitrary use of political power, they carried out constructive changes designed to make the system more responsive to popular demands and less subject to control by political elites once democratic rule is restored.

These problems of modernization raise a core question: Can the economic development demanded by all Brazilians be achieved under political democracy and with social justice?

Ithiel de Sola Pool writes that most studies on political development support the classical view that political participation and public order are hard to reconcile.[2] In a modern context this means that the more political power the people have the more they demand for themselves without regard to the long range effects of immediate consumption as opposed to national savings. If their demands are not met order may break down. This view accurately describes virtually all developing nations although it runs counter to recent American political experience and particularly to widely held assumptions that popular government is good government and that elitist government is bad government. The contradiction may be more apparent than real: the classical view may be accurate for developing societies and the popular American view true for developed nations.

The experience of the developed nations indicates quite clearly that industrialization cannot be achieved under the type of mass democracy characteristic of the developed world today. This will be discussed at greater length but it suffices to say that an argument can be made for the thesis that optimum economic development and social justice are not compatible in a developing nation.

This theoretical statement, based on the investigations of A. F. K. Organski,[3] is at the heart of the heated controversy over the road Brazil has taken since 1964 to national development. The controversy is based on income distribution data made available from the 1970 census indicating that the great boom is favoring a small segment of the population. The level of income of all classes rose in the decade but the difference between rich and poor markedly increased. Critics hold that the system has led to gross social injustice for the poor while the already rich have become wealthier. Supporters of the government's strategy, notably its architect, Finance Minister Delfim Netto, complain that the critics fail to point out how better distribution can be brought about without stopping or seriously slowing down economic growth.

Furthermore, government planners point to a new danger on the horizon: the national market is expanding at so heavy a rate in some sectors as to threaten exports which are vital for sustained growth. The heart of the argument of the developmentalists is that "You can't distribute what doesn't exist." In other words, their thesis is that much wider distribution of income will simply decrease the savings which make investment and the creation of new wealth possible. Brazilians would then be frozen at a much lower status than if they were willing to await the availability of considerably higher income levels.

Brazilian distribution (5 percent of the population earns 38 percent of the total income) is comparable to that in the United States in the late 1920's, with the difference that the per capita GNP in the United States was considerably higher than Brazil's. The subsequent change to a consumer's democracy in the United States improved distribution in favor of the less privileged.* No such change has begun in Brazil and it would undoubtedly be premature to think in terms of

---

*Nevertheless, data from the 1970 census indicate a reversal of the improved income distribution pattern in the United States. The gap between rich and poor in recent years has widened rather than narrowed, but still the top 20 percent of male wage earners took in 40 percent of total income compared to only 5 percent in Brazil.

mass democracy, but better distribution would not be premature. The real question is the degree of change, or the balance between social justice and economic growth. Whether as a result of the criticism or because of the realization that deprivation of the masses will eventually slow down the boom because of the want of consumers, Médici ordered several measures in 1972 designed to give a larger share of income to the lower class. Among these were worker salary increases over and above inflationary levels, greater educational opportunities for workers to increase their earning capacity and renewed efforts at agrarian reform.

Despite the foregoing arguments, authoritarian government is not an imperative for developing nations. Several countries, including Colombia, have made satisfactory if not spectacular economic growth under democratic regimes and with better balanced income distribution than Brazil, that is, with more social justice. It is possible for a capable and charismatic political leader to bring the Brazilian people through crucial stages of the modernizing process in a democratic society. The record shows that it would not be easy but it would be possible. Vargas was effective in promoting constructive modernization largely during his dictatorship, not during his legal presidency. His legal period in office was in many respects a failure, despite his prodigious leadership qualities.

Kubitschek probably did as much as one man could to advance development in a five year period, but the weakness of his administration was the failure to hold the economy within manageable confines by taking restrictive monetary measures. Such measures would have been politically difficult. Jãnio Quadros contends that full democracy and economic development in Brazil are incompatible and that this fact forced his resignation. These three are the only Brazilian presidents of recent history who had the qualities of leadership necessary to inspire the nation in difficult times, asking and receiving short-term sacrifices for long-term growth. As the Castello Branco government showed later, all presidents could have worked more effectively for development and necessary reform within a democratic system that gives the executive more power than did the 1946 Constitution. It is difficult to say whether the people did not want the executive to have more power or whether intrenched self-interest groups in congress prevented change. In any event, the people's representatives refused to surrender their powers to one man. Vargas did not ask; he seized power. Kubitschek did not ask for nor seek extra powers but he fell short of some of his goals. Quadros asked and was refused. In 1964, the military seized full powers and has held most of them since.

Two problems faced by most developing nations, and from which Brazil is not immune, are high population growth rates and bureaucratic administration. Brazil's population growth rate is somewhere around 2.8 percent per annum. This means that a 6 percent economic growth rate is necessary to meet the minimum standard of 2½ percent per capita set by the Alliance for Progress. After 1961 Brazil did not achieve a 6 percent economic growth rate until 1968. In terms of people, as has been noted, a 2.8 percent population growth rate means that over half the population is under nineteen years of age and that a million new jobs must be created each year just to absorb the new eligibles on the labor market. Brazil, at a less than 6 percent economic growth rate, cannot create a million new jobs each year. The result is unemployment and underemployment, mostly in the cities.

Most of the developed nations have solved the population problem without government intervention. As urbanization and industrialization increase, population growth rates tend to decline. The underdeveloped nations seem unable to do so. The obvious answer would be birth control and family planning, to avoid negation of such economic gains as can be made. Quite apart from religious conviction, this answer is not today acceptable to Brazilians who believe, by and large correctly, that Brazil is underpopulated. Brazil needs more hands to work its land and to man its expanding industrial complex. Obviously, it does not need the hands of gravely undernourished or starving people, which the Northeast, in particular, produces. The question then is by no means exclusively a religious one. The military strongly opposes birth control because a national objective is to settle and develop unpopulated or thinly populated border areas. Brazil's problem in truth has been less one of overpopulation than of slow development, particularly in the agricultural sector. When the country's tremendous agricultural potential is better utilized, many millions more could be adequately supported. Meanwhile, the danger is that the economy will turn into little more than a treadmill operation even with a 6 percent growth rate. A sustained 9 percent economic growth rate, like that reached in 1968 and subsequently, would relegate the population problem to a law priority position, but this is far from assured.

The other major problem that retards modernization is the bureaucracy. Brazil has had a civil service from the time of the Empire. It was institutionalized under Vargas, but this institutionalization did as much to systematize dispensation of political favors as to improve the efficiency of government services. A prime target of the Castello Branco regime was to improve the operations of the badly swollen bureaucracy. The administrative reform decree-law that went into effect only one month before Castello Branco left office in March 1967 had long been promised, and it had as long bogged down over the inability of even an authoritative government to make deep surgical changes in the incrusted, constitutionally protected body of nearly three-quarters of a million public workers.

The importance of administrative reform and efficiency is difficult to overestimate in a government that in recent years had been responsible for 65 percent of new fixed-capital formation and over the past decade had entered into new enterprises, many of them run by semi-autonomous agencies. Government expenditures for current items, a large proportion of which were salaries, in 1966 ran to 13 percent of GNP, but investment reached only 12 percent. This, for example, compared to 5 percent and 16 percent, respectively, in Mexico. The government decreed bans on hiring by independent agencies and made cuts in employees of the central government. It took other measures aimed at making more capital available for investment, most of which did not come out of either industry or labor but from government itself. One important measure was to reduce the share given the states from tax revenues which would, indirectly at least, raise the contribution of the rural sector to industrialization. By 1972 the position had improved. Savings had reached 20 percent of GNP, and expenditures for current items held steady under 12 percent.

Statutory government reorganizations and less legal but more heroic methods to bring the bureaucracy under control have met with varying success. Nonetheless, there is sound basis for believing that administrative reform is not a precondition to development as has been shown in many countries whose bureaucracy improved only after modernization. The problem in Brazil may be less technical than political. Since most power centers in 1970 were still linked to large land-owners, who traditionally controlled or strongly influenced the mech-anism of government, the shift in balance slowly taking place will inevitably bring a changed political and administrative system.

Of a different order are the newly created problems rising out of the military regimes and their determination to reform the political system. The adventure of the military into a governing role has within it the seeds of one of the most serious institutional crises Brazil has ever faced. The inability of the military to govern under normal give-and-take conditions of democracy led to confrontations with the Church and with students and intellectuals, in addition to the traditional poli-ticians. The authoritarian state installed by the military in 1964, made somewhat bland by the 1967 Constitution but again hardened in December 1968, will probably survive long enough to give time for the change in the system to eliminate most of the old politicians of the pro-Vargas/anti-Vargas dichotomy. Since that dichotomy was an important factor in the paralysis of the decision-making process before 1964, new faces and new interests will have a better chance to work out the politics of Brazilian development. But what the role of the military will be in the new polity was still far from clear in 1973.

The new symbol of military control, "National Security and De-velopment," is no more than an updated version of the old slogan "Order and Progress," adopted by the military Positivists before the fall of the Empire. In 1969, defining the new role of the armed forces, Minister of the Army, General Lyra Tavares, credited Comte's writings more than a century before with concepts which today serve as the army's philosophical bases.[4] Positivism as postulated by Comte would not be a danger to Brazilian institutions, but "National Security" has acquired a more foreboding context than the simple "Order" of an earlier day. National security (by the *Escola Superior de Guerra* definition, adopted by the national government) penetrates virtually every phase of Brazilian life, most of which are normally the concern of civilian government, and not of the armed forces.

This disproportionately heavy military input in decision making, if continued, could annul the real reforms carried out since 1964 and indefinitely delay the return to normal political procedures. The ex-treme form this military preponderance could take would be nationa-listic-socialism in a military-controlled society, possibly one similar to a Nassarist regime. A small but determined group of military officers—hardliners—believe that something akin to Nassarism is needed to reform the political and social system in order to set Brazil on the road to greatness. They do not, however, control national decisions but have in certain crises decisively influenced them.

Through 1970 the Brazilian military was still able to enjoy a favorable image among the mass of the Brazilian people, if not the upper middle class and the intellectuals, because of its past largely constructive role in society and the failure of civilian political leaders. It is questionable that this image could survive a prolonged period of repression that blocked necessary change.

U. S. military collaboration with Brazil postulates as one of its objectives the example of the limited function of the military in a democratic society, as opposed to the common concept in several Latin American countries of the military as the most stable element in the society and the only one with sufficient authority to be able to govern effectively. The foundation of the *Escola Superior de Guerra* was one of the results of U. S. military collaboration with Brazil, and one of its models was the United States National War College. In the United States, however, the War College serves a very different purpose than does the *Escola Superior de Guerra* because the military plays a less prominent role in U. S. society.

The deformation of Brazilian society through this route is by no means preordained. The military has its traditions, of which most of its officers are very conscious. As a guardian of the constitution and as a moderator of serious civilian political quarrels, it has a history of responsiveness to public opinion. In fact, the dilemma faced by the military has within it some of the qualities of a tragic drama. As a body the military recognizes the need for social justice and for the reforms required to reach the national goal. But it has yet to demonstrate the political ability to effect the required changes. With few exceptions, the military would be happy to turn back the government to civilians if it could be convinced that the old corrupt personalist-centered government that had failed to modernize the nation would not return. In a democratic society, of course, they can never have this assurance.

Several other problems of a more technical nature, capable of blocking rapid economic growth, will have to be solved if present perform ance is to continue. Perhaps most important among them is the need to expand exports in order to avoid a future payments crisis which could develop as a result of the mounting public debt. The debt is large by any standard and growing, but is being held to 17 percent of GNP. Another is the question of national savings. They are not yet at what developmentalists would call satisfactory levels but have improved substantially. Savings in 1969 were only 10.5 percent of GNP but by 1972 had doubled thanks to a number of imaginative measures aimed at creating confidence in continuance of "the economic miracle." Principal among these is monetary correction which compensates for many negative influences of inflation. Stimulation of investment in the stock market and industrial enterprises in backward areas, has also effectively inspired the entire economy.

The Brazilian experience has been that any given situation controlled by man is never as bad as external factors indicate. Important in this phenomenon is the irrelevance to the Brazilian dynamic of factors important in other societies. Nevertheless, granting that "instant social justice" is not compatible with sustained economic growth, a way will have to be found to modernize the social system more rapidly. If the commitment of the people is needed for building the nation, then concern must be shown for its welfare. As Dom Helder Camara, Archbishop of Recife, put it with a poet's insight when attacking the political repression of mid-1968; "If the Brazilian cannot be carried along skillfully (*con jeito*), and with love, he will even less be carried along with violence."[5]

The military may be logically correct; certain officers are respected as honest, hard working, trained technicians. The technocrats also may be correct in their economic diagnoses of what is best for the people in the long view, but both Castello Branco and Costa e Silva failed to bring stability because most policy makers have too little experience with the political factors to which people respond. Paternalism is still a marked characteristic of the Brazilian social and political fabric, and although it must one day make way for more impersonal social justice, it contains those elements, primarily a human concern, to which the Brazilian people will continue to respond. This accounts in no small part for their nonviolent nature. Revolution could more easily come from the coldness of efficient technocrats than from the injustices of paternalism.

Macro-Politics

The foregoing particulars may help in understanding how the nation reached its present point in history and the major problems it faces. They include factors that influence its functions as a nation and should make it possible to see the future potential more accurately. It is impossible to plot the immediate future with any degree of accuracy, as the Brazilian system still depends too heavily on the political capacity of its chief executive, over whom the people and the congress have little control. Political science has still to learn to cope with the unpredictability of individuals who can change the immediate course of nations. It knows a good deal, however, about the larger forces that shape nations. It will thus be helpful to turn from the micro-politics of the particular—to the larger view of macro-politics —the forest.

In 1960 Brazil was well on its way to industrializing in the pattern set by the Western democracies when the political system, weakened by fumbling leadership, proved unequal to supporting the tensions created by a changing society. The demands for more rapid development than could be produced in a democratic context and with social justice was one of the causes of collapse. Another was the failure of leadership that might have preserved most of the democratic forms while engaging the imagination and efforts of Brazilians in what Kalman Silvert calls a "voluntaristic human mobilization of democratic development." [6] A new system was being constructed on the ruins of the old democracy, and by 1972 Brazil was again moving toward economic development but in the very different context of an authoritarian state in which "voluntaristic human mobilization," although improving over the first years, is still largely absent because of the persistence of paternalistic patterns and concomitant failure to encourage popular participation in the political and social as well as the economic process.

Other, more concrete aspects of development can be examined with a view to anticipating the Brazilian future. The best known of these forecasts, and at the same time the best example of how precarious such exercises can be, is that constructed by members of the Hudson Institute, published in the volume *The Year 2000.*[7] Taking 1965 as a base, the authors, Herman Kahn and Anthony J. Wiener, reached the conclusion that it would take Brazil until the end of the century to lift per capita GNP to $506, the present level in Argentina. The Kahn and Wiener assumptions were that economic growth would move along at the average rate of 4.5 percent and that population would increase beginning at the 1965 rate of 3.1 percent until 1985 when it would have dropped to 2.4 percent.

The Kahn prophecy, which could not be ignored because of the high reputation of the Hudson Institute, was proved all but useless in a matter of a few years. Actual economic growth rates were among the highest in the world. Neither Kahn nor Brazilian futurologists could anticipate the present economic boom, any more than anyone can predict with certainty that it will continue. But Kahn could take credit for stirring up sometimes complacent Brazilians who believed that their country's march to great nationhood was pre-ordained and automatic. Not only did *The Year 2000* provoke deep soul searching within the government, but officials rushed into print to attempt to refute the figures which seemed to relegate Brazil permanently to the status of a tropical slum.[8] The refutation, of course, has been actual growth, but note should be taken of Brazilian projections. The most authoritative of these was issued early in 1969 by João Paulo Reis Veloso, Minister of Planning.

If a rate of 6.5 percent economic growth is coupled with an optimistic population growth rate of 1 percent for the last decade of the century, by the year 2000 Brazil would have a per capita GNP of $1,463, which would place it in the middle or upper grouping of industralized countries. If an average of somewhat higher than 7 percent growth is maintained—which is not impossible in light of the astonishing 9.3 percent in 1968; 9 percent in 1969; 9.5 percent in 1970; and 11.3 percent in 1971—Brazil would rank high among the ten leaders, with an absolute GNP of something near $250 billion.[9]

Some will assume that having reached this level of economic development, social and political development would have caught up and many of Brazil's more nettlesome problems of modernization would have disappeared. But what kind of society can really be anticipated?

As already noted, Brazil is one of the older developing nations. Having resolved key problems of ethnic divisions and regional independence from central control, problems which usually block modernization, it has entered the second industralizing stage of development. Many similarities to classic Western bourgeois demo-cratic development are apparent; at least as many differences are to be found.

Brazil still preserves many aspects of a traditional society. The rural lower class can hardly be said to participate in national life; the govern-ment has done very little to improve the welfare of these people and not a great deal more in behalf of the welfare of the urban lower class, at least as compared to some of the more advanced nations. The interest of the majority to contribute to efforts toward national purposes is correspondingly reduced. The traditional elites are united in opposi-tion against key moderninzing changes, except those with economic gains. New strata are growing between the lower and upper classes, but almost exclusively in urban areas. The bourgeoisie is nationalistic; the rural elite is still far less so.

By the foregoing criteria, common to traditional and industrializing societies of Western Europe, Brazil would have far to go to modernize. But as in most things, differences from the classic pattern are important. Thus, the paternalistic character of society has made differences be-tween upper and lower rural classes less relevant to modernization than in the Eupropean societies. Society has been able to develop with less conflict between the classes because relations were made blander by the *patrão* system. As for the urban lower classes, the hierarchic system still has considerable influence, and paternalism has operated to improve the workers' lot far more rapidly than in the industrializing nations of the nineteenth century.

It is questionable whether the rural elite sees a dichotomy in in-dustralization and its own survival. Most see no contradiction between a rural society still retaining near feudal (for them paternalistic) aspects and an otherwise modern society. The *fazendeiro* sees the threat to his survival as coming more from urban, demagogic, and "Communist influenced" politicians and, recently, also more from the Catholic Church, his ertswhile ally, than from industrialization. He may have had to fight increasing numbers of lawmakers from urban areas, but they have not greatly reduced his ability to protect his interests. Changes in the distribution of power have come about so gradually as to cause a mini-mum of conflict. Two factors may be at work here. The extraordinary blandness of social relations in Brazil extends not only between upper and lower classes but also between rural and urban elites, whose in-

terests often conflict in industrializing societies. Few urban elites see
the destruction of the rural aristocracy as a precondition to modernization. Agrarian reform may be accepted as a desideratum, but it is
not seen as a *sine qua non* of development. The all but universal inclination to avoid conflicts of the kind that tore society apart in many
modernizing societies may have operated to convince Brazilians that
their goals can be reached without resort to this type of violence. The
question is whether this diagnosis is correct and conflict can be avoided
or whether the full implications of industrialization have not been
accepted.

Patent as are the traditional features of Brazilian society, as many or
more features of a modern society are present. Many writers have
pointed out that Brazil is two countries, that what is valid for the
modern urban part is not valid for the traditional rural part. Yet the
country is so large and so sparsely occupied that the usual conflicts that
arise over competitiveness within a more compact system are muted
or nonexistent. It was probably during Vargas's second term, 1950-
1954, or the succeeding one of Kubitschek when a crucial modernization milestone was passed. The new economy had grown in importance enough to change its status from a welcome supplement to a
static agrarian economy to an expanding industrial economy on which
more and more of the population depended. The state itself became
dependent on the new economy for income needed to carry out domestic
and foreign responsibilities.

To keep Brazilian development in perspective, it is well to recall
some of the more important aspects of the process among the world's
developed nations. Earlier development under bourgeois politics predicated three principal problems which all polities must solve: How
to put power in the hands of the industrializing managers; how to assist
and encourage the accumulation of capital needed to industrialize;
and how to facilitate the migration of rural labor to urban areas in order
to satisfy the industrial labor requirements.

This developmental process would not have been carried out in developing nations without help from a revolutionary lower class, but
once power had been seized from the aristocracy the state ignored the
needs and aspirations of the masses while it used its powers to facilitate
industrialization. Industrialization, in the beginnng at least, did not
entail improving the lot of the workers. To the contrary, in order to

accumulate necessary capital it not only forced the rural aristocracy to share the burden through taxation and other means but it also derived most of the capital from savings made by keeping wages and consumption low. The savings, or in this case profits, were then made available for reinvestment. Labor paid the price by what today seems brutal living and working conditions, repression, and lack of a voice in the government. This was true in Western Europe and the United States no less than the Stalinist-Communist Soviet Union and the fascist countries that succeeded in making the transition to an industrial society. It was a successful industrializing policy, albeit an inhuman one. Bourgeois politics were anything but democratic. The various elites contended for control of the decision-making machinery. Only several generations after the nations modernized did mass democracies come into being.

Brazil's politics until 1964, with some aberrations, fitted a description of bourgeois politics with reasonable accuracy. With two exceptions, successive governments since 1930 have effectively stimulated industrialization by such conventional means as increasing the availability of capital through credit facilities and capital loans as well as through expanding the currency. Tariff protection was given to new and old industries.

By and large, Brazilian governments were less efficient than the Western bourgeois democracies in preventing increased production from going to improved living conditions in urban centers. The demands of the workers were by no means fully satisfied, but the exploitation of labor was not comparable to what it had been during the industrializing period in Western Europe and the United States, or to take a more recent example, the Soviet Union. In fact, several interrptions in the economic growth pattern in Brazil have been ascribed to the failure to adopt stringent measures to limit mass consumption enough to accumulate capital.

Here is an essential difference in the pattern of development among many nations in the twentieth century from that of the nations which developed during the nineteenth century. Those which industrialized earlier could depend only on their internal resources and such little private capital as ventured in. More capital had to be accumulated by underpaying workers. In the twentieth century private foreign capital has been available in large quantities. Also, international institutions, like the World Bank and the Inter-American Development

Bank, as well as government development agencies, like the U. S. Government's Agency for International Development, have made it possible to hasten the developmental process without the kind of sacrifices forced on labor in an earlier era.

Labor was repressed in Brazil, but with a lighter hand; only unions approved by the government (and effectively controlled by it) were given legal status. Capital was given a free hand in such areas as price fixing and in making labor contracts, and strikes were often declared illegal by the government and were broken with police power. However, all these privileges and facilities accorded to capital had limitations not as severe as those on labor but nonetheless real. Employers were allowed to establish associations, but the government maintained some control over them. It occasionally instituted price controls over items of prime necessity. Labor courts were established to assure that real wages did not fall too far behind. But of farthest reaching consequences was the direct responsibility the government assumed for economic development. In this respect the Brazilian experience parallels the Japanese, as outlined by A. F. K. Organski [10], more than it does that of the Western democracies, whose development was guided largely by laissez-faire doctrines.

In Brazil, as in Japan, direction of the industrialization process was taken over by the government, not left to private capital. An elite of government bureaucrats in both countries (the technocrats in Brazil) made the principal decisions as to which industries were to be favored— even deciding which new industries were to be established; which infrastructure projects were to have priority; and when credit was to be tightened or expanded. In Brazil, as well as in Japan, the state left the bulk of industry in private hands, in both cases much of it concentrated in the large industrial family empires. Japan was apparently successful in preserving many of the old political, social, and economic forms during its transition to an industrial nation. Brazil will try to preserve some of its social forms deriving from the hierarchic-paternalistic bases of an earlier day.

Differences in the industrializing experiences of the two countries, however, are by no means inconsiderable. Because of the failure of Brazilian private enterprise to enter certain areas vital to industrialization, such as steel, petroleum, electric power, and the merchant marine, the Brazilian government owns and runs an important part of the economy. In one other respect the Brazilian and Japanese experiences have varied. The Japanese removed the rural aristocracy from power and thus did not have to make compromises to provide for the rural elite to share power with the industrial and bureaucratic elites. Japanese industrialization was consequently more rapid and efficient than that in the Western democracies, where shifting power from the rural to the urban sectors was a more painful and prolonged process. The problem has yet to be resolved in Brazil, but measures taken by military-controlled governments after 1964 left little doubt that a change in the *status quo* is the goal.

The objective of the military rulers is a system that will permit controlled change to modernization without the instability that has usually accompanied such change in the modern world. Or, as they would say, without danger to national security. After a decade a new "Brazilian model" which military intelligentsia favor had yet to be devised. Discussions at the *Escola Superior de Guerra,* however, have given attention to a one party system, similar to the Mexican. To date purely pragmatic political action has been pursued to change the bourgeois democracy, eliminating most of the former principal actors. Ronald Schneider describes the government as "a modernizing authoritarian regime," and devotes a considerable part of his discussion to comparative formulations based on his own observations and the analysis of other leading political scientists.[11]

The tentative nature of these studies as applied to Brazil and recent events, particularly the successful economic revolution, tend to confirm the uniqueness of the Brazilian system and the failure of political scientists to typify it. Nevertheless, for this discussion I have found it helpful to use as a comparative model what A. F. K. Organski defines as "the syncratic state." Organski uses a broader brush than other scholars here noted, dividing developing nations into bourgeois democracies, the Stalinist-Communist state and, finally, the syncratic state. The syncratic state is a facist-type government like those in Spain, Portugal, and Italy at the time of Mussolini (but not Hitler's Germany, which was already industrialized).[12] Various Latin American governments at times seem to fit the description, as does Brazil since 1964. A number of differences will become apparent, however, because basic conditions are different and also because the army, rather than a syncratic political party, has taken control. On the other hand, the fact that military rule is corporate, that is, all important decisions are collective rather than personal, adds to the validity of the comparison.

The syncratic model postulates that activities begin when the nation is well on the way to industrialization.[13] Syncratic politics may occur at a time when power among the various elites is shifting but its eventual locus is still undetermined, and conflicts, particularly between industrial and rural elites, are present. In Italy one such conflict led to alienation between the industrial north and the agricultural south. A somewhat similar situation developed between the industrial south and agrarian north in Brazil, though in less radicalized form. Other major conflicts develop between each of the elites and their respective workers, which may become so serious as to cause the two opposing elites to unite against the threat from below. Under the Goulart administration the threat from the urban and rural workers was allowed to grow almost without restraint until virtually all the elites sought military intervention to head it off.

A rather important difference from the Organski model is that in Brazil the industrial elite had become more powerful than the rural elite before 1964. As has been noted, the rural elite has been able to block modernizing reforms, but its influence is confined largely to the legislature and some government departments that remain relatively isolated from modernizing influences. It is not clear as yet how far the syncratic-military government will go in modernizing the rural areas. Perhaps, as is characteristic of such governments, each elite is to be given considerable freedom within its own economic and social sector. Through 1972, despite halting moves toward agrarian reform (which were not intended to wipe out the power of the rural elite), the government seemed more concerned about the possible disruption of agricultural production through reform measures than in finding permanent solutions or in improving social conditions. Its principal efforts were being channeled into industrializing the Northeast under forced draft rather than to modernizing agriculture. 1969, however, saw the beginnings of a confrontation when the central government moved to force rural areas to make a larger contribution to industrialization by reducing the states' share of certain tax revenues.

The Brazilian case fits that part of the syncratic model which postulates the protection of the agricultural sector, a basic difference from both the bourgeois and Stalinist methods of industrialization. Capital accumulations will come out of the governmental sector through greater efficiency and less waste, from the industrial sector through increased productivity, and from labor in lagging wages. The rural contribution is still minimal. The unavoidable result will eventually be to slow down industrialization.

The Brazilian past suggests that the syncratic form of government in Brazil, if it continues for long, is likely to be atypical. It would be the first time a nation so large had tried it as a method of industrialization. One important factor suggesting that it may be discarded for some more efficient method is that in other countries it has proved to be a slower way to reach developed status and is likely to be found wanting in Brazil as well. The syncratic state has some elements of Positivism in it, but Positivism as such is not a system of government. More idealistic than the syncratic state and more attuned to the Brazilian character, its influence will be substantial in any government in which the military has a voice. Its influence is likely to be more enduring than the syncratic model.

Foreign Relations and the New Nationalism

Brazil's international relations continue to be of less importance than national affairs. Like the United States until it started on the road to world prominence during and after World War II, Brazil continues to be absorbed by the development of the country, a purpose that consumes most of the thought and energies of its leaders. Its size, wealth, and geopolitical position, which effectively protect it from most extrasocietal influences, makes its external environment of secondary importance. An obvious exception is the matter of economic assistance which will strongly influence the rate of economic development. The United States today is important to Brazilian development. Over the longer run Brazil may be even more important to the United States. Equally significant as Brazil's potential as a major power is its position as a key element in any hemisphere policy. A hemisphere in serious disarray will mean a weakened United States and a weakened Latin America and a weakened Brazil. A look at the particulars is in order.

It is not difficult to discern the likely course of some political events in Brazil's near future. A nationalism that now manifests itself in extreme and immature forms will mature with the gradual realization of the nation's potential.

Relations with the United States will become more stable as it becomes more widely understood that although the northern country may sometimes err in its strategy for assisting Brazil to major nationhood, its motives are clear. It should be evident to those willing to read the record that the United States does not want either to absorb or to make a satellite of the Latin American country with which it has the most parallel interests. Since extreme nationalism has strong connotations of defense mechanism against feelings of insecurity and inferiority, Brazilian achievements will serve to disarm the nationalist extremists. Those inspired by more dubious motives, who have made a profession of anti-Americanism, will find less and less support.

One other more consequential and reasoned aspect of nationalism that will affect relations between Brazil and all developed countries is the one related to the nativist-oriented thesis expounded by the historian José Honório Rodrigues. He has carried Gilberto Freyre's thesis of a new world in the tropics beyond its original concept. To Rodrigues, Brazil is a unique and original creation—a mestizo republic, neither European nor Latin American. He grounds his argument for an independent foreign policy, run strictly in the national interest, on this fact of the Brazilian condition as well as on its underdevelopment. His thesis served as the rationale for the Quadros-Goulart policy of rapprochement with Africa and Asia as well as a radical loosening of ties with the United States and Portugal.

The Rodrigues thesis is important because it reflects a strong current in today's Brazil that seeks to establish a philosophical base for a new, more firmly grounded nationalism. It recalls the São Paulo modern art show of 1922, which marked the start on the road to national self-awareness and away from its concentration on solely European ideals. However, other Brazilian realities are as strong as, or stronger than, that of "a mestizo republic." The modernizing and fast industrializing south is preponderantly white. Although it contains large numbers of non-Portuguese European immigrants and their sons, Portuguese white culture remains the ideal for most of the population, as it does in the less white tropical coastal areas. Brazil is a racial democracy, but Portuguese white culture continues to be an ideal to which not only the upper class but the middle and even lower classes aspire. This ideal could change, but short of a racial revolution it is unlikely.

The likelihood then is that this thesis, basically one of national identity, will not alter relations between Brazil and the United States in the foreseeable future. Other factors, linked with problems of far wider scope and affecting hemisphere and world policies of the United States will assume more significance. These relate directly to the question of trade versus aid and to the larger question of relations between the developed and developing nations. Equally important is the matter of the position of the United States in the hemisphere.

As has been noted the Brazilian dilemma over trade versus aid can be summed up by the claim that coffee prices a few cents higher would be more valuable than total aid. This is a facile oversimplification of a complex issue. A more cogent complaint concerns restrictions placed by the United States and other developed nations on the importation of Brazilian manufactures and semimanufactures. U. S. doctrine on foreign aid programs has long preached that industrialization cannot be attained unless manufactures can compete in world markets. Exports of manufactures are needed to supplement exports of raw materials. Yet entry into the United States of soluble coffee, certain textiles, meat, and even revolvers has been blocked or greatly restricted by the Department of State or Congress through action taken in response to pressures from manufacturers unable to compete with imported products.[13] This is one of the causes of the widening gap between the developed and underdeveloped nations which threatens to create a defensive alliance of alienated nations. An alliance of this nature could cause as many problems on the international front as alienated groups are capable of causing nationally.

The prominent British author and philosopher, C. P. Snow, suggested in 1968 that frustrated, hungry, underdeveloped countries would have the advanced nations in a "state of siege" within twenty years if measures were not taken to narrow the gap between them. To meet the problem he urged that the developed nations undertake a coordinated program, devoting 20 percent of their GNP to economic assistance each year for the next ten to fifteen years. Raul Prebisch, Secretary General of the U. N. Conference on Trade and Development (UNCTAD) from 1963 to 1969 and Latin America's most active and articulate pleader for economic planning and assistance for the underdeveloped nations, is more modest, believing that "Disaster is avoidable . . ." provided the Latin American nations undertake necessary changes in their social and economic structures, and the advanced nations contribute one percent of GNP to stimulate sufficient development to thrust them into self-sustained economic growth.[14] Few industrialized nations come close to that level today.

Portents of alienation are already visible in Latin America. The growing number of governments in Latin America seeking extremist solutions to their problems, beginning with Cuba and continuing with Peru, Bolivia, and Chile (two leftist and two military regimes) may well be the handwriting on the wall. Latin Americans are losing patience not only with their own ineffectual political leaders but also with the major powers who have set the terms of trade at will and whom they hold responsible for maintaining Latin America is a "colonial status." In Brazil the rationale for this alienation is to be found in arguments for an "independent foreign policy in the national interest," which draw on instances of U. S. discrimination and disinterest or simply on instances of predatory private capital, principally from the United States, interested only in profits. Some subtle and some not-so-subtle changes in relations with the United States reflect a growing alienation that will accelerate if aid from the United States is reduced and the United States does not devote the attention to the area that is demanded. This is the economic side of the problem; the political is equally important.

The number of meetings among Latin American nations to which the United States was not invited increased after Castello Branco left office. Problems between the two countries, which under Castello Branco had been kept in low key and out of the public glare, shortly became material for public debate in line with policies of a more nationalistic government. As we have seen, a more serious portent came out of the visit of President Eduardo Frei of Chile to Brazil in 1968, well before the installation of the Allende Socialist government. The meaning of the communiqué issued after the visit was that the United States is an outsider among the Latin American nations and is welcome in some of their councils because of the economic assistance it can provide, not because it has a common past or common destiny. Its seriousness is difficult to overestimate, representing as it does a long step toward achieving a principal goal of the more bitter opponents among the Spanish American countries of U. S. policy in the hemisphere. Until 1960, Brazil's role of mediator or interpreter between Sapnish-America and Anglo-America helped prevent polarization of ideas in the north and south to the point of creating irremediable differences. Brazil's policy shift toward Latin American integration and away from hemisphere integration   has grave portents for the hemisphere. Not only will the United States be weakened, but the other American nations will also suffer.

The trend away from hemisphere unity is a negation of the Western Hemisphere Idea that a special relationship among all the countries in the hemisphere sets them apart from the rest of the world. The concept of a special relationship has been recognized and cultivated not only by Latin American statesmen but by statesmen of greatest vision in the United States, beginning with Thomas Jefferson and including James Monroe, Henry Clay, James Blaine, Elihu Root, Franklin D. Roosevelt, and John F. Kennedy. Yet at this dangerous stage in United States history and Latin American development, when innovating leadership is most needed, neither the United States nor the other countries of the hemisphere have brought forth renovative ideas to bridge the growing gap between north and south. *Ad hoc* adjustment by the U.S. to Latin American outbursts of nationalistic fervor, the normal policy under President Nixon, is not leadership. It will not improve a relationship that once served as a model for other areas of the world. While the United States seeks new relationships to meet changes on the world scene in its recent role of keeper of world peace, it has allowed its firmest and most fruitful relationship to wither.

The failure of the United States to maintain and improve on the inter-American relationship is at the base of the Brazilian decision to alter its traditional relationship with the United States and the other Latin American countries. The long-term objective henceforth will be Latin American integration under Brazilian leadership. The meeting between Presidents Nixon and Medici in 1971, as vital as it was in Brazilian eyes in bestowing important nation status on Brazil, will be only a palliative if more substantive action does not follow. Only an effective hemisphere policy and a concomitantly effective relationship with Brazil is likely to modify that objective. In today's world such a relationship would have to be based on some form of hemisphere common market. Its ultimate political objective could be an American commonwealth of nations, one to be worked out slowly as the weaker nations become more assured as they grow economically and less fearful of dominance by the strongest powers.

Regardless of the outcome of the more difficult problems, some adjustments will inevitably have to be made in relations between the United States and Brazil.

As long as the United States continues to be the principal importer of Brazilian coffee, the country's most important export, and remains a principal supplier of economic and financial assistance, relations will continue on an acceptable if less than satisfactory level. However, as even the favorably disposed General Golbery de Couto e Silva suggested more than a decade ago in his study of Brazilian geopolitics, concessions made to meet military requirements can no longer be expected in return for "a plate of lentils." U.S. defense planners learned this, presumably to their shock, when Brazil joined other Latin American nations in extending its offshore limits to 200 miles and thereby jeopardized U. S. worldwide defense concepts. As for commercial relations, it is probable that friction between the two governments over policy concerning the treatment of U. S. private enterprise will increase, because Brazil has changed from a country with an essentially colonial economy to a partially industrialized, modernizing nation; and as a consequence its national priorities have changed.

Because it is so deeply concerned over Brazilian development and reform, the United States is also likely to find itself a target for the bitterness of one or another of the growing modernizing forces, as they seek to change the power structure by reducing the role of the traditional ruling elites. If U. S. actions do not encourage reform, the modernizing forces will feel betrayed by the nation that created the Alliance for Progress. If reform is effected, the traditional groups that have been most friendly to the United States in the past will feel betrayed. Temporary misunderstandings are inevitable between countries that are so closely concerned with the policies of each other. It is vital for the United States to show sympathy and concern for a longtime friend and ally, even under adverse circumstances. This becomes easier when it is understood that at the root of many of the misunderstandings are problems growing out of the travails of a modernization process. More difficult to deal with on a reasonable plane are problems arising out of political repression whose victims arouse the concern of Americans. No matter how justified Brazilian authorities believe themselves to be in meeting terrorism and other subversive activities with force, such repression, often visited on the innocent, inevitably raises voices of protest in the United States, as elsewhere among democratic countries. When press and other censorship accompanies political repression, it becomes virtually impossible for the government to defend its policies before world opinion. These are political problems which the nation's leaders have yet to solve.

New World in the Tropics

It is essential to remember that as complex and difficult as are its problems, Brazil nonetheless continues to grow and modernize. Military control and political repression have continued for almost a decade but the prospect is good for a return to bourgeois democracy, whether within a few years, when the present administration is due to end, or in ten years, the maximum claimed by extremists to be needed to clear away the political underbrush for a better ordered society. Brazil is fast becoming a model of how private enterprise, under able state guidance, can contribute effectively to economic development. It is not hard to point out failures in the system, particularly in the social area. Yet economic resources are being generated on a scale that will make the problems of social inequities far easier to deal with in the future. It remains to be seen how these resources are eventually distributed.

If, on the other hand, some variety of the syncratic way of development is maintained, and economic growth is sustained at 1968-1972 rates, the return to democracy could be delayed until the transformation is made at the advanced stage of a mass or consumer democracy. Development will not stop unless, of course, anomic movements are successful in creating a polity so unstable as to frighten off new internal investment and foreign private and institutional capital. Even Brazil's past record of nonviolence at the institutional level does not make it immune to social upheaval, but violence remains highly unlikely so long as social progress continues. The military, which is second to none in wanting a great nation, is aware of this need for social progress, as is shown by its inclusion among Brazil's formal national objectives. Because of pressures from the Church, students, intellectuals, and even some within military ranks, social change could come faster than the ordered, rational, nondisruptive pace favored by most of the higher ranking military men. Some of the younger and more radical officers understand the anachronistic nature of Brazilian society and believe that a modified democratic system is a more effective way than the old to social change and great-nation status.

The long view of history shows that all syncratic states are temporary. They are eventually replaced because the industrial managers soon become aware that their erstwhile protector from the masses is a drag on development and that they fare better under a mass democracy, with all its disruptions, than under the artificial restraints of authoritarianism.

Brazil is well on its way to industrialization, and a welfare state, an outgrowth of the modernizing process, is within view. To believe Brazilian experts, a mass consumption economy will be possible by the year 2000. Barring national disasters, Brazil as a tropical slum is highly improbable. Its future seems most likely to be that of a modern industrial nation, with a combination of geography, culture, and social heritage that gives it a unique character and an increasing role in a world long accustomed to leadership from temperate-zone and colder countries. Brazil will thus become the world's first great tropical nation of modern times.

What role the United States will play in this development depends largely on the vision of its leaders. They must be able to build constructively on the distinction between short-term gains and long-term interests, as well as between ephemeral annoyances and the demands of a difficult but essential responsibility for aiding nation building in the Western Hemisphere neighborhood.

REFERENCES

CHAPTER I

1. This view, expounded in Golbery do Couto e Silva, *Geopolítica do Brazil,* Rio de Janeiro, José Olympio, 1967, concedes that in its present stage of development the Amazon is a negative influence because of difficulties of communication and dense vegetation. The book was written before the concentration of effort to open up the Amazon which began in 1968.

2. A good recent history in English is E. Bradley Burns, *A History of Brazil,* New York, Columbia University Press, 1970. Other standard basic books, limited in scope and uneven in quality, include: Américo Jacobins Lacombe, *Brazil, A Brief History,* Rio de Janeiro, 1954; João Pandia Calógeras, *A History of Brazil,* Chapel Hill, University of North Carolina Press, 1939; José Maria Bello, *A History of Modern Brazil,* Stanford, Stanford University Press, 1966. Two of the best histories in Portuguese are Pedro Calmon, *História do Brasil* (7 vols.), Editôra José Olympio, Rio de Janeiro,, 1955-1961; and *História geral da civilização brasileira,* edited by Sérgio Buarque de Holanda, São Paulo, 1960—.

3. One French king is credited with observing that he had not been shown Adam's testament that bequeathed the world to the Spanish and the Portuguese.

4. The best account of the *bandeirantes* epic can be found in Richard M. Morse, *The Bandeirantes,* New York, Alfred A. Knopf, 1965.

5. João Ribeiro, *História do Brasil,* 19th ed., Rio de Janeiro, Libraria Francisco Alves, 1966, p. 29. Although not as well known as other more modern historians, Ribeiro has special importance for the student of Brazil today because his history is a leading college textbook in Brazil and thus important in its influence on the country's future leaders. His interpretation of English exploitation of Brazilian gold has doubtless contributed to nationalist sentiment.

6. Karl Lowenstein, *Brazil Under Vargas,* New York, Macmillan, 1942, p. 7.

7. Rollie E. Poppino, *Brazil: The Land and People,* New York, Oxford University Press, 1968. See particularly Chapter V.

8. In 1835, 24.2 percent of the population was white; in 1872 the figure had risen to 38.1 percent; in 1890 to 43.9 percent; and in 1940 to 63.4 percent. Source: Rollie E. Poppino, *Brazil: The Land and People,* p. 198.

9. José-Itamar de Freitas, *Brasil, Ano 2000, O Futuro sem Fantasia,* São Paulo, Artes Graficas Gomes de Souza, S.A., 1968, p. 88. Since 14.53 percent are unaccounted for, it may be presumed that they are unemployed. See also Florestan Fernandes, *The Negro in Brazilian Society,* New York, Columbia University Press, 1970; and Jean-Claude Garcia-Zamor, "Social Mobility of Negroes in Brazil," *Journal of Inter-American Studies,* vol. XII, no. 2, 1970.

10. Nonetheless, more government officials and technocrats are speaking out, e.g., Rubens Costa, President of the Bank of the Northeast of Brazil, a government-controlled institution, recently observed: "No people has performed the miracle of developing with vegetative growth rates of its population higher than 2

percent per annum for long periods." (*Visão,* March 14, 1970). These are challenging words in Brazil, where the growth rate is just less than 3 percent

11. Anthony Leeds, "Brazilian Careers and Social Structure: An Evolutionary Model and Case History," *American Anthropologist,* vol. 66, December, 1964 (no. 6, part 1).

12. Gabriel A. Almond and G. B. Powell, *Comparative Politics: A Developmental Approach,* Boston, Little, Brown & Co., 1966, p. 62.

CHAPTER II

1. Quoted in Freitas, *Ano 2000,* p. 2.
2. Poppino, *Land and People,* p. 5.
3. Freitas, *Ano 2000,* p. 5.
4. James L. Busey in an essay, "Brazil's Reputation for Political Stability," in Richard Graham (ed.) *A Century of Brazilian History Since 1865,* New York, Alfred A. Knopf, 1969, disputes the accuracy of the nonviolence thesis in Brazilian history. It may, indeed, be true that many writers fail to mention the many instances of violence in history while emphasizing the nonviolent. Nevertheless, compared to that of most Spanish American countries, most of Brazil's national life has been tranquil. The author notes that ". . . violence was never far from the surface." This is perhaps the notable aspect of Brazilian political life. When matters have deteriorated to the explosive point, Brazilians have almost always found a conciliatory formula to keep the situation dampened down. Civil war has been averted many times under such circumstances.
5. Vianna Moog, *Bandeirantes e Pioneiros,* 8th ed., Rio de Janeiro, Editora Civilização Brasileira, 1966, p. 122.
6. Nathaniel H. Leff, *Economic Policy-Making and Development in Brazil, 1947-1964,* New York, John Wiley, 1968. See chap. VII.
7. Data from Charles Daugherty, James Rowe, and Ronald Schneider, *Brazil Election Factbook,* Washington, D.C., Institute for the Comparative Study of Political Systems, 1965; and *Anuário Estatístico do Brasil, 1968,* Rio de Janeiro, Instituto Brasileiro do Estatística, 1968.
8. Robert E. Scott, "Nation Building in Latin America," in Karl W. Deutch and William J. Foltz, *Nation Building,* New York, Atherton Press, 1966.
9. Gabriel A. Almond and Sidney Verba, *The Civic Culture,* Princeton, Princeton University Press, 1963.
10. Conducted by the Instituto de Estudos Speciaes e Econômicos, for the U.S. Agency for International Development, September, 1965, interviews in January, February and March, 1965.

CHAPTER III

1. The constitutional power of the president to intervene in a state gives him the right to remove the governor (and other state officials) and replace him with an intervertor of his own chosing. The power is limited, and the extent of its use has always been one of the great constitutional issues in Brazil.
2. The 1967 Constitution did, however, incorporate changes in the judiciary already made by the executive through Institutional Act No. Two, which established additional federal courts to handle cases involving certain types

of federal law. Previously, infractions of this type had been judged in state courts, not always to the satisfaction of the central government.

3. Among sources of information on the 1967 Constitution and amendments to it are *Embaixada do Brasil,* "Boletim Especial," nos. 199-201, Washington, D.C., October 21, 22, and 23, 1969; and *Jornal do Brasil,* Rio de Janeiro, October 18 and 19, 1969.

4. Subsequent legislation formally named these municipalities in which industries must be predominantly Brazilian in captal and labor.

5. Carlos Castello Branco, "O Congresso Nacional," *Cadernos Brasileiros,* Rio de Janeiro, no. 41, May-June 1967.

6. As noted elsewhere a transitory provision of the amended 1967 Constitution permits the suspension of a number of individual rights, including the use of *habeas corpus.*

7. Article VI of the extralegal Institutional Act No. five of December 13, 1968, changed this provision (probably temporarily), suspending constitutional guarantees related to life tenure and nontransferability and stability in office, making all justices (among others) subject to dismissal or retirement.

8. Institutional Act No. six of January 31, 1969, reduced the number from sixteen to eleven, which number was subsequently incorporated into the Amendment to the Constitution. The same Act removed the competence of the supreme court to review ordinary writs of security appeals and ordinary appeals against military court decisions related to crimes against national security committed by civilians.

9. The 1969 Amendment to the Constitution provides that governors are to be indirectly elected in 1970 and directly elected thereafter. This provision was subsequently changed to extend indirect elections through 1974.

10. "Municipality" is not a good translation of *"município,"* but "municipality" and "municipal" are used for convenience; the Brazilian *município* is comparable to a county or township in the United States.

CHAPTER IV

1. Frank Bonilla, *Rural Reform in Brazil,* American Universities Field Staff Reports, East Coast South America Series, vol. VIII, no. 4, October 1961.

2. Since the proportion of registered voters to total population in 1966 did not increase over 1955, it is apparent that the new regulation was not yet operative.

3. The superior electoral court has a large staff to attend to its judiciary and administrative functions. The court is made up of two justices of the supreme court (who serve as the president and vice president and change rather frequently), two justices from the highest court of appeals, and one from the Federal District court. Two others are appointed by the President of the Republic.

4. Douglas A. Chalmers, "Parties and Society in Latin America," a paper delivered at the 1968 Annual Meeting of the American Political Science Association, Washington, D. C.

5. The literature on Brazil makes repeated reference to the weakness of political parties because of lack of ideological content and motivation, as does this work, but this generalization should be viewed with caution. Brazilians

are not unlike the people of the United States in their pragmatic approach to politics. As even ideologically based countries have found, economic growth and social justice mean more than ideology does to the electorate. Developmentalism, as a means for bringing material benefits, is perhaps the nearest thing to an ideology that attracts Brazilians today.

6. Comments about the newly decreed Complementary Act No. 54 establishing primary elections made by the Brazilian jurist, João de Oliveira Filho, a past President of the Brazilian Institute of Lawyers, gives some indication of how the party nominating machinery actually functioned under the old party statutes. *Jornal do Brazil,* June 25, 1969, reports him as saying that the most important effect of the Act is to deprive the party leadership of the competence to select party candidates. "The situation will now improve," he was quoted as saying, "because the candidates will no longer be named by political chieftains, but rather through popular convention. Heretofore the party (directorate) did as it pleased. Anything could happen, even corruption in the selection." Once chosen the proportional representation system made it relatively easy for candidates with no popular backing to be elected.

7. Leonido Basbaum, *História Sincera da Republica,* 1889-1930, vol. II, São Paulo, Editôra Edaglit, 1958, p. 314.

CHAPTER V

1. From Dr. Teixeira's study for the Instituto Nacional de Estudos Políticos and the Pan American Union, reported in Leeds, "Brazilian Careers and Social Structure," *American Anthropologist,* December, 1964.

2. *Ibid.,* p. 1341.

3. *Visão* devotes its entire March 29, 1968, issue to a thorough study of the Brazilian administration, including some aspects of civil service reform under Decree-law 200.

4. Civil Service employment may not have increased during the short period under Quadros, who prided himself on getting rid of excess personnel.

5. Nelson Mello e Souza, quoted in Robert T. Daland, *Brazilian Development,* Chapel Hill, University of North Carolina Press, 1967, p. 213.

5a. Ronald Schneider, *The Political System of Brazil,* Columbia University Press, New York, 1971, p. 43.

5b. Alfred Stepan, *The Military in Politics,* Princeton University Press, New Jersey, 1971, pp. 64-65.

5c. *Ibid.,* p. 31.

6. Ledo Ivo, "A escola que mudou o Brasil," *Manchete,* September 6, 1969. His article was written with the collaboration of the *Escola Superior de Guerra.*

7. *Ibid.*

8. MBD Deputy Amaral Peixoto, formerly president of the majority party, the PSD, who was given rsponsibility by President Goulart to draw up a broad administrative reform law, told a journalist that the draft decree-law establishing "security zones" in 235 municipalities throughout Brazil, making their mayors no longer elective, originated in the *Escola.* He said that he had been approached in 1963 by representatives of the *Escola* to include such zones in the reform measure then being drawn up. On the same occasion, he said that the decree-law, granting broader powers to the National Security Council and weighting it with

more military representatives, originated in the *Escola*. He was quoted in the *Jornal do Brasil* of February 6, 1968, as saying "We are witnessing no more than the de-pigeonholing of the old ideas of the ESG."

9. Federal University of Minas Gerais, *Revista Brasileira de Estudos Políticos,* July 1966. The entire issue of this review is devoted to the *Escola Superior de Guerra* and national security.

10. *Cadernos Brasileiros,* November-December 1966.

11. Ivan Vallier, "Religious Elites," in Seymour M. Lipset and Aldo Solari (eds.), *Elites in Latin America,* New York, Oxford University Perss, 1967.

12. See the summary of Brazilian Catholicism by the French sociologist Roger Bastide, "Religion and the Church in Brazil," in T. Lynn Smith and Alexander Marchant, *Brazil: Portrait of Half a Continent,* New York, 1951.

13. From "A Religião," in *Livro do Centenario,* Rio de Janeiro, 1900, quoted in João Cruz Costa, *Panorama of the History of Philosophy in Brazil,* Washington, D. C. Pan American Union, 1962.

14. Data on the Church hierarchy can be found in Winfredo Plagge, A. A., *A Igreja do Brasil,* Rio de Janeira, CERIS, 1965. Current data are from *Jornal do Brasil,* July 21, 1968.

15. Vallier, "Religious Elites" in Lipset and Solari, *Elites in L.A.,* pp. 204-206.

16. See David E. Mutchler, S. J., "Roman Catholicism in Brazil," *Studies in Comparative International Development,* St. Louis, Washington University, vol. I, no. 8, 1965, for a study made shortly after the 1964 revolution when the conflict between Church and State first became apparent for all to see. Father Deelen's typology was printed in *Jornal do Brasil,* July 21, 1968.

17. Conferencia Nacional dos Bispos do Brasil, *Plano de Pastoral de Conjunto, 1966-1970,* Rio de Janeiro, Livraria Dom Bosco, Editora, 1967, p. 13.

18. Mutchler, "Roman Catholicism" in *Comparative International Development,* p. 109.

19. *The Washington Post,* February 14, 1970.

20. *Jornal do Brasil, July 28, 1968.*

21. Thomas G. Sanders, "Catholicism and Development: The Catholic Left in Brazil," Kalman H. Silvert, (ed.) *Churchs and States: The Religious Institution and Modernization,* New York, American Universities Field Staff, Inc., 1967. Sanders gives sympathetic treatment to the Catholic Left, including the far left extremists.

22. Many Brazilians and foreign observers believed Goulart was either a crypto-Communist or was under Communist control, a judgment which known facts did not support.

22a. *Miami Herald,* November 22, 1970.

22b. *La Prensa Libre,* San José, Costa Rica, October 20, 1970.

22c. *La Nación,* San José, Costa Rica, October 20, 1970.

22d. *Ibid.,* November 1, 1971.

22e. *Ibid.,* October 18, 1971.

23. *Ibid.,* November 5, 1971.

24. As in other parts of the world, recruiting of priests in Brazil is still a serious problem, but the causes are related more to the universal than the national Church.

25. Quoted in *Jornal do Brasil,* October 21, 1969.

26. *Ibid.*

27. Vallier, "Religious Elites" in Lipset and Solari, *Elites in L.A.*

28. For some considerations on the size and importance of non-Catholic religious movements in Brazil, see Emilio Williams, "Religious Mass Movements and Social Changes in Brazil," Eric N. Baklanoff, (ed.) *New Perspectives in Brazil,* Nashville, Vanderbilt University Press, 1966. Reliable statistics on the size of non-Catholic movements are not available. The count of Protestants in *Anuário Estatístico* was 2,484,968 at the end of 1965. However, Pentacosts estimated their numbers alone to be 2 million in 1961, of a total of more than 4 million Protestants in the country. It is possibly more difficult to estimate the number of Spiritualists, the other important religious movement. The "Scientific Spiritualists." followers of Kardec, by official count numbered 732,784 at the end of 1965. Umbandista Spiritualists, who are an offshoot of the African Macumba (disowned by the Kardecists), were numbered at a little more than 100,000. Catholic sociologists, on the other hand, believe the number of Umbandistas to be much higher, since many of them (to the despair of the hierarchy) consider themselves to be Catholics practicing a variation of folk Catholicism, and they classify themselves accordingly to census takers. The Church has noted the rapid growth of Spiritualism in the backward Northeast states, where Catholic proselytising is least effective. The *Boletim Informativo* of CERIS (July/September 1966, pp. 77-79) estimated that Spiritualists in Brazil had increased by 78 percent from 1940 to 1950, and Protestants by 62 percent. The total population increased only 26 percent, while Catholics increased by 24 percent. However, Pentacostalism and Spiritualism are largely urban phenomena, explained principally by the failure of the Catholic Church to fill the need of recent arrivals from the rural areas for a substitute for the family, community, and *patrão* they left behind.

29. Federative Republic of Brazil—Prospectus 1972. For issue of bonds on the Frankfurt Stock Exchange, Brasilia, February 1972, p. 14.

30. In 1968 only 0.29 percent of the Brazilian population attended institutions of higher learning, compared to 3.5 percent in the United States in that same year.

31. Poll cited in Leonard D. Therry, "Dominant Power Components in the Brazilian Student Movement Prior to April 1964," *Journal of Inter-American Studies,* January 1965.

32. Sanders, "Catholicism and Development" in Silvert, *Churches and States,* p. 90.

33. *Autarquías* are more or less independent administrative agencies whose functions are often similar to regulating commissions and government corporations in the United States.

34. See Paulo Ayres Filho, "The Brazilian Revolution," in Norman A. Bailey, *Latin America: Politics, Economics and Hemisphere Security,* New York, Praeger, 1965; James W. Rowe, "Revolution and Counterrevolution in Brazil," part I, American Universities Field Staff Reports Service, East Coast South America Series, vol. XI, no. 4, June 1964; and Norman Blume, "Pressure Groups and Decision-Making in Brazil," *Studies in Comparative International Development,* St. Louis, Washington University, vol. III, no. 11, 1967-68, who gives a useful analysis of the structure and functions of IPES. See also Stepan, *The Military in Politics,* pp. 154 and 186.

35. Leff, *Economic Policy-Making,* pp. 113-118.

36. Blume, "Pressure Groups," in *Comparative International Development,* p. 217.

37. Leff, *Economic Policy-Making*, p. 113.

38. Blume, "Pressure Groups," in *Comparative International Development*.

39. Glaucio Ary Dillon Soares, "Intellectual Identity and Political Ideology among University Students," in Lipset and Solari, *Elites in Latin America*.

40. Frank Bonilla, "A National Ideology for Development: Brazil," in Kalman H. Silvert, *Expectant Peoples: Nationalism and Development*, New York, Random House, 1963.

41. Hélio Jaguaribe, *O Nacionalismo na Atualidade Brasileira*, Rio de Janeiro, Ministerio de Educaçao e Cultura, ISEB, 1958.

42. A poll taken in Rio de Janeiro for a U. S. Government agency in 1965 showed that even in a city with a relatively high literacy rate, radio competed with, if it did not supersede newspapers as a preferred medium. Among an equal number of "better off and modest" respondents, 31 percent favored newspapers, 24 percent television, and 18 percent radio. Among the "poor," however, 29 percent favored radio, 15 percent newspapers, and only 6 percent television.

CHAPTER VI

1. See Gabriel A. Almond and James S. Coleman, *The Politics of the Developing Areas*, Princeton, Princeton University Press, 1960.

2. Calculated from data from *Anuário Estatístico do Brasil*, 1968.

3. *Veja*, São Paulo, No.207, August 23, 1972.

4. Data in this section from *Anuário Estatístico do Brasil*, 1967 and 1968, and *Visão*, March 15, 1968.

5. Data from a United States Embassy report of May 12, 1967.

6. Hélio Jaguaribe, *Economic and Political Development*, Boston, Harvard University Press, 1968, p. 136.

7. See particularly Leff, *Economic Policy-Making;* and Joel Bergsman, *Brasil's Industrialization and Trade Policies*, Brazil Development Assistance Progrem, Berkeley, University of California, 1968. A more popularly written but wider ranging study is contained in *The Economist*, London, September 2, 1972.

8. Robert E. Scott, "Political Parties and Policy-Making in Latin America," in Joseph La Palombara and Myron Weiner, *Political Parties and Political Development*, Princeton, Princeton University Press, 1966, p. 333.

9. Silvert, *Expectant Peoples*, p. 360.

10. Unless otherwise indicated data are from "Fifteen Years of Economic Policy in Brazil," *Economic Bulletin for Latin America*, vol. IV, no. 2, November 1964 and *Conjunctura Económica*, published annually by the Fundaçao Getúlio Vargas and the *Anuário Estatístico do Brasil*. Most recent data are from *The Economist*, September 2, 1972 and *Brazil, Prospectus*.

11. Sources for data in this section are the *Anuario Estatístico do Brasil*, 1967 and 1968; a special supplement of *Visao*, July 18, 1969, *Política dos Transportes do Brazil*, which contains a thorough review of all aspects of transportation, except air transport; and *O Brasil Cresce*, a special supplement of *Realidade*, São Paulo, July 1970, prepared by the Getúlio Vargas Foundation.

12. Data from Getúlio Vargas Foundation in *O Brasil Cresce*, July, 1970.

13. *Ibid.*

14. *Brazil, Prospectus*.

15. Although attention to agriculture under Kubitschek is generally agreed to

have been inadequate, most of the target goals were reached, e.g., storage facilities for agricultural products were increased 500 percent, fertilizer production topped the goal by over 30 percent, and more than 20,000 tractors were imported for farm use, pending installation of manufacturing facilities.

16. Data from Inter-American Development Bank, (IADB), *Socio-Economic Progress in Latin America,* 1967, and United States Embassy Telegram No. 5843 of May 12, 1967 to Department of State.

17. It is difficult to estimate how much of the change can be ascribed to the law and how much to normal change in a modernizing state, because a good deal of the law's potential effect was negated by leaving its administration to municipal authorities, notoriously subject to influence by large landowners.

18. Data in this section are from various sources including *Anuário Estatístico do Brasil;* the *Three-Year Economic and Social Development Plan, 1963-1965;* the *Seventh Annual Report of the Social Progress Trust Fund of the IADB, 1967;* Charles Wagley, "The Brazilian Revolution," in *Social Change in Latin America Today,* New York, Harper & Brothers, 1960; and reports of the U. S. Agency for International Development Mission in Brazil. See also Robert J. Havinghurst and J. Roberto Moreira, *Society and Education in Brazil,* Pittsburgh, University of Pittsburgh Press, 1965.

19. *Visão,* March 15, 1968.

20. Primary school usually ends with the fourth grade. For those continuing to secondary school a fifth grade is offered although this requirement may be waived for pupils able to pass entrance examinations for higher status.

21. Data from U. S. Agency for International Development Mission in Brazil, 1967.

CHAPTER VII

1. The one notable exception, in a somewhat different context, was Brazilian involvement in Uruguayan affairs, sometimes forced by Rio Grande do Sul's independent minded *caudilhos* (leaders of irregular military forces).

2. Principal among these are Mario Travassos' *Projeção Continental do Brazil,* Rio de Janeiro, 1937, and Lt. Col. Carlos de Meira Mattos' *Projeção Mundial do Brasil,* São Paulo, Grafica Leal (undated, c. 1955), whose objective is to extend Travassos' hemisphere thesis worldwide. See also Golbery, *Geopolítica do Brasil.*

3. Delgado de Carvalho in his *História Diplomática do Brasil,* São Paulo, Cia, Editôra Nacional, 1959, pp. 297-298, quoted from the Chilean writer B. Monteagudo, *Colección de Ensayos Relativos a la Unión y Confederacion,* Santiago, 1862. "We should not look with confidence on the new Brazilian Empire . . . Everything leads us to believe that the Imperial Cabinet of Rio de Janeiro will lend itself to further the ambitions of the Holy Alliance against the Republics of the New World . . ." A Brazilian diplomat, Ambassador Meira Penna, put it another way when he wrote in 1967 that the highly dynamic quality of Brazilian diplomacy, particularly during the Empire period, gained it the not entirely unmerited reputation of "South American imperialism."

4. J. D. de Meira Penna, *Política Externa, Segurança e Desenvolvimento,* Rio de Janeiro, 1967, pp. 23-24.

5. If it is not yet necessary to divide the hemisphere into four areas, thereby

giving the predominantly black former European colonies separate status, it soon will be.

6. Cuba's temporary exclusion currently (1973) brings the number down to 17.

7. Meira Penna, *Política Externa*, p. 90.

8. The rubber boom made the Amazon region a major subject for planning in the early 1900's. Its subsequent hibernation, which followed the collapse of the rubber industry, shifted communications efforts to Mato Grosso. Efforts to develop the Amazon basin, begun in 1967, could again open up the region as an outlet for Bolivia and other neighboring nations.

9. Meira Penna, *Política Externa*, pp. 110-111.

10. Ramón J. Cárcano, *Mis primeros 80 anos*, Buenos Aires, 1943, pp. 282-283. Quoted in Alvaro Lins, *Rio-Branco*, 2nd ed., São Paulo, Cia. Editôra Nacional, rev. 1965, p. 461.

11. Carvalho, *História Diplomática*, pp. 315-316.

12. Meira Penna, *Política Externa*, p. 100.

13. Good grounds exist for the report that during the brief Quadros administration (1961) the President ordered the military to prepare contingency plans for an invasion of Guyana, then a British colony, because of an alleged threat in the colony from the leftist leader, Cheddi Jagan. Even the Communist-conscious armed forces refused to give much importance to this project.

14. Meira Penna, *Política Externa*, p. 149.

15. Meira Mattos, *Projeção Mundial*, p. 25.

16. Carvalho, *Historia Diplomatica*, pp. 331-332.

17. See E. Bradford Burns, *The Unwritten Alliance, Rio-Branco and Brazilian American Relations*, New York, Columbia University Press, 1966, for an account of this interesting period.

18. It is not possible to quantify how much responsibility for the political deterioration in Brazil and elsewhere in Latin America is chargeable to the Eisenhower administration's failure to grant assistance until the Communist threat became more imminent, but that it was considerable it is hard to deny.

19. José Honório Rodrigues, *Interêsse Nacional e Política Externa*, Rio de Janeiro, Editôra Civilização Brasileira, 1966, pp. 3-4.

20. Arthur Schlesinger, Jr., *A Thousand Days: John F. Kennedy in the White House*, Boston, Houghton-Mifflin, 1965, p. 201.

21. Gilberto Freyre considers Brazil a Portuguese community in the sense that some writers consider the United States an Anglo-Saxon community. Most scholars today separate the two—as in the field of Luso-Brazilian studies, Luso being the Portuguese part of the whole.

22. Relative values, according to these nationalists, are illustrated by the witticism: "Did you know that Brazil is the only country in the Western Hemisphere with a colony in Europe?"

23. José Honório Rodrigues, *Brazil and Africa*, Berkeley, University of California Press, 1965, translated from *Brasil e Africa: Outro Horizonte*, 2nd ed., Rio de Janeiro, Editôra Civilização Brasileira, S.A., 1964.

24. Jânio Quadros, "Brazil's New Foreign Policy," *Foreign Affairs*, 40(1), October 1961. Although written before his resignation, this article was not published until he left office.

25. An opinion poll taken among Brazilian legislators in 1961 showed a strong neutralist sentiment as well as approval for expanded diplomatic relations

that the United States viewed with alarm. Thus, 80 percent favored renewed diplomatic relations with the Soviet Union, and 74 percent with Communist China.

26. Rodrigues, *Interêsse Nacional*.

27. *Política Externa Independente*, vol. 1. no. 1, Rio de Janeiro, May 1965. The rationale is outlined in some detail in this chapter because it appears to have exerted far greater influence on policy makers than they would be willing to admit. Most of the policy recommendations formulated by these nationalistic diplomatic "outcasts" parallel policies pursued today.

28. This and the following quotations are from the "Introduction," *Política Externa Independente*, May 1965, pp.3-8.

29. This thesis is a frontal rejection of the traditional view held by military and civilian leaders of the *Escola Superior de Guerra* that bases military security policy on the assumption of continued East-West antagonism and the cold war.

30. Even the moderate General Golbery in *Geopolítica do Brasil*, referring to favored treatment accorded some countries by the United States, observed: "it seems just to us to make use of our highly valuable assets to obtain the means for carrying out a mission and a duty . . . We too can invoke a 'manifest destiny'. . . ." (p. 54).

31. Meira Penna, *Política Externa*, pp. 195-196.

CHAPTER VIII

1. Seymour Lipset, "Values, Education and Enterpreneurship," in Seymour Martin Lipset and Aldo Solari, (eds.) *Elites in Latin America*, New York, Oxford University Press, 1967, pp. 17-18.

2. Ithiel de Sola Pool, (ed.) *Contemporary Political Science*, New York, McGraw-Hill, 1967, p. 26.

3. Organski, *Stages of Political Development*. Much of the analysis of the development process in the Western democracies and Japan is drawn from this work. Although Organski does not consider Brazil in his study, many of his observations are pertinent.

4. Speech at commencement of the school year at the Command and General Staff School, Rio de Janeiro, reported in *Jornal do Brasil*, March 4, 1969.

5. Quoted in *Visão*, May 24, 1968.

6. Silvert (ed.), *Expectant Peoples*, p. 360.

7. Herman Kahn and Anthony J. Wiener, *The Year 2000*, New York, Macmillan Company, 1967.

8. An indication of part of this soul-searching can be found in Freitas, *Brasil Ano 2000*, pp. 141-145. To support its thesis that a great Brazil of the future is not a categorical imperative, the book quotes a lengthy confidential memorandum prepared in the Foreign Office calling for "inflexible determination and great sacrifices" to bring per capita GNP to $1500, "the *present* standard of GNP of Western Europe." This memorandum is remarkable for the candor with which it faces the possibility of failure to meet the challenges of modernization. A scholarly rebuttal to the Kahn-Wiener projection can be found in Mario Enrique Simonson, *Brasil 2001*, Rio de Janeiro, Apec Editôra, S. A., 1969. A more popular approach is in Murilo Melo Filho, *O Desafio Brasileiro*, Bloch, Rio de Janeiro, 1972.

9. From *Jornal do Brasil*, Rio de Janeiro, April 22, 1969.

10. See Organski, *Stages of Political Development*, pp. 90-96.

11. Schneider, *The Political System of Brazil*. Schneider leans most heavily on Samuel P. Huntington, *Political Order in Changing Societies*, New Haven, 1968; José Nun, "A Latin American Phenomenon: The Middle Class Military Coup," in James Petras and Maurice Zeitlin (eds.), *Latin America: Reform or Revolution*, New York, 1968; Hélio Jaguaribe, *Political Strategies of National Development in Brazil*, Washington University, St. Louis, *Studies in Comparative International Development*, III, No. 2 (1967-1968); David E. Apter, *The Politics of Modernization*, Chicago, 1965; and *Some Conceptual Approaches to the Study of Modernization*, Englewood Cliffs, N. J., 1968. All contain useful descriptions and analyses.

12. The use of "fascist" is not intended to be pejorative; the repressive aspects of military-controlled government in Brazil are dealt with elsewhere; here the term is employed simply to describe a pattern of development, not to make comparisons of ideologically competitive systems.

13. The problem here is oversimplified for brevity, but it is essentially as stated.

14. Quoted in the *Washington Post*, March 23, 1969.

INDEX

Act of Roboré, 191
Administrative reform, 12, 61-62, 102, 200, 231
Africa, 5, 9, 196-197, 210-212, 215, 217
Agency for International Development, 135, 203, 206
Agrarian reform, 145, 157, 180-182, 238
Agriculture, 6-7, 10, 13, 178-180, 257-258
Alagados, 160
Alagoas, 80
Alliance for Progress, 144, 166, 198, 204
Amapá, 70
Amazon Basin, 2-4, 6, 10, 61, 166, 172, 251, 259
Amazon River, 3, 8
Amazonas, João, 95
Andreazza, Mário David, 171
Anti-Americanism, 47, 201, 205, 207, 218, 244
Arantes, Aldo, 137
Argentina, 4, 12-13, 104, 107, 177, 187, 190-193, 195, 200, 206
Atomic Energy Commission, 61, 174
Autarquías, 139, 141, 256
Auto industry, 175-176
Aviation, 170

Bahia, 9-10, 28
Bandeirantes, 9-10, 28
Bank of Brazil, 61
Barbosa, Rui, 109
Barros, Adhemar de, 71, 78, 89
Basbaum, Leonido, 94
Belem, 173
Belo Horizonte, 1
Birth control, 230
Bolivia, 187, 246
Bolívar, Simón, 193-194
Borders, 4, 10, 69, 167, 186
Brasil, Ano 2000, 34, 260
Brasilia, 3, 21, 158-159, 166, 223

Brazilian character, 31-36
Brazilian Democratic Movement, 92. See also Political parties.
Brazilian Labor Party, 20, 86-91, 130. See also Political parties
Brazilian Rural Confederation, 141, 144
Brazilian Rural Society, 144
Brazilian Socialist Party, 89-90
Buenos Aires, 10, 173
Buffer states, 187, 190-193

Cabral, Pedro Alvares, 7
Cacao, 178-180
Café Filho, João, 20
capitanias (captaincies), 8-9
Camara, Dom Helder Pessoa, 117-118, 125, 127
Camara, Jaime de Barros, 117
Camara, Sette, 198
Campos Sales, Manuel Ferraz de, 16
Cardonnel, Thomas, 136
Carvalho, Delgado de, 195
Casserite, 174
Castello Branco, Humberto, 22, 54, 81, 135, 201, 205
Caste system, 30, 225
Catholic Church, 14, 24, 38, 112, 114-121, 232, 255-256
Catholic Action, 122
Catholic Electoral Leagues, 121
Catholic Left, 122-123, 136-137, 139
Catholic University Youth, 122
Cattle, 9-10
Cement, 175
Censorship, 24, 150, 153, 207
Centralism, 70-73
Chamber of deputies, 63, 83
Chile, 4, 45, 107, 190-191, 193, 218, 246
Christian Democratic Party, 89-90, 121. See also Political parties
Civil household, 59
Civil service, 62, 100-102, 231
Class structure, 29-30, 161-163

263